Hope you & enjoyment in the study of Ps 119.

Blessed are the undefiled in the way, who walk in the law of the Lord. Blessed are they that keep his testimonies, and that seek him with the whole heart.
Psalm 119:1-2

Your testimony & example have been a blessing to me over the years. Keep pressing on!

Love in Christ,
Angie

The GOLDEN Alphabet

Register This New Book

Benefits of Registering*

- ✓ FREE **replacements** of lost or damaged books
- ✓ FREE **audiobook** – *Pilgrim's Progress*, audiobook edition
- ✓ FREE information about new titles and other **freebies**

www.anekopress.com/new-book-registration

*See our website for requirements and limitations.

The GOLDEN Alphabet

AN EXPOSITION OF PSALM 119

CHARLES H. SPURGEON

ANEKO PRESS

We love hearing from our readers. Please contact us at www.anekopress.com/questions-comments with any questions, comments, or suggestions.

The Golden Alphabet – Charles H. Spurgeon
Revised Edition Copyright © 2018
All rights reserved. No part of this book may be reproduced, stored in a retrieval system, or transmitted in any form or by any means – electronic, mechanical, photocopying, recording, or otherwise, without written permission from the publisher.

Unless otherwise marked, scripture quotations are taken from the Jubilee Bible, copyright © 2000, 2001, 2010, 2013 by Life Sentence Publishing, Inc. Used by permission of Life Sentence Publishing, Inc., Abbotsford, Wisconsin. All rights reserved.

Cover Design: Jonathan Lewis
Editors: Donna Sundblad, Ruth Zetek, and Paul Miller

www.anekopress.com
Aneko Press, Life Sentence Publishing, and our logos are trademarks of
Life Sentence Publishing, Inc.
203 E. Birch Street
P.O. Box 652
Abbotsford, WI 54405

RELIGION / Biblical Commentary / Old Testament
Paperback ISBN: 978-1-62245-511-9
eBook ISBN: 978-1-62245-512-6

10 9 8 7 6 5 4 3 2

Available where books are sold

Contents

Preface ix
Introduction xiii
Psalm 119:1-8 1
Psalm 119:9-16 23
Psalm 119:17-24 39
Psalm 119:25-32 53
Psalm 119:33-40 67
Psalm 119:41-48 83
Psalm 119:49-56 97
Psalm 119:57-64 109
Psalm 119:65-72 123
Psalm 119:73-80 135
Psalm 119:81-88 147
Psalm 119:89-96 157
Psalm 119:97-104 167
Psalm 119:105-112 177
Psalm 119:113-120 187
Psalm 119:121-128 199
Psalm 119:129-136 211
Psalm 119:137-144 221
Psalm 119:145-152 229
Psalm 119:153-160 239
Psalm 119:161-168 249
Psalm 119:169-176 259
Charles H. Spurgeon – A Brief Biography 269
Similar Titles 273

Preface

The *Treasury of David*, a Bible commentary I've written on the book of Psalms, is found in thousands of libraries in seven large volumes, but it is too large a work to be found among the general population of Christians. For this reason, I decided to publish certain parts of it in smaller books so that many more people might profit from it. The 119th psalm is of such a size as to stand out from all the rest and claim separate treatment. It is known among the Germans as "The Christians' golden ABC of the praise, love, power, and use of the Word of God," and from them I've borrowed the title for this book. Each portion of the psalm begins with a letter of the Hebrew alphabet. For example, the first eight verses may be rendered as to begin in each case with the letter *A* (*Aleph*).

> *A blessing is on them that are undefiled in the way, and walk in the law of Jehovah;*
>
> *A blessing is on them that keep His testimonies, and seek Him with their whole heart;*
>
> *Also on them that do no wickedness, but walk in His ways.*
>
> *A law You have given unto us, that we should diligently keep Your commandments.*

Ah, Lord! that my ways were so directed that I might keep Your statutes!

And then shall I not be confounded, while I have respect unto all Your commandments.

As for me, I will thank You with a sincere heart, when I shall have learned Your righteous judgments.

An eye will I have unto Your statutes: O forsake me not utterly.

Psalm 119 is a wonderful composition. Its expressions are as many as the waves of the sea, but its testimony is as singular as the ocean. The entire psalm deals with only one subject, although it consists of a considerable number of verses. Although some verses are very similar to others, the exact thought is not repeated throughout its 176 verses. There is always a shade of difference, even when the color of the thought appears to be the same.

Some have said it lacks variety, but that is merely the observation of those who haven't studied it. I have weighed each word and looked at each syllable with extended meditation, and I bear witness that this sacred song has no redundancy in it, but is charmingly varied from beginning to end. Its variety is like that of a kaleidoscope – from a few objects, innumerable variations and combinations are produced. In the kaleidoscope, you look once and see a strangely beautiful form. You shift the glass a little and another shape, equally delicate and beautiful, is displayed before your eyes. It is the same here. What you see is the same, yet never the same. It is the same truth, but it is always placed in a new light or connection, or in some way or other infused with freshness.

I do not believe that any subject other than a heavenly one would have allowed for such a psalm to be written about it, because the themes of this world are narrow and shallow. A mind less than divine could not have handled such a writing, even with a sacred subject. Inspiration alone can account for the fullness and freshness of this psalm.

The best compositions of men are soon depleted, for they are cisterns and not springing fountains. You enjoy them very much when you first come across them, and you think you could hear them a hundred times over; but you cannot actually do so, for you soon find them wearisome. A man very quickly eats too much honey, and even children are sickened by sweets eventually.

In the same way, all human books grow stale after a time, but with the Word of God, the desire to study it increases, while the more you know of it, the less you think you know. The Book grows on you. As you dive into its depths, you have a fuller perception of the infinity which remains unexplored. You are still longing to enjoy more of that which it is your delight to taste. All this is true even of this psalm, which is in itself nothing more than the commendation of the Word of God.

> *How manifold are the words and thoughts of God!*

This wonderful psalm, from its great length, helps us to marvel at the immensity of Scripture. As it keeps to the same subject, it helps us adore the unity of Scripture. Yet, from the many turns it brings to that one subject, it helps us see the variety of Scripture. How manifold are the words and thoughts of God! In His Word, just as in creation, the wonders of His skill are displayed in many ways.

I admire the singular blending of testimony, prayer, and praise in this psalm. In one verse, the psalmist bears witness; in a second verse, he praises; in a third verse, he prays. It is an incense made up of many spices, but they are wonderfully mixed and worked together to form one perfect sweetness. The blending greatly increases the value of the whole. You would not like to have the first third of the psalm composed of prayer, then second third made up exclusively of praise, and the third portion entirely made of testimony. It is best to have all these divinely sweet ingredients intermixed and worked together into a sacred unity, as you have them in this thrice-hallowed psalm. Its prayers bear witness, and its testimonies are fragrant with praise.

Charles Bridges wrote a peculiarly delightful work based upon this psalm.[1] I do not seek to rival him, but I would attempt to edify the Lord's people in the same way as he has done, for he has made no effort to display his learning, but his goal was to promote devotion. Several notable authors have written on this psalm before Mr. Bridges, and I am one of those who follow after him. The succession will not end until the Lord comes.

I commit my work to my Lord's acceptance, and pray that His Holy Spirit may make these praises of Holy Scripture ring like sweet bells in the ears of His own people forevermore.

Dear reader, pray for your brother in Christ,

C. H. Spurgeon
Westwood, July 1887

---

[1] Charles Bridges, *Exposition of Psalm CXIX: As Illustrative of the Character and Exercises of Christian Experience*. First published in 1827. This was written by Bridges (1794-1869) when he was thirty-three years old. By the time of his death in 1869, the book had gone through at least twenty-four editions.

Introduction

This psalm has no special title, nor is any author's name mentioned. It is the longest psalm, and this is a sufficiently distinctive name for it. In size, it equals twenty-two psalms of the average length of the Songs of Degrees.[2] It is not just long, though, for it equally excels in breadth of thought, depth of meaning, and height of passion. It is like the celestial city whose height and breadth are equal. *The city lies foursquare, and the length is as large as the breadth* (Revelation 21:16). Many superficial readers have supposed that it harps upon one string and abounds in pious repetitions and redundancies, but this perspective arises from the shallowness of the reader's own mind.

Those who have carefully studied each line of this divine hymn are amazed at the variety, insight, and depth of thought. Using only a few words, the writer has produced variations and combinations of meaning that display his holy familiarity with his subject and the sanctified ingenuity of his mind. He never repeats himself, for if the same sentiment occurs, it is used in a fresh way and exhibits another interesting shade of meaning. The more one studies it, the fresher it becomes. As those who drink the water of the Nile like it better every time they take a drink, so this psalm becomes fuller and more fascinating the more you turn to it.

This psalm contains no unnecessary word. The grapes of

---

[2] This is the title given to Psalms 120-134, also called the Song of Ascents.

this cluster are almost bursting full with the new wine of the kingdom. The more you look into this mirror of a gracious heart, the more you will see in it. Calm on the surface, like the sea of glass before the eternal throne, it yet contains within its depths an ocean of fire. Those who devoutly gaze into it will not only see the brightness, but will also feel the glow of the sacred flame. It is loaded with holy wisdom, and it is as weighty as it is bulky.

Again and again while studying it, we have cried, *O the depth of the riches!* (Romans 11:33). Yet these depths are hidden beneath an apparent simplicity, as Augustine has well and wisely said, which makes the exposition all the more difficult. Its obscurity is hidden beneath a veil of light, and so the only ones who discover it are those who sincerely and earnestly not only look on the Word, but like the angels, also look into it.

The psalm is alphabetical. Eight stanzas begin with one letter, the following eight stanzas begin with the next letter, and so the whole psalm proceeds by eights through the entire twenty-two letters of the Hebrew alphabet. Along with this, there are multitudes of parallel phrases and other word structures and patterns with which the Hebrew mind is pleased – formalities very similar to those in which our older poets indulged.

The Holy Spirit in this way spoke to us in styles attractive to the mind and helpful to the memory.

The Holy Spirit in this way spoke to us in styles attractive to the mind and helpful to the memory. The psalmist is often plain or elegant in his manner, but he doesn't avoid being unconventional or formal if by doing so his manner of instruction can be more easily understood. He does not scorn even abbreviated and contrived modes of speech if he can firmly set his teaching upon the mind by their use.

be by getting our minds into intense harmony with its subject. In order to do this, we would do well to commit it to memory. Philip Henry was a Nonconformist minister in the 1600s. His daughter wrote in her diary, "I have of late taken some pains to learn by heart Psalm CXIX, and have made some progress therein." She was a sensible, godly woman.

Having gone over the subject matter of this golden psalm, we should consider further still the fullness, certainty, clearness, and sweetness of the Word of God, since by such reflection we are likely to be stirred up to a warm affection for it. What favored beings are those to whom the eternal God has written a letter in His own hand and style! What intensity of devotion, what diligence of composition can produce a worthy tribute for the divine testimonies! If ever one such work has fallen from the pen of man, it is this 119th psalm, which might well be called the holy soul's soliloquy before an open Bible.

This sacred poetic song is a little Bible, the Scriptures condensed, a unified collection of Holy Writ rewritten in holy emotions and actions. The Germans called it "The Christians' golden ABC of the praise, love, power, and use of the Word of God." Blessed are they who can read and understand these pious precepts. They will find golden apples in this true Hesperides,[4] and come to consider that this psalm, like the whole Scripture which it praises, is a pearl island, or better still, a garden of sweet flowers.

The study of this sacred song has often proved helpful to holy men. Henry Martyn mentions it again and again in his diary.[5] For instance: "I experienced a solemn gladness in learning this part, MEM, of the 119th Psalm." During a time

---

4   In Greek mythology, the Hesperides were goddess-maidens entrusted with the care of a tree that produced golden apples. The garden in which this tree grew was called the Garden of the Hesperides.

5   Henry Martyn (1781-1812) was a missionary to India, and his diary and letters would be beneficial to be read by all who desire to read the life of a holy servant of God.

of political trouble, William Wilberforce wrote: "Walked from Hyde Park Corner repeating the 119th Psalm in great comfort." Pascal, in the reading of this holy song, seemed to pass out of himself in holy rapture.

May those who read this psalm and accept the help of our exposition feel their hearts burn within them. To this purpose, at the very beginning let our prayer ascend to God, that His Holy Spirit might rest on us while we devoutly examine this sacred psalm.

Psalm 119:1-8

ALEPH

Blessed are those who walk in the perfect way, who walk in the law of the LORD.

Blessed are those that keep his testimonies and that seek him with their whole heart.

For those who do no iniquity walk in his ways.

Thou hast commanded us to keep thy precepts diligently.

O that my ways were ordered to keep thy statutes!

Then I shall not be ashamed, when I have insight unto all thy commandments.

I will praise thee with uprightness of heart when I shall have learned thy righteous judgments.

I will keep thy statutes; O do not utterly forsake me.

These first eight verses are taken up with a contemplation of the blessedness that comes from keeping the statutes of the Lord. The subject is treated in a devotional manner rather than in a teaching style. Heart fellowship with God is enjoyed through love of His Word, which is God's way of communicating with the soul by His Holy Spirit. Prayer, praise, and all sorts of devotional acts and feelings gleam through these verses like beams of sunlight through an olive grove. You are not only instructed to devout feelings, but these verses influence you and help you to express those holy emotions that derive from being near God and His Word.

Those who love God's Holy Word are blessed, because they are preserved from defilement (verse 1), because they are made practically holy (verses 2 and 3), and because they are led to follow after God sincerely and intensely (verse 2). It is made clear that walking in holiness must be desirable, because God commands it (verse 4). Therefore, the devout soul prays for it (verse 5) and feels that its comfort and courage must depend upon obtaining it (verse 6). In the expectation of answered prayer, even while the prayer is being answered, the heart is full of thankfulness (verse 7) and is fixed in solemn resolve not to miss the blessing if the Lord will give enabling grace (verse 8).

The changes are made evident with these words: (1) *way – who walk in the perfect way, walk in his ways,* and *O that my ways were ordered*; (2) *keep – keep his testimonies, keep thy precepts diligently, ordered to keep,* and *I will keep*; and (3) *walk – walk in the law,* and *walk in his ways*. Yet there is no redundancy of word or thought, though it may seem so to the careless reader.

The change from statements about others and about the Lord to a more personal dealing with God begins in the fourth verse and becomes clearer as we move forward, until in the later verses, the communion becomes most intense and soul moving. *I will praise thee. I will keep thy statutes. O do not utterly forsake me.* I wish every reader would feel the glow of personal devotion while studying this first section of the psalm!

> 1. *Blessed are those who walk in the perfect way, who walk in the law of the LORD.*

Blessed. The psalmist is so enraptured with the law of the Lord that he considers being conformed to it to be his highest ideal of blessedness. He has gazed on the beauties of the perfect law, and as if this verse were the sum and outcome of all his emotions, he exclaims, "Blessed is the man whose life is the practical record of the will of God."

True Christianity is not cold and dry. It has excitement and delight. We not only consider the keeping of God's law to be a wise and proper thing, but we are also warmly captivated by its holiness, and we cry out in adoring wonder, *Blessed are those who walk in the perfect way!* By this we mean that we eagerly desire to become such people ourselves. We wish for no greater happiness than to be perfectly holy. It may be that the writer labored under a sense of his own faults, and therefore envied the blessedness of those whose walk had been more pure and clean. In fact, the very contemplation of the perfect law of the Lord was quite enough to make him lament his own imperfections and long for the blessedness of an undefiled walk.

> *True Christianity is not cold and dry.*

True Christianity is always practical, for it doesn't allow us to delight ourselves in a perfect rule without producing in us a longing to be conformed to that rule in our daily conduct. A blessing belongs to those who hear and read and understand the Word of the Lord; yet it is a far greater blessing to be actually obedient to it and to carry out in our daily walk and lives what we learn in our searching of the Scriptures. Purity in our way and walk is the truest blessedness.

This first verse is not only an introduction to the whole psalm, but it can also be regarded as the text which the rest of the psalm discusses. It is similar to the benediction of the first psalm, which is set at the beginning of the entire book of Psalms. There is a similarity between this 119th psalm and the entire book of Psalms, and this is one example of it – that it begins with a benediction.

We also see some foreshadowing of the Son of David, who began His great Sermon on the Mount in the same way David began his great psalm. We do well to open our mouth with blessings. When we can't bestow them, we can show the way of obtaining them, and even if we do not yet possess them ourselves, it may be profitable to contemplate them so our desires can be stirred up and our souls moved to seek after them. Lord, if I am not yet so blessed as to be among *those who walk in the perfect way*, I will think much about the happiness which such people enjoy, and I will set it before me as my life's ambition.

Young people should begin their lives in the same way David begins his psalm. New converts should begin their profession of Christ Jesus in this manner, and this is how all Christians should begin each day. Settle it in your hearts as a fact and as a certain rule, that holiness is happiness and that we are wise to seek *first the kingdom of God and his righteousness* (Matthew 6:33). Well begun is half done. To start with a true idea of blessedness is important beyond measure. Man began with being blessed in his innocence, and if our fallen race is ever to be blessed again, it must find blessedness where it lost it at the beginning; that is, in conformity to the command of the Lord.

The perfect way. They are undefiled in the way, the right way, the way of the Lord, and they keep that way, walking with holy carefulness and washing their feet daily, so that they will not be defiled by contact with the world. They enjoy great blessedness in their own souls. In fact, they have a foretaste of heaven where blessedness depends much on being absolutely undefiled. If they could continue completely and altogether without defilement, their days would no doubt often seem like heaven on earth. Outward evil would hurt us very little if we were entirely rid of the evil of sin – the attainment of which the best of us still desire, but haven't yet fully reached. However, we eagerly press toward that goal because we have such a clear view of it that we see it to be blessedness itself.

He whose life is, in a gospel sense, undefiled, is blessed, because he never could have reached this point if a thousand blessings hadn't already been bestowed on him. By nature, we are defiled and out of the way, and therefore we must have been washed in the atoning blood to remove defilement. We must have been converted by the power of the Holy Spirit, or we would not have been turned to the way of peace nor be undefiled in it. This is not all, for the continual power of grace is needed to keep a believer in the right way and to preserve him from the contamination of sin and the world. All the blessings of the covenant must have been in some measure poured upon those who have been enabled from day to day to perfect holiness in the fear of the Lord. Their way is the evidence of their being the blessed of the Lord.

David speaks about a high degree of blessedness, for some who are in the way and are true servants of God are still flawed in many ways and bring defilement on themselves. Others who walk in the light more fully and maintain closer fellowship with God are enabled to keep themselves unspotted from the world. These people enjoy far more peace and joy than their less vigilant brothers and sisters. Without question, the more complete our sanctification, the more intense our blessedness. Christ is our way, and we are not only alive in Christ, but we are also to live in Christ. Sadly, we blemish His holy way with our selfishness, self-exaltation, willfulness, and worldliness. As a result, we miss the full measure of blessedness which is in Him as our way. A believer who errs is still saved, but he does not experience the joy of his salvation. He is rescued, but not improved; greatly tolerated, but not greatly blessed.

How easily defilement can come upon us, even in our holy

activities, and even when we are in *the way*! We can even come from public or private worship with defilement on our conscience, gathered when we were on our knees. The tabernacle had no floor but the desert sand, and so the priests at the altar frequently had to wash their feet. By the kind foresight of their God, the laver stood ready for their cleansing, just as our Lord Jesus still stands ready to wash our feet so we can be every bit clean. Thus, our text sets forth the blessedness of the apostles in the upper room when Jesus had said of them, *Ye are clean* (John 15:3).

What blessedness awaits those who follow the Lamb wherever He goes, and who are preserved from the evil which is in the world through lust! These people will be the envy of all mankind *in that day* (Matthew 7:22-23). Though now they despise them as fanatics and Puritans, the most prosperous of sinners will wish that they could change places with them at that time. My dear reader, seek your blessedness in following hard after your Lord, who was holy, harmless, and undefiled; for you have found peace there until now, and you will find peace there forever.

Who walk in the law of the LORD. Habitual holiness is found in those *who walk in the law of the LORD*. Their walk, their public everyday life, is lived in obedience to the Lord. The command of the Lord God rules their lives. Whether they eat, or drink, or whatsoever they do, they do all in the name of their great Master and Example (1 Corinthians 10:31). To them, Christianity is nothing out of the ordinary, but is their everyday way of life. It molds their public behavior as well as their private devotions. This ensures blessedness. He who walks in God's law walks in God's company, and he must be blessed. He has God's smile, God's strength, and God's secret with him, so how can he be anything but blessed?

The holy life is a walk, a steady progress, a quiet advance, and a lasting continuance. Enoch walked with God. Good people always want to be better, and so they go forward. Good people are never idle, and so they do not lie around lazily or waste time, but they are continually walking onward to their desired end. They are not hurried, worried, or flurried, and so they keep the even tenor of their way, walking steadily toward heaven. They are not perplexed about how to conduct themselves, for they have a perfect rule by which they are happy to walk. The law of the Lord is not disagreeable to them. Its commandments are not burdensome to them, and they do not view its restrictions as drudgery.

> *Good people are never idle, and so they do not lie around lazily or waste time, but they are continually walking onward to their desired end.*

It does not appear to them to be an impossible law that is theoretically admirable but practically absurd, but they walk by it and in it. They do not wander around aimlessly and then consult God's law occasionally to see if they are on course, but they use it as a chart for their daily sailing, a map of the road for their life journey. Nor do they ever regret that they have entered upon the path of obedience, or else they would easily leave it, for a thousand temptations offer them the opportunity to return to their old ways.

Their continued walk in the law of the Lord is their best testimony to the blessedness of such a way of life. Yes, they are blessed even now. The psalmist himself bore witness to this fact. He had tried and proved it to be true, and he wrote it down as a fact which defied all denial. Here it stands in the forefront of David's *magnum opus*, written on the topmost line of his greatest psalm: "BLESSED ARE THOSE WHO WALK IN THE LAW OF THE LORD."

The way might be rough, the commandments strict, and the disciplined life might be hard; all this we know, and more, but a thousand heaped-up blessings are still found in godly living, and we bless the Lord for all of them.

We have in Psalm 119:1 blessed people who enjoy five blessed things: a blessed way, blessed purity, a blessed law, given by a blessed Lord, and a blessed walk in them. To this we can add the blessed testimony of the Holy Spirit given in this very passage – that they are indeed the blessed of the Lord.

We must aim at the blessedness which is set before us in this way, but we must not think that we can obtain it without earnest effort. David has much to say about it. His discourse in this psalm is long and solemn, and it hints to us that the way of perfect obedience is not learned in a day. There must be precept upon precept, line upon line (Isaiah 28:10), and after efforts long enough to be compared with the 176 verses of this psalm, we may still have to cry, *I have gone astray like a lost sheep; seek thy slave; for I have not forgotten thy commandments* (Psalm 119:176).

It must, however, be our plan to keep the Word of the Lord much upon our minds, for this discourse about blessedness has the testimony of the Lord for its guiding principle. Only by daily communion with the Lord, through His Word, can we hope to learn His way, to be purged from defilement, and to be made to walk in His statutes. We set out on this exposition with blessedness before us. We see the way to it, and we know where its law is to be found. Let us pray that as we pursue our meditation, we will grow into the habit and walk of obedience, and so feel the blessedness of that which we read.

2. Blessed are those that keep his testimonies and that seek him with their whole heart.

Blessed are those that keep his testimonies. What! A second blessing? Yes, those whose outward life is supported by an inward zeal for God's glory are doubly blessed. In the first verse, we had an undefiled way, and it was assumed that the purity in the way was more than a mere superficial work, but was accompanied by the inward truth and life that comes from divine grace.

In verse two, that which was implied is now expressed. Blessedness is attributed to those who treasure up the testimonies of the Lord. This implies that they search the Scriptures, that they come to understand and love them, and they then continue to practice them. We must first obtain something before we can keep it. In order to keep it well, we must get a firm grip on it. We cannot keep in the heart that which we have not wholeheartedly embraced by our affections. God's Word is His witness or testimony to great and important truths concerning Himself and our relation to Him. We should desire to know this, and when we know it, we should believe it. Once we believe it, we should love it, and loving it, we should hold it tightly against all who try to take it away from us.

There is a doctrinal keeping of the Word by which we are ready to die for its defense, and a practical keeping of it when we actually live under its power. Revealed truth is as precious as diamonds and should be kept or treasured in the memory and in the heart like jewels in a strongbox, or like the law was kept in the ark of the covenant.

This, however, is not enough, for it is meant to be used practically, and so must be kept or followed in the same way that people keep to a path or to a certain occupation. If we keep God's testimonies, they will keep us. They will keep us right in opinion, comfortable in spirit, holy in conversation, and hopeful in expectation. If they were ever worth having (and no thoughtful person will question that), then they are worth keeping. Their designed effect does not come by temporarily seizing them, but by perseveringly keeping them. *In keeping them there is great reward* (Psalm 19:11).

We are bound to carefully keep the Word of God, because it contains His testimonies. He gave them to us, but they are still His. We are to keep them as a watchman guards his master's house, as a steward manages his lord's goods, and as a shepherd takes care of his employer's flock. We will have to give an account, for we are entrusted with the gospel, and woe to us if we are found unfaithful.

We cannot fight a good fight or finish our course unless we keep the faith. To accomplish this, the Lord must keep us, for only those who are kept by the power of God unto salvation will ever be able to keep His testimonies. What a blessedness is therefore shown and testified to by a careful belief in God's Word and a continual obedience to it. God has blessed them, is blessing them, and will bless them forever. That blessedness that David saw in others he realized for himself, for in verse 168 he says, *I have kept thy precepts and thy testimonies,* and in verses 54-56 he traces his joyful songs and happy memories to this same keeping of the law. He confesses, *This I had, because I kept thy precepts* (verse 56). We should experience for ourselves the doctrines that we teach to others.

And that seek him with their whole heart. Those who keep the Lord's testimonies are sure to seek after God. If His Word is precious, we can be sure that He is more precious still. Personal dealing with a personal God is the longing of all who have allowed the Word of God to have its full effect upon them. Once we really know the power of the gospel, we must seek the God of the gospel. *Oh, that I knew where I might find him!* (Job 23:3) will be our wholehearted cry.

See the growth indicated in these sentences. First, one is *in* the way, then one *walks* in the way, and then one finds and keeps the treasure of truth; to crown it all, one seeks after the Lord of the way Himself. Also, note that the further a soul advances in grace, the more spiritual and divine are its longings.

An outward walk isn't enough to satisfy the gracious soul. Not even the treasured testimonies are enough, because in due time, such a soul reaches out after God Himself, and when it finds Him in part, it still yearns for more of Him and seeks Him still.

Seeking after God signifies a desire to commune with Him more closely, to follow Him more fully, to enter into more perfect union with His mind and will, to promote His glory, and to realize completely all that He is to holy hearts. The blessed person already has God, and for this reason he seeks Him. This may seem like a contradiction, but there is really no conflict here.

God is not really sought by cold inquiries of the brain. We must seek Him with the heart. Love reveals itself to love. God manifests His heart to the heart of His people. In vain we try to comprehend Him by reason, for we must understand Him through love. If we are to seek the Lord, our hearts must not be divided with many different things. God is one, and we will not know Him until our heart is one. A broken heart does not need to be distressed by this, for no heart so completely seeks after God as a heart that is broken, for every fragment sighs and cries after the great Father's face.

> *God is one, and we will not know Him until our heart is one.*

It is the divided heart that the doctrine of this verse condemns. This might seem strange to say, but in scriptural terms, a heart can be divided and not broken, and it can be broken but not divided; it can be broken and still be whole, but it can never be whole until it is broken. When our whole heart seeks the holy God in Christ Jesus, it has come to Him about whom it is written that all who touched the hem of His garment were made perfectly whole (Matthew 14:36).

That which the psalmist admires in this verse he claims in the tenth verse, where he says, *With my whole heart I have sought thee*. It is good when admiring a virtue leads to attaining it. Those who do not believe in the blessedness of seeking the Lord will not be likely to arouse their hearts to seek Him, but the one who calls someone else blessed because of the grace that he sees in him is on the way to gaining the same grace for himself.

If those who seek the Lord are blessed, what will be said about those who actually dwell with Him and know that He is theirs?

> "To those who fall, how kind thou art!
> How good to those who seek!
> But what to those who find? Ah! this
> Nor tongue nor pen can show:
> The love of Jesus, what it is,
> None but His loved ones know."[6]

3. *For those who do no iniquity walk in his ways.*

For those who do no iniquity. Blessed indeed would those people be about whom this could be unreservedly said with no explanation needed. We will have reached the state of pure blessedness when we cease from sin altogether. Those who follow the Word of God do no iniquity. His Word is perfect, and if it is constantly followed, no fault will result.

To the outward observer, life consists much in doing; he who never swerves from being just and fair in all that he does, toward both God and man, has hit upon the way of perfection, and we can be sure that his heart is right. Observe that a pure heart leads to avoiding evil. The psalmist says, *For those who do no iniquity walk in his ways.* We know that no one can claim to be absolutely without sin, and yet we believe there are many who do not purposely, willfully, knowingly, and continuously

---

[6] From the twelfth-century hymn by Bernard of Clairvaux, "Jesus, the Very Thought of Thee," translated by Edward Caswall.

do anything that is wicked, ungodly, or unjust. Grace keeps the life seeking to be righteous, even when the Christian laments transgressions of the heart. Judged properly by their fellow men, according to such just rules as people make for each other, the true people of God do no iniquity. They follow the law. They are honest, upright, and chaste, and are blameless regarding justice and morality, and therefore they are happy.

They *walk in his ways.* They do not just pay attention to the great main highway of the law, but they also follow the smaller paths of specific precepts. Not only do they want to remain free from committing sin by doing that which is wrong, but they want to be certain that they do not neglect doing that which is right. It is not enough to them to be blameless, but they also want to be actively righteous. A hermit can escape into solitude so that he will do no iniquity, but a saint lives in society so he may serve his God by walking in His ways. We must be positively as well as negatively right. We will not long keep the second unless we take care of the first, for people walk one way or another. If they do not follow the path of God's law, they will soon fall into iniquity. The surest way to abstain from evil is to be fully occupied in doing good.

> *It is not enough to them to be blameless, but they also want to be actively righteous.*

This verse describes believers as they live among us. Although they have their faults and weaknesses, they still hate evil and will not allow themselves to do it. They love the ways of truth, righteousness, and true godliness, and they habitually walk in them. They do not claim to be absolutely perfect except in their desire to follow and please God, and in this desire they are indeed pure. They long to be kept free from all sin and to walk in holiness. If they could always walk according to the desire of their renewed hearts, they would follow the Lord Jesus in every thought, word, and deed of life. Their whole being would embody holiness.

4. *Thou hast commanded us to keep thy precepts diligently.*

When we follow God, this is simply doing our duty, since God commands us to keep His commandments. *So likewise ye, when ye shall have done all those things which are commanded you, say, We are unprofitable slaves: we have done that which was our duty to do* (Luke 17:10).

God's precepts require careful obedience; there is no keeping them by accident. Some people offer careless service to God, a sort of hit-or-miss obedience, but the Lord has not commanded, nor will He accept such service. His law demands the love of all our heart, soul, mind, and strength (Mark 12:30), and a careless kind of Christianity has none of these.

We are also called to zealous obedience. We are to obey the precepts fully. Vessels of obedience should be filled to the brim, and the command should be carried out to the full extent of its meaning. We are to be as eager to serve the Lord as much as possible, just as a diligent businessman works to gets as much business as he can.

We must not rule out the necessary difficulties to do so, for a diligent obedience will also be laborious and self-denying. Those who are diligent in business rise up early, stay up late, and deny themselves much comfort and leisure. They are not soon tired, or if they are, they persevere even with an aching head and weary eyes. This is the manner in which we should serve the Lord, for such a Master deserves diligent servants. He demands such service and will be content with nothing less. How seldom people give Jesus the service and dedication that He deserves! Consequently, many miss the double blessing spoken of in this psalm through their negligence.

Some people are diligent in superstition and worshiping their own wills, but our diligence ought to be in keeping God's precepts. There is no use traveling quickly if we are not on the right road. People have been diligent in a losing business, and the more they have traded, the more they have lost. This is bad enough in commerce, but we cannot afford to have this happen in our Christianity.

God has not commanded us to be diligent in making precepts, but in keeping them. Some people bind yokes upon their own necks and make chains and rules for others, but the wise path is to be satisfied with the rules of Holy Scripture and to strive to keep them all, in all places, towards all people, and in all respects. If we don't do this, we may become eminent in our own religion, but we will not have kept the commands of God and will not be accepted by Him.

The psalmist began with the third person: *Blessed are those who walk in the perfect way.* Now he is closer to home and has already reached the first person plural. *Thou hast commanded us* (verse 4). We will soon hear him crying out personally and for himself: *O that my ways were ordered!* (verse 5).

As the heart glows with love toward holiness, we desire to have a personal interest in it. The Word of God is a book that affects the heart, and when we begin to sing its praises, it soon comes home to us and starts us praying to be conformed to its teachings. Dear reader, you would do well to pause here, and by devout meditation, impress your heart with the divine authority of the Scriptures so you can personally devote yourself to the careful, prayerful, constant, prompt, and cheerful keeping of the precepts of the Lord.

5. *O that my ways were ordered to keep thy statutes!*

Divine commands should guide us in the subject of our prayers. We cannot in our own strength keep God's statutes as He wants them kept, and yet we long to do so. What course of action do we have but prayer? We must ask the Lord to work our works in us, or we will never work out His commandments.

This verse is a sigh of regret because the psalmist feels that he has not kept the precepts diligently. It is a cry of weakness appealing for help to the God who can help. It is a request of perplexity from one who has lost his way and would gladly be directed in it. It is a petition of faith from one who loves God and trusts in Him for grace.

Our ways are by nature opposed to the way of God, and they must be turned by the Lord's guidance in another direction or they will lead us down to destruction. God can direct the mind and will without violating our ability to make our own choices, and He will do so in answer to prayer. In fact, He has already begun the work in those who are wholeheartedly praying after the manner shown in this verse. It is the longing for present holiness that causes the desire to arise in the heart. Oh, I wish it were like that with me now! However, this verse also involves future holiness that preserves us, for David here longs for grace to keep the statutes of the Lord now and forever.

The deep yearning of the text is really a prayer, though it does not exactly take that form. Desires and longings are the substance of supplication, and it matters very little what shape they take. *O that* is as acceptable a prayer as *Our Father*.

One would not have expected a prayer for direction here, but we would have thought that David would have had a prayer to be enabled to keep the commandments. After all, can't we direct ourselves? If we cannot row, we can steer. The psalmist here confesses that even for the smallest part of his duty, he felt unable without grace. He longed for the Lord to influence his will, as well as to strengthen his hands. We need a rod to point out the way as much as a staff to support us in it.

The longing evident in this text is prompted by admiration for the blessedness of holiness, by the contemplation of the righteous man's beauty of character, and by a reverent awe of the command of God. It is a personal application of David's own case of the truths he had been considering.

O that my ways were ordered to keep thy statutes! It would be good if all who hear the Word would imitate this example and turn all that they hear into prayer. We would have more keepers of the statutes if we had more people who longed and cried for the grace which alone can keep them from wandering.

6. *Then I shall not be ashamed, when I have insight unto all thy commandments.*

Then I shall not be ashamed. David had known shame, and here he rejoices in the prospect of being freed from it. Sin brings shame, and when sin is gone, the reason for being ashamed is gone, too. What a deliverance this is, for to some people, death is preferable to shame!

> Sin brings shame, and when sin is gone, the reason for being ashamed is gone, too.

When I have insight unto all thy commandments. When he respects God, he will respect himself and be respected. Whenever we err, we prepare ourselves for shame and disappointment of heart. If no one else is ashamed of me, I will be ashamed of myself if I sin. Our first parents never knew shame until they made the acquaintance of the old serpent, and the shame never left them until their gracious God covered them with sacrificial skins. Disobedience made them naked and ashamed.

We will always have cause for shame until every sin is

vanquished and every duty toward God is followed. When we show continual and universal respect for the will of the Lord, then we will be able to look ourselves in the face in the mirror of the law, and we won't feel ashamed at the sight of men or devils, no matter how eager their hateful intentions may be to accuse us of wrong.

Many are not confident enough to take any action in this area, and this verse suggests a cure. An abiding sense of obligation will make us bold and we will be afraid to be afraid. No shame in the presence of man will hinder us when the fear of God has taken full possession of our minds. When we are on the king's highway by daylight and engaged on royal business, we don't need to ask anyone's permission.

It would be a dishonor to a king to be ashamed of the garments he has provided or of being in his service. Such shame should never make a Christian blush, nor will it if he has the proper reverence for the Lord his God. There is nothing to be ashamed of in a holy life. A man may be ashamed of his pride, ashamed of his wealth, and even ashamed of his own children, but he will never be ashamed of regarding the will of the Lord his God in all things.

It is worthwhile to mention that David promises himself no immunity from shame until he has carefully paid homage to all the precepts. Pay attention to that word *all*, and don't leave one command out of your consideration. Partial obedience still leaves us liable to be called to account for those commands which we have neglected. A person may have a thousand virtues, and yet a single failing may cover him with shame.

To a poor sinner who is buried in despair, it may seem a very unlikely thing that he could ever be delivered from shame. He blushes, is confounded, and feels that he can never lift up his face again. Let him read these words: *Then I shall not be ashamed*. David isn't dreaming or picturing an impossible situation. Be assured, dear friend, that the Holy Spirit can renew the image of God in you, so you can again look up without fear. Oh, for sanctification to direct us in God's way, for then we will have boldness toward both God and His people, and we will no longer be ashamed and confused.

Isaac Watts turns this passage into an admirable poem. Let us sing with him:

> "Then shall my heart have inward joy,
>   And keep my face from shame,
> When all thy statutes I obey,
>   And honor all thy name."

7. I will praise thee with uprightness of heart when I shall have learned thy righteous judgments.

I will praise thee. It is never a long or a difficult journey from prayer to praise. You can be certain that he who prays for holiness will one day praise God for happiness. Shame will have vanished, silence will be broken, and the formerly silent person will declare, "I will praise thee." He cannot do otherwise than promise praise while he seeks sanctification. Notice how well he knows upon what head to set the crown. *I will praise thee.* He himself could be praiseworthy, but he signifies God alone as worthy of praise. By the sorrow and shame of sin he measures his obligations to the Lord, who wants to teach him the art of living so he can completely escape his former misery.

With uprightness of heart. His heart can be upright if the Lord teaches him, and then it will praise its teacher. There is such a thing as false and pretended praise, and the Lord abhors this; but there is no music like that which comes from a pure soul which stands in its integrity. Heart praise and uprightness in the heart are required, accompanied by the Lord's teaching to make the heart upright. An upright heart is sure to bless the Lord, for grateful adoration is a part of its uprightness. No one can be right unless he is upright towards God, and this involves giving Him the praise which is His due.

When I shall have learned thy righteous judgments. We must learn to praise, learn that we can praise, and praise when we have learned. If we are ever to learn, the Lord must teach us, and especially on such a subject as His judgments, for they are very deep. While these pass before our eyes and we learn from them, we ought to praise God, for the original doesn't say, "when I shall have learned," but, "in my learning."

While I am still a student, I will be part of the choir; my upright heart will praise God's uprightness. My purified judgment will admire His judgments. God's providence is a book full of teaching, and to those whose hearts are right, it is a music book out of which they chant Jehovah's praise. God's Word is full of the record of His righteous care and actions, and as we read it we feel compelled to burst forth into expressions of holy delight and enthusiastic praise. When we read about God's judgments and become joyful partakers in them, we are twice as much moved to sing – singing in which there is neither formality nor hypocrisy nor lukewarmness, for the heart is upright in the presentation of its praise.

8. *I will keep thy statutes; O do not utterly forsake me.*

I will keep thy statutes. A calm resolve. When praise calms down into solid resolution, it is well with the soul. Zeal that spends itself in singing and leaves no practical residue of holy living is worth little. Many go to church and sing praises to God, and then live for the world and sing to the world the rest of the week. "I will praise" should be coupled with "I will keep."

This firm resolve is by no means boastful, like Peter's *Though*

I should die with thee, yet will I not deny thee (Matthew 26:35), because it is followed by a humble prayer for divine help: *O do not utterly forsake me.* Feeling his own inability, he trembles for fear that he could be left to himself, and this fear is increased by the fear that he has of falling into sin.

The *I will keep* sounds suitable enough now that the humble cry is heard with it. This is a happy combination of resolution and dependence. We meet people who to all appearance humbly pray, but there is no strength of character, no decision in them, and consequently the pleading of the closet is not embodied in their life.

On the other hand, we meet people with an abundance of resolve accompanied by complete absence of dependence upon God, and this makes as poor a character as the former example. May the Lord grant to us such a blending of excellences that we can be *perfect and entire, not lacking in anything* (James 1:4).

> *This prayer is certain to be heard, for certainly it must be highly pleasing to God to see someone set on obeying His will.*

This prayer is certain to be heard, for certainly it must be highly pleasing to God to see someone set on obeying His will. For this reason, it must be most agreeable to Him to be present with such a person and to help him in his endeavors. How can He forsake someone who does not forsake His law?

The peculiar fear that tinges this prayer with a feeling of gloom is the fear of being utterly forsaken. The soul may well cry out against such a calamity. It is a sufficient enough trial to be left alone so that we will discover our weakness, but to be altogether forsaken would be ruin and death. For God to hide His face from us in a moment of His wrath brings us very low, but if He were to absolutely desert us, it would plunge us ultimately into the lowest hell. However, the Lord never has utterly forsaken His servants, and He never will; blessed be His name. If we desire to keep His statutes, He will keep us. Yes, His grace will keep us keeping His law.

There is quite a steep descent from the mount of benediction of the first verse to the almost cry of despair in this eighth verse, yet this is spiritually and practically a noticeable and gracious growth. We have moved from an admiration of goodness to a burning longing after God, hungering after communion with Him, with an intense fear that we might not realize our desire. The yearning of verse 5 is now replaced by an actual prayer from the depths of a heart that is conscious of its lack of merit and is sensible about its entire dependence upon divine love.

The two "I wills" – *I will praise thee* and *I will keep thy statutes* – needed to be seasoned with some other humble request, or it might have been thought that the good man's dependence was to some extent based upon his own resolve. He presents his resolutions like a sacrifice, but he cries to heaven for the fire. The desire is present in him, but he cannot perform that which he wants unless the Lord will abide with him.

This last verse of the first octave has a link with the first verse of the next octave in this way: Lord, do not forsake me, for how can I cleanse my way if You are gone from me and Your law ceases to have power over me?

Psalm 119:9-16

BETH

With what shall a young man cleanse his way? when he shall keep thy word.

With my whole heart I have sought thee; O let me not err from thy commandments.

Thy spoken word have I hid in my heart that I might not sin against thee.

Blessed art thou, O LORD: teach me thy statutes.

With my lips I have declared all the judgments of thy mouth.

I have rejoiced in the way of thy testimonies as above all riches.

I will meditate in thy precepts and consider thy ways.

I will delight myself in thy statutes; I will not forget thy words.

These verses start at the beginning of life. Though written by an old man, they were written for all young men. Only he who begins with God in the greenness of youth will be able to write like this from experience in the ripeness of age. No sooner did David introduce his subject with one octave of verses, then he felt compelled to look after young men in the next set of eight stanzas. How much he thought of youthful piety! In the Hebrew, each verse in this section begins with *B*. If thoughts on the Blessed Way make up his *A*, then thoughts on Blessed Young Men will fill up the next letter. Oh, to be with God early in life! To give Him the dew of the day of life is to make the most of life.

9. *With what shall a young man cleanse his way? when he shall keep thy word.*

With what shall a young man cleanse his way? How will he become and remain practically holy? He is just a young man, full of hot passions and lacking in knowledge and experience. How will he get on the right path and stay there? There was never a more important question for any man, and never a better time to ask it than at the start of life.

It is by no means an easy task that the wise young man sets before himself. He wants to choose a clean way, to be himself pure in it, to cleanse it of any filthiness that might arise in the future, and to end by showing a clear course from the first step to the last. However, his way is already unclean by actual sin that he has already committed, and he already has within his nature a tendency towards that which defiles.

The difficulty, then, is to be sure to first of all begin in the right way. Next, one needs to always be able to know and choose what is right, and of continuing in the right way until spiritual maturity is ultimately reached. This is difficult for any man, so how will a youth accomplish it? The way, or life, of a man has to be cleansed from the sins of his youth that are behind him, and it must be kept clear of the sins that temptation will place before him. This is the work; this is the difficulty.

No nobler ambition can lie before a young man, none to which he is called by so sure a calling – but none in which greater difficulties can be found. Do not let him, however, be reluctant to pursue the glorious undertaking of living a pure and gracious life. Rather, let him inquire of the way by which all obstacles can be overcome. Do not let him think that he knows the road to easy victory. Let him not dream that he can keep himself by his own wisdom. Instead, he will do well to follow the psalmist and become an earnest inquirer asking how he may cleanse his way. Let him become a practical disciple of the holy God, who alone can teach him how to overcome the world, the flesh, and the devil – that trinity of defilers by which many hopeful lives have been spoiled. He is young and unaccustomed to the road, so let him not be ashamed to often ask his way of Him who is ready and able to instruct him in it.

> *You must study your Bible so you can pay careful attention to your daily life.*

Our *way* is a subject which deeply concerns us, and it is far better to inquire about it than to speculate upon mysterious themes that puzzle rather than enlighten the mind. Among all the questions which a young man asks, and they are many, let this be the first and most important: *With what shall a young man cleanse his way?* This is a question suggested by common sense and pressed home by daily events, but it is not to be answered by unaided reason. When the question is answered, the answer is not to be carried out by unsupported human power. It is our duty to ask the question, but it is God's task to give the answer and enable us to carry it out.

When he shall keep thy word. Young man, the Bible must be your map, and you must exercise great carefulness that your way may be according to its directions. You must pay careful attention to your daily life, as well as study your Bible. In fact, you must study your Bible so you can pay careful attention to your daily life.

Even with the greatest care, a man will go astray if his map misleads him, and even with the most accurate map, he will still lose his road if he doesn't follow it. The narrow way was never arrived at by chance, nor did any careless man ever lead a holy life. We can sin without thought and neglect the great salvation and ruin our souls, but to obey the Lord and walk uprightly will require all our heart, soul, and mind. Let the careless remember this.

Yet the *Word* is absolutely necessary, for otherwise care will darken into unhealthy concern, and conscientiousness may become superstition. A captain may watch from his deck all night, but if he knows nothing about the coast and has no pilot on board, he may be carefully rushing on to shipwreck. It isn't enough to desire to be right, because ignorance can make us think we are doing God a service when we are actually provoking Him, and the fact of our ignorance will not reverse the nature of our action, however much it may lessen its severity.

If someone carefully measures out what he believes to be a dose of beneficial medicine, he will die if it turns out that he has picked up the wrong bottle and has poured out a deadly poison. The fact that he did it ignorantly won't change the result. Even so, a young man may surround himself with ten thousand problems by carefully using foolish judgment and refusing to receive instruction from the Word of God. Willful ignorance is in itself willful sin, and the evil that comes of it is without excuse.

Let each person, whether young or old, who desires to be holy have a holy watchfulness in his heart and keep his Bible open and read. In the Bible he will find every turn of the road marked down, every bog and miry place pointed out, along with the way to go through unblemished. In the pages of the Bible, he will find light for his darkness, comfort for his weariness, and company for his loneliness, so that by its help he will reach the benediction of the first verse of Psalm 119, which suggested the psalmist's inquiry and awakened his desires.

Note how the first section of eight verses has for its first verse, *Blessed are those who walk in the perfect way*, and the second section runs parallel to it, with the question, *With what shall a young man cleanse his way?* The blessedness that is set before us in a conditional promise should be practically sought for in the way appointed. The Lord says, *I will yet be enquired of by the house of Israel, to do it for them* (Ezekiel 36:37).

The sooner we avail ourselves with a promise of God the better, especially as our early days enjoy special encouragement; for Wisdom has said, *Those that seek me early shall find me* (Proverbs 8:17). It is a pity to miss the blessedness of holiness for a year, or even for a day or an hour.

10. *With my whole heart I have sought thee; O let me not err from thy commandments.*

With my whole heart I have sought thee. His heart had gone after God Himself. He not only desired to obey His laws, but he also desired to commune with Him. This is a proper royal search and pursuit, and it may well be followed with the whole heart. The surest method of cleansing the way of our life is to seek after God Himself and to make every effort to abide in fellowship with Him. Up to the good hour in which he was speaking to his Lord, David had been eagerly seeking after the Lord, and even when weak, he was still pursuing. If he had not sought the Lord, he would never have been so anxious to cleanse his way.

It is pleasant to see how the writer's heart turns distinctly and directly to God. He had been considering an important truth in the preceding verse, but here he so powerfully feels the presence of his God that he speaks to Him and prays to Him as to one who is near. A faithful heart cannot live long without fellowship with God.

His prayer is based upon his life's purpose. He is seeking the Lord, and he prays to the Lord to prevent his going astray in or from his search. It is by obedience that we follow after God; thus the prayer, *O let me not err from thy commandments*. If we leave the ways of God's appointments, we certainly won't find the God who appointed them. The more a person's whole heart is set on holiness, the more he fears falling into sin. He is not so fearful of deliberate sin as he is of unintentionally wandering from the right way. He cannot endure a wandering look or a rambling thought that might stray outside the boundaries of the precept.

We are to be such wholehearted seekers that we have neither the time nor the will to wander, yet with all our wholeheartedness we are still to cultivate a jealous fear, so that even with a whole heart, we might not wander from the path of holiness.

Two things may be very similar and yet altogether different. Saints are "strangers" – *I am a stranger in the earth* (verse 19), but they are not wanderers. They are passing through an enemy's country, but their route is direct. They seek their Lord while they travel this foreign land. Their way is hidden from others, yet they haven't lost their way.

The man of God exerts himself, but he does not trust himself. His heart is in his walking with God, but he knows that even his whole strength is not enough to keep him right unless his King will be his keeper. He who made the commands will make him steady in obeying them, and this is why we have the prayer, *O let me not err*. Still, this sense of need was never turned into an argument for idleness, for while he prayed to be kept on the right road, he took care to run in it, with his whole heart seeking the Lord.

Note how the second part of the psalm keeps step with the

first. Whereas verse 2 pronounces that person to be blessed who seeks the Lord with his whole heart, verse 10 claims the blessing by pleading, *With my whole heart I have sought thee.*

11. *Thy spoken word have I hid in my heart that I might not sin against thee.*

When a godly man requests a favor from God, he should carefully use every means for obtaining it. Accordingly, as the psalmist had asked to be kept from wandering, here he shows us the holy precaution he took to keep from falling into sin. *Thy spoken word have I hid in my heart.* His heart would be kept by the Word because he kept the Word in his heart. All that he had of the written Word and all that had been revealed to him by the voice of God – all, without exception – he had stored away in his affections, like a treasure to be preserved in a strongbox, or like a first-rate seed to be buried in fruitful soil. What soil is more fruitful than a renewed heart wholly seeking the Lord?

> What soil is more fruitful than a renewed heart wholly seeking the Lord?

The Word was God's own, and therefore was precious to God's servant. He didn't wear the text on his heart like a charm, but he hid it in his heart as a command. He laid it up in the place of love and life, and it filled the chamber with sweetness and light. We must imitate David in this, copying his heart-work as well as his outward character. We must take care that what we believe is truly God's Word, and then we each must hide or treasure it for ourselves. We must see that this is done, not like a mere accomplishment of the memory, but as the joyful act of the affections.

That I might not sin against thee. This is the goal. As one has said well: "Here is the best thing – *thy word*; hidden in the best place – *in my heart*; for the best of purposes – *that I might not sin against thee.*" This was done by the psalmist David as carefully as a man hides away his money when he fears thieves. In this case, the dreaded thief was sin. Sinning against God is the believer's view of moral evil. Other people only care when they do wrong against their fellow men and women. God's Word is the best preventive against offending God, for it tells us His mind and will, and it tends to bring our spirit into conformity with the divine Spirit. No cure for sin in one's life is equal to the Word in the seat of life, which is the heart.

A very pleasant variety of meanings is obtained by stressing the words *thy* and *thee*. He speaks to *God*, he loves the Word because it is *God's* Word, and he hates sin because it is sin against *God* Himself. If he irritated others, he didn't mind as long as he didn't offend his God. If we do not want to displease God, we must treasure up His Word.

The personal way in which the man of God did this is also noteworthy: *With my whole heart I have sought thee*. Whatever others might choose to do, he had already made his choice. He had already placed the Word in his innermost soul as his dearest delight. No matter how others might sin, his aim was for holiness, *that I might not sin against thee*. This was not what he proposed to do, but it was what he had already done. Many people are great at promising, but the psalmist had been true in performing, and so he hoped to see a definite result. When the Word is hidden in the heart, the life will be hidden from sin.

The parallelism between the second octave and the first continues. Verse 3 speaks of doing no iniquity, while verse 11 deals with the method of not sinning. When we form an idea of a blessedly holy man (verse 3), then it is right to make a sincere effort to attain the same sacred innocence and divine happiness. This can only come through heart piety that is based on the Scriptures.

12. *Blessed art thou, O LORD: teach me thy statutes.*

Blessed art thou, O LORD. These words of adoration arise out of an intense admiration of the divine character, which the writer is humbly aiming to imitate. He blesses God for all that He has revealed to him and worked in him. He praises God with warmth of reverent love and depth of holy wonder. These are also words of appreciation written from contemplating the great Jehovah's infinite happiness within himself. The Lord is and must be blessed, for He is the perfection of holiness. This is probably the reason this is used as a plea at this point. It is as if David said, "I see that my way to happiness lies in my conformity to You, Lord, for You are supremely blessed. If I am conformed to You in holiness, then I will also partake of Your blessedness."

No sooner is the Word in the heart than a desire arises to discern and learn it. When food is eaten, the next thing is to digest it. When the Word is received into the soul, the first prayer is "Lord, teach me its meaning." *Teach me thy statutes,* because only in this manner can I learn the way to be blessed. You are so blessed that I am sure You will delight in blessing others, and I crave this benefit from You, that I may be instructed in Your commands."

Happy men usually rejoice to make others happy, and surely to the happy ones God will willingly impart the holiness that is the fountain of happiness. Faith prompted this prayer, and based it not on anything in the praying person, but solely on the perfection of the God to whom he made supplication: Lord, You are blessed; therefore, bless me by teaching me.

We need to be disciples or learners – *teach me* – but what an honor to have God Himself for a teacher! How bold David is to beg the blessed God to teach him! Yet the Lord put the desire into his heart when the sacred Word was hidden there, and so we can be sure that he wasn't too bold in expressing it. Who would not wish to enter the school of such a Master to learn from Him the art of holy living? We must submit ourselves to this Instructor if we want to practically keep the statutes of righteousness. The King who ordained the statutes knows their meaning best, and since they are the outcome of His own nature, He can best inspire us with their spirit. The petition presents itself to all who wish to cleanse their way, since it is very practical and asks for teaching, not on obscure legends, but upon statute law. If we know the Lord's statutes, we have the most essential education.

Let each of us say, *Teach me thy statutes*. This is a sweet prayer for every day. It is a step above that of verse 10, *O let me not err*, in the same way that verse 10 is a rise above that of verse 8, *O do not utterly forsake me*. It finds its answer in verses 98 to 100: *Thou through thy commandments hast made me wiser than mine enemies, for they are eternal unto me. I have more understanding than all my teachers, for thy testimonies have been my meditation. I understand more than the elders because I keep thy precepts.* This was the third time that we hear this message in this psalm, as it was given before in the *Teach me* of verses 33 and 66, all of which I hope you will examine. Even after this third time, the prayer occurs again in so many words in verses 124 and 139, and the same longing comes out near the close of the psalm in verse 171: *My lips shall overflow with praise when thou hast taught me thy statutes.*

13. With my lips I have declared all the judgments of thy mouth.

The one who is being taught in verse 12 is here in verse 13 a teacher himself. What we learn in secret we are to proclaim on the housetops. This is what the psalmist has done. As much as he had learned, he declared. God has revealed many of His judgments by His mouth; that is, by a plain and open revelation, and it is our duty to repeat them, becoming many echoes of His one infallible voice. There are judgments of God which are very deep, which He does not reveal, and it is not wise for us to interfere with these. What the Lord has veiled, it would be presumption for us to uncover; but on the other hand, what the Lord has revealed, it would be shameful for us to conceal. It is a great comfort to a Christian in times of trouble when he can look back on his life and can claim to have done his duty according to the Word of God.

> *It is a great comfort to a Christian in times of trouble when he can look back on his life and can claim to have done his duty according to the Word of God.*

To have been, like Noah, a preacher of righteousness, is a great joy when the floods are rising and the ungodly world is about to be destroyed. Lips that have been used in proclaiming God's statutes are sure to be acceptable when pleading God's promises. If we have had such high regard for the words that come out of God's mouth that we have proclaimed it far and wide, we can rest quite assured that God will have respect for the prayers that come out of our mouths.

It will be an effective approach of cleansing a young man's way if he devotes himself continually to preaching the gospel. One whose whole soul is occupied in setting forth the judgments of the Lord cannot go far wrong in judgment. By teaching, we learn. By training the tongue in holy speech, we master the whole body. By familiarity with the divine procedure, we are made to delight in righteousness. Even so, in a threefold manner, our way is cleansed by our proclaiming the way of the Lord.

What a joy for anyone to be able to look back on a faithful testimony to divine truth! When weary with Sunday services, how sweet to feel that we have not spoken our own words, but the teachings of divine revelation. When we come to die, it will be much consolation that we have kept the faith. Christ will surely plead for those whose lives are spent in pleading for Him.

14. *I have rejoiced in the way of thy testimonies as above all riches.*

Delight in the Word of God is a sure proof that it has taken effect on the heart, and so is cleansing the life. The psalmist not only says that he does rejoice, but also that he has rejoiced. For years, it was his joy and delight to give his soul to the teaching of the Word. His rejoicing not only arose out of the Word of God, but also out of its practical elements. The way was as dear to him as the Truth and the Life. There was no picking and choosing with David, or if he actually made a selection, he chose the most practical first.

Above all riches. He compared his intense satisfaction with God's will with that of a man who possesses large and varied estates and the heart to enjoy them. David knew the riches that come with power and authority and that grow out of conquest. He valued wealth obtained from hard work or acquired by inheritance. He knew *all riches*. The gracious king had been glad to see the gold and silver poured into his treasury so he could devote vast amounts of it to the building of the temple of Jehovah on Mount Zion. He rejoiced in all sorts of riches consecrated and laid up for the noblest uses, and yet the way of God's Word had given him more pleasure than even these. Observe that his joy was personal, distinct, remembered, and abundant. Do not wonder that in the previous verses he glories in having spoken much about the things he enjoyed so much, for a man may well talk about that which is his delight.

15. *I will meditate in thy precepts and consider thy ways.*

I will meditate in thy precepts. He who has an inward delight in anything will not stop thinking about it for very long. Just as the miser returns often to look on his treasure, so the devout believer, by frequent meditation, turns over the priceless wealth that he has discovered in the Book of the Lord. Meditation is a task to some people, but to the one of a cleansed way it is a joy. He who has meditated will meditate; he who says, "I have rejoiced" is the same person who adds, "I will meditate."

No spiritual exercise is more profitable to the soul than that of devout meditation, so why are many of us so exceedingly lazy in it? It is worthy of observation that the parts of God's Word dealing with precepts and commands were David's special subject of meditation. This was natural because the question was still on his mind as to how a young man should cleanse his way. Practical godliness is vital godliness.

And consider thy ways; that is to say, I will think much about them so I can know what Your ways are, and next, I will think much about them, in order to hold Your ways in great reverence and high esteem. I will see what Your ways are towards me, so I can be filled with reverence, gratitude, and love. Then I will observe those ways which You have advised for me – Your ways by which You want me to follow You. I will observe these ways carefully, so I can become obedient and prove myself to be a true servant of such a Master.

Note how the verses grow more inward as they proceed. From the speech of verse 13 we advanced to the revealed joy of verse 14, and now we come to the secret meditation of the happy spirit. The richest graces are those which dwell deepest.

16. *I will delight myself in thy statutes; I will not forget thy words.*

I will delight myself in thy statutes. Delight follows meditation in this verse, from which it is the true flower and outgrowth. When we have no other comfort but are quite alone, it will make the heart glad to turn upon itself and sweetly whisper, "I will delight myself. If I hear no one else sing, I will delight myself. If the time of the singing of birds has not yet arrived, and the voice of the turtledove is not heard in our land, yet I will delight myself" (see Song of Solomon 2:12).

This is the most excellent and noblest of all rejoicing. In fact, it is the good part which can never be taken from us (Luke 10:42), but there is no delighting ourselves with anything below that which God intended to be the soul's eternal satisfaction. The statute book is intended to be the joy of every loyal subject. Once the believer examines the sacred pages, his soul burns within him as he turns first to one and then to another of the royal words of the great King – words full and firm, unchanging and divine.

I will not forget thy words. People don't readily forget what they have treasured up (verse 14), what they have meditated on (verse 15), or what they have often spoken about (verse 13). Yet since we have unreliable memories, it is best to bind them well with the knotted cord of *I will not forget.*

Note how two "I wills" (verses 13 and 14) follow two "I haves." We may not dare to promise for the future if we have failed altogether in the past, but where grace has enabled us to accomplish something, we may hopefully expect that it will enable us to do more.

A repeated action becomes habit, and when habits are well formed we may without boasting resolve to maintain them, and even to use them to achieve other and higher habits. Yet it is good never to let our *I wills* of resolve exceed the *I haves* of our actual performance.

It is curious to note how this sixteenth verse is modeled upon verse 8. It is based on the same words, but the meaning is quite different, and there is no suspicion of a vain repetition. The same thought is never repeated in this psalm, and those who think so are not very wise. Something in the position of each verse affects its meaning, so even where the words are almost identical with those of another verse, the sense is delightfully varied. If we do not see an infinite variety of fine shades of thought in this psalm, we might conclude that we are color blind. If we do not hear many sweet harmonies, we can judge our ears to be dull of hearing, but we cannot suspect the Spirit of God of monotony.

Psalm 119:17-24

GIMEL

Deal bountifully with thy slave that I may live and keep thy word.

Open my eyes, and I shall behold the wonders of thy law.

I am a stranger in the earth; hide not thy commandments from me.

My soul is broken from desiring thy judgments at all times.

Thou hast reprehended the proud; cursed are those who err from thy commandments.

Remove from me reproach and contempt, for I have kept thy testimonies.

Princes also sat and spoke against me as thy slave spoke according to thy statutes.

For thy testimonies are my delight and my counsellors.

In this section, the trials of the way appear to be plain in the psalmist's mind, and he prays accordingly for the help that will meet his situation. Just as he prayed in the last eight verses as a youth newly come into the world, so here he pleads as a servant and a pilgrim who increasingly finds himself to be a stranger in an enemy's country. His appeal is to God alone, and his prayer is especially direct and personal. He speaks with the Lord like a man speaks with his friend.

17. Deal bountifully with thy slave that I may live and keep thy word.

Deal bountifully with thy slave. He takes pleasure in acknowledging his duty to God, and he considers it the joy of his heart to be in the service of his God. From his situation he makes a plea, for a servant has some sway with a master; but in this case, the wording of the plea shuts out the idea of any legal claim, since he seeks generosity rather than reward.

The psalmist is asking God to let his wage be according to God's goodness and not according to his own merit. Reward me according to the largeness of your generosity, and not according to the meagerness of my service. All the hired servants of our Father have enough bread and more to spare, and He will not let one of His household perish with hunger. If the Lord will only treat us as He treats the least of His servants, we can be well content, for all His true servants are sons, princes of the blood, and heirs of life eternal.

David felt that his great needs required a bountiful provision, and that the little that he deserved would never earn such a big supply. So, he had to throw himself upon God's grace and look for the great things he needed from the great goodness of the Lord. He begs for a liberality of grace, after the style of one who prayed, "O Lord, you must give me great mercy or no mercy, for little mercy will not serve my purpose."

That I may live. Without abundant mercy, David could not live. It takes great grace to keep a saint alive. Even life is a gift of divine abundance to such undeserving people as we are. Only the Lord can keep us alive, and it is mighty grace which preserves the life that we have forfeited by our sin. It is right to desire to live, it is proper to pray to live, and it is just to attribute prolonged life to God's favor. Spiritual life, without which this natural life is nothing more than existence, is also to be sought from the Lord's bounty, for it is the noblest work of divine grace, and through which the abundance of God is gloriously displayed. The Lord's servants cannot serve Him in their own strength, for they cannot even live unless His grace abounds towards them.

And keep thy word. This should be the standard, the goal, and the joy of our life. We may not want to live and sin, but we can pray to live and keep God's Word. Being is a poor thing if it is not well-being. Life is only worth keeping while we can keep God's Word. Indeed, there is no life in the highest sense apart from holiness, for life while we break the law is life in name only.

> *There is no life in the highest sense apart from holiness, for life while we break the law is life in name only.*

The prayer of this verse shows that it is only through divine bounty or grace that we can live as faithful servants of God and demonstrate obedience to His commands. If we serve God, it is because He gives us grace. We work *for* Him because He works *in* us. Accordingly, we can link together the opening verses of the three first octaves of this psalm. Verse 1 blesses the holy man, verse 9 asks how we can attain to such holiness, and verse 17 traces such holiness to its secret source and shows us how to seek the blessing. The more a person values holiness and the more earnestly he strives after it, the more he will be driven towards God for help in this, for he will plainly perceive that his own strength is insufficient, and he will realize that he cannot even so much as live without the generous assistance of the Lord his God.

18. *Open my eyes, and I shall behold the wonders of thy law.*

Open my eyes. This is a part of the bountiful dealing for which he asked. No bounty is greater than that which benefits our person, our soul, our mind, and such an important organ as the eye. It is far better to have the eyes opened than to be placed in the midst of the noblest prospects and remain blind to their beauty.

And I shall behold the wonders of thy law. Some people cannot perceive any wonders in the gospel, but David felt sure that there were glorious things in the law. He didn't have even half the Bible, but he treasured it more than some people cherish the whole thing. He felt that God had laid up great benefits and rewards in His Word, and he begs for power to perceive, appreciate, and enjoy them. We do not so much need God to give us more benefits, as we need the ability to see what He has already given.

The prayer implies a conscious darkness, a dimness of spiritual vision, a powerlessness to remove that defect, and a full assurance that God can remove it. It also shows that the writer knew there were vast treasures in the Word which he had not yet fully seen, marvels he had not yet beheld, and mysteries which he had scarcely believed. The Scriptures are full of marvelous things. The Bible is a land of wonder. It not only relates miracles, but is itself a world of wonders.

Yet what are these to closed eyes? And what person who is born blind can open his own eyes? God himself must reveal revelation to each heart. Scripture needs opening, but not half as much as our eyes do. The veil is not on the book, but on our hearts. What perfect precepts, what precious promises, what priceless privileges are neglected by us because we wander among them like blind men among the beauties of nature. They are to us as a landscape shrouded in darkness.

The psalmist had a portion of spiritual perception, or he would never have known there were wondrous things to be seen; nor would he have prayed, *Open my eyes*. What he had seen made him long for a clearer and wider sight. This longing proved the genuineness of what he possessed, for it is a test of the true knowledge of God that it causes its possessor to thirst for deeper knowledge.

David's prayer in this verse is a good sequel to verse 10, which corresponds to it in position in its octave. There he said, *O let me not err from thy commandments*, and who is so likely to err as a blind man? There, too, he also declared, *With my whole heart I have sought thee*, and this is the reason for his desire to see the One for whom he is searching. The way the branches of this huge tree of a psalm are interlaced are very remarkable and contain many wonders within itself, if our eyes are open to see them.

19. *I am a stranger in the earth; hide not thy commandments from me.*

I am a stranger in the earth. This is meant as a plea. By divine command, people are compelled to be kind to strangers, and what God commands for others, He will demonstrate in Himself. The psalmist was a stranger for God's sake; otherwise, he would have been as much at home as worldly people are. He was not a stranger to God, but was a stranger to the world. He was as an exiled man as long as he was out of heaven.

Therefore he pleads, *Hide not thy commandments from me.* If these are gone, what else do I have? Since nothing around me is mine, what can I do if I lose Your Word? Since no other people around me know or care to know the way to You, what will I do if I fail to see Your commands, by which alone I can guide my steps to the land where You dwell?

David implies that God's commands were his comfort in his exile. They reminded him of home and they showed him the way there, and so he begged that they might never be hidden from him, by his being unable to understand or obey them. If spiritual light is withdrawn, the command is hidden, and a gracious heart greatly dislikes this. Of what use are opened eyes if the best object of sight is hidden from view? While we wander here in this world, we can endure all the troubles of this foreign land with patience if the Word of God is applied to our hearts by the Spirit of God. However, if the heavenly things that grant us peace are hidden from our eyes, we will find ourselves in a troubling situation; in fact, we would be out to sea without a compass, in a desert without a guide, and in an enemy's country without a friend.

This prayer is a supplement to *Open my eyes*, and as verse 18 contains a prayer to see, verse 19 contains a prayer against not seeing – that God's commands would not be hidden from us. It is best for us to look at both sides of the blessing we are seeking and to plead for it from every point of view. The prayers are appropriate to the characters mentioned. Since he is a servant, he asks for opened eyes so that his eyes would always be toward his Lord, like the eyes of a servant should be. As a stranger, he begs that he will not be a stranger to the way in which he is to walk toward his home. In both cases, his entire dependence is upon God alone.

Note how the third verse of the second octave (verse 11) has the same keyword as this third verse of the third octave (verse 19): *Thy spoken word have I hid* and *hide not thy commandments from me*. This invites a meditation on the different meanings of hiding *in* and hiding *from*.

20. *My soul is broken from desiring thy judgments at all times.*

True godliness lies very much in desires. Just as we are not currently what we will be, so also we are not what we want to be. The desires of gracious people seeking after holiness are intense, and they can wear on the heart and strain the mind until it feels ready to snap with the heavenly pull. Placing a high value on the Lord's commandment leads to a pressing desire to know it and to do it, and this so weighs on the soul that it is ready to break in pieces under the pressure of its own longings. What a blessing it is when all our desires are after the things of God! We may rightly yearn for such longings.

> *God's judgments are His decisions upon points that would otherwise be in dispute.*

God's judgments are His decisions upon points that would otherwise be in dispute. Every precept is a judgment of the highest court on a point of action – an infallible and unchangeable decision on a moral or spiritual question. The Word of God is a code of justice from which there is no appeal.

> "This is the Judge which ends the strife
>   Where wit and reason fail;
> Our guide through devious paths of life,
>   Our shield when doubts assail."
>   – Isaac Watts

David had such reverence for the Word and such a desire to know it and to be conformed to it, that his longings caused him a sort of heartbreak, which he pleads here before God. Longing is the soul of praying, and when the soul longs until it breaks, it cannot be long before the blessing will be granted. The most intimate communion between the soul and its God is carried on by the process described in verse 20. God reveals His will, and our heart longs to be conformed to it. God judges, and our heart rejoices in the verdict. This is a most real and thorough fellowship of heart.

Notice carefully that our desire after the mind of God should be constant. We should feel holy longings *at all times*. Desires which can be put off and on like our garments are at best only mere wishes, and might not even be true enough to be called desires. Rather, they are temporary emotions born from excitement, doomed to die when the heat which created them has cooled down. The person who always longs to know and do what is right is the truly right man. His judgment is sound, for he loves all God's judgments and follows them faithfully. His times will be good since he longs to be good and to do good at all times.

Observe how this fourth verse of the third group of eight harmonizes with the fourth verse of the fourth eight. *My soul is broken* and *My soul melts* (verse 28). Surely there is some little-known poetic art about all this, and it is good for us to carefully study what the psalmist was so vigilant in composing.

21. *Thou hast reprehended the proud; cursed are those who err from thy commandments.*

Thou hast reprehended the proud. This is one of God's judgments. He is sure to deal out a terrible portion to those who are arrogant. God rebuked Pharaoh with severe plagues, and at the Red Sea *the foundations of the world were discovered at thy rebuke, O LORD* (Psalm 18:15). Through the arrogant Egyptian, God taught all the proud that He will certainly humble them.

Cursed are those who err from thy commandments. Proud people are cursed people. Nobody blesses them, and they soon become a burden to themselves. In itself, pride is a plague and a torment. Even if no curse came from the law of God, there seems to be a law of nature that proud people should be unhappy people. This led David to abhor pride. He dreaded the rebuke of God and the curse of the law. The proud sinners of his day were his enemies, and he felt happy that God was in the quarrel as well.

Only humble hearts are obedient, for they alone will yield to rule and government. The arrogant looks of the proud are too high to observe their own feet and to keep the Lord's way. Pride lies at the root of all sin. If people were not arrogant, they would not be disobedient.

God rebukes pride, even when many people applaud it, for He sees it as rebellion against His own majesty and as the seeds of still further rebellion. It is the sum of sin. People talk about an honest pride, but if they were candid, they would see that it is the least honest of all sins and the least attractive sin in a person – especially in a fallen person. Still, proud people know so little regarding their own true condition under the curse of God that they set out to condemn the godly and express contempt for them, as can be seen in the next verse. While they are themselves contemptible, they are scornful toward those who are better than they are.

If people were not arrogant, they would not be disobedient.

We may well love the judgments of God when we see them so decisively leveled against the arrogant people who would gladly lord it over righteous people, and we may well take comfort in the rebukes of the ungodly, since their power to hurt us is destroyed by the Lord Himself. "The Lord rebuke thee" is answer enough for all the accusations of people or devils (Jude 9).

In the fifth verse of the former octave, the psalmist wrote, *With my lips I have declared all the judgments of thy mouth* (verse 13), and here he continues in the same manner, giving a particular instance of the Lord's judgments against arrogant rebels. In the next two portions, the fifth verses deal with lying and vanity, and pride is one of the most common forms of those evils.

22. *Remove from me reproach and contempt, for I have kept thy testimonies.*

Remove from me reproach and contempt. These are painful things to tender minds. David could bear them for righteousness' sake, but they were a heavy yoke from which he longed to be free. To be slandered and then despised as a result of a vile accusation is an awful affliction. No one likes to be misrepresented or despised. He who says, "I don't care about my reputation" isn't a wise man, for in Solomon's view *a good name is better than precious ointment* (Ecclesiastes 7:1).

The best way to deal with slander is to pray about it. God will either remove the slander or remove its sting. Our own attempts at clearing ourselves usually result in failure. We are like the boy who wanted to remove the blot from his picture, but by his clumsy attempts made it ten times worse. When someone lies about us, it is better to pray about it than to take them to court or even to confront them and demand an apology. You who are reproached, take your matters before the highest court and leave them with the Judge of all the earth. God will rebuke your proud accuser. You be quiet and let your Advocate plead your cause.

For I have kept thy testimonies. Innocence may justly ask to be cleared from reproach. If there is truth in the charges alleged against us, what can we plead with God? If, however, we are wrongfully accused, our appeal has a right to be heard in the court and cannot be refused. If through fear of reproach we forsake the divine testimony, we will deserve the coward's doom. Our safety lies in sticking close to what is true and right. God will keep those who keep His testimonies. A good conscience is the best security for a good name. Reproach will not abide with those who abide with Christ, and neither will contempt remain upon those who remain faithful to the ways of the Lord.

This verse stands as a parallel both in sense and position to verse 6, and it has the catchword of *testimonies*, by which it corresponds with verse 14.

> *Our safety lies in sticking close to what is true and right.*

23. *Princes also sat and spoke against me as thy slave spoke according to thy statutes.*

Princes also sat and spoke against me. David was a big target, and the great ones of the earth went hunting after him. Princes saw in him a greatness that they envied, and so they mistreated him. On their thrones, they might have found something better to consider and speak about, but they turned the seat of judgment into the seat of the scorner (Psalm 1:1).

Most people covet a prince's good word about them, and so to be spoken of unfavorably by a great man is a great discouragement to them. However, the psalmist bore his trial with holy calmness. Many of the lordly ones were his enemies, and they made it their business to speak unfavorably about him. They held sessions for scandal and slander and parliaments of falsehood, yet he survived all their attempts upon him.

Thy slave spoke according to thy statutes. This was brave indeed. David was God's servant, and so he attended to his Master's business. He was God's servant, and therefore felt sure the Lord would defend him. He paid no attention to his princely slanderers. He did not even allow his thoughts to be disturbed by the knowledge of their secret plotting. Who were these malicious people that they would rob God of His servant's attention or deprive the Lord's chosen of a moment's communion? The pack of princes was not worth five minutes' thought if those five minutes had to be taken from holy meditation. It is very beautiful to see the two sittings: the princes sitting together to reproach David, and David sitting with his God and his Bible, answering his slanderers by never answering them at all. Those who feed upon the Word grow strong and peaceful and are by God's grace hidden from the strife of tongues.

Note that in the close of the former octave David had said, *I will meditate* (verse 15), and here he shows how he redeemed his promise – even under great incitement to forget it. It is a praiseworthy thing when we fittingly carry out in our seasons of difficulty what we had resolved in our happy times.

24. *For thy testimonies are my delight and my counsellors.*

God's testimonies were not just topics for meditation; they were also sources of delight and means of guidance. While his enemies took counsel with each other, the holy man took counsel with the testimonies of God. The fowlers could not drive the bird from its nest with all their noise. It was *their* delight to slander and *his* delight to meditate.

The words of the Lord serve us for many purposes. In our sorrows, they are our delight. In our difficulties, they are our guide. We derive joy from them and discover wisdom in them. If we desire to find comfort in the Scriptures, we must submit ourselves to their counsel; when we follow their counsel, it must not be with reluctance, but with delight. This is the safest way of dealing with those who plot for our ruin. Let us give more attention to the true testimonies of the Lord than to the false witness of our enemies. The best answer to give to accusing princes is the word of the justifying King.

In verse 16 David said, *I will delight myself in thy statutes*, and here he says, they *are my delight*. Resolutions formed in God's strength come to fruition, and spiritual desires ripen into actual achievements. Oh, that it might be so with all who read these lines!

Psalm 119:25-32

DALETH

My soul cleaves unto the dust; quicken me according to thy word.

I have declared my ways, and thou didst hear me; teach me thy statutes.

Make me to understand the way of thy precepts; so I shall meditate of thy wondrous works.

My soul melts for heaviness; strengthen me according to thy word.

Remove from me the way of lying, and from thy law grant me mercy.

I have chosen the way of truth; I have laid thy judgments before me.

I have stuck unto thy testimonies; O LORD, put me not to shame.

I will run the way of thy commandments when thou shalt enlarge my heart.

It seems to me that here we have the psalmist in trouble, lamenting the bondage to earthly things in which he finds his mind to be held. His soul cleaves to the dust, melts for heaviness, and cries to be released from its spiritual prison.

In these verses, we will see the influence of the divine Word on a heart which laments its downward tendencies and is filled with mourning because of its deadening surroundings. The Word of the Lord evidently arouses prayer (verses 25-29), confirms choice (verse 30), and inspires renewed resolve (verse 32). It is the surest source of help in all troubles, whether of body or mind.

This portion has *D* for its alphabetical letter. It sings of depression, in the spirit of devotion, determination, and dependence.

25. *My soul cleaves unto the dust; quicken me according to thy word.*

My soul cleaves unto the dust. In part, he means he was full of sorrow, for mourners in the east threw dust on their heads and sat in ashes, and the psalmist felt as if these symbols of woe were glued to him, and his very soul was made to cleave to them because of his powerlessness to rise above his grief. Does he not also mean that he felt ready to die? Did he not feel his life absorbed and held fast by the grave's mold, half choked by the dust of death? It isn't straining the language if we imagine that he also felt and lamented his earthly-mindedness and spiritual deadness. There was a tendency in his soul to cling to earth, which he greatly lamented.

Whatever the cause of his complaint, it wasn't just a surface evil, but was a matter of his inmost spirit. His soul cleaved to the dust, and it was not a casual accidental falling into the dust, but a continuous and powerful tendency, or cleaving, to the earth. What mercy that the good man could feel and deplore whatever there was of evil in the cleaving!

The serpent's seed can find their food in the dust, but the seed of the woman will never be degraded in this manner. Many people are *of the earth, earthy* (1 Corinthians 15:47), and never lament it. Only the heaven-born and heaven-soaring spirit grieves at the thought of being fastened to this world and trapped by its sorrows or its pleasures.

Quicken me according to thy word. The cure for all our ailments is more life, and only the Lord can give it. He can impart it at once, and He can do it according to His Word without departing from the usual course of His grace, as we see it mapped out in the Scriptures. It is good to know what to pray for. David seeks to be quickened, or made alive.[7] One would have thought he would have asked for comfort or lifting up, but he knew that these would come out of increased life, and therefore he sought that blessing that is the root of the rest.

> *The cure for all our ailments is more life, and only the Lord can give it.*

When a person is depressed in spirit, weak, and with his head bent down, the main thing is to increase his stamina and put more life into him; then his spirit revives and his body stands straight. When life is revived, the whole person is renewed. Shaking off the dust is a little thing by itself, but when it follows after quickening, it is a blessing of the greatest value, just as a good frame of mind flows from established health; it is among the most excellent of our mercies.

The phrase *according to thy word* means according to Your revealed way of giving life to Your saints. The Word of God shows us that He who first made us must keep us alive, and it tells us about the Spirit of God, who through the ordinances pours fresh life into our souls. We ask the Lord to act towards us in this, His own regular method of grace.

Perhaps David remembered the Word of the Lord in Deuteronomy 32:39, where Jehovah claims both to kill and to make alive, and he begs the Lord to exercise that life-giving power on His servant who is at death's door. Certainly, the

---

7   The word "quicken" (or quickening, quickened, etc.) is used much in this book, and refers to make alive or revive, to make one's life even more alive.

man of God did not have as many rich promises to rest upon as we have, but even a single word was enough for him, and he rightly sincerely urges *according to thy word*. It is a wonderful thing to see a believer in the dust and yet pleading the promise – a man at the grave's mouth crying, "Quicken me," and hoping it will be done.

Notice how this first verse of the fourth octanary corresponds with the first of the third (verse 17) – *That I may live* and *Quicken me*. While in a happy state, he begs to be dealt with bountifully, and when in a hopeless condition, he prays for quickening. In both cases, life is the object of pursuit – that he *might have life and that they might have it in abundance* (John 10:10).

Truly, this is wisdom. Fools hunger for food and yet lose life, but the wise know that life is more than food. It is a common sin of unbelievers to yearn for riches and neglect the soul, while the prudent course of the believer is to seek true riches in an increase of life. Life – eternal life – is true treasure. Our Lord has come not only that we may have life, but that we may have it more abundantly. Lord, pour Your life-floods into us forevermore, that we may be made alive to the fullness of our strength and filled with all the fullness of God.

> 26. *I have declared my ways, and thou didst hear me; teach me thy statutes.*

I have declared my ways. Open confession is good for the soul. Nothing brings more ease and more life to someone than a direct acknowledgment of the evil that has caused the sorrow and weariness. Such a declaration proves that the person knows his own condition and is no longer blinded by pride. Our confessions aren't meant to make God know our sins, but to make us know them.

And thou didst hear me. His confession had been accepted.

It was not wasted effort. God had drawn near to him in it. Pardon follows penitent confession, and David felt that he had obtained it. It is God's way to forgive our sinful way when we confess the wrong from our hearts.

Teach me thy statutes. Being truly sorry for his wrong and having obtained full forgiveness, he is anxious to avoid offending again and so he begs to be taught obedience. He was not willing to sin through ignorance, so he wished to know all the mind of God by being taught it by the best of teachers.

He longed for holiness. Justified people always long to be sanctified. When God forgives our sins, we are all the more fearful of sinning again. Mercy, which pardons our offense, causes us to long for grace, which prevents wrongdoing. We can boldly ask for more when God has given us much. He who has washed away the past stain will not refuse that which will preserve us from present and future defilement. This cry for teaching is frequent in Psalm 119. In verse 12, it follows a sight of God; here it follows a sight of self. Every experience should lead us to plead with God in this way.

27. *Make me to understand the way of thy precepts; so I shall meditate of thy wondrous works.*

Make me to understand the way of thy precepts. Give me deep insight into the practical meaning of Your Word. Let me get a clear idea of the tone and tenor of Your law. Blind obedience only has small beauty; God would rather have us follow Him with our eyes open.

To obey the letter of the Word is all that the ignorant can hope for. If we wish to keep the spirit of God's precepts, we must come to understand them, and that can be gained nowhere but at the Lord's hands. Our understanding needs enlightenment and direction. He who made our understanding must also make us understand.

The last part of the previous verse was *teach me thy statutes*, and the words *make me to understand* are an instructive expansion and explanation of that sentence. We need to be taught so that we understand what we learn. It is to be noted that the psalmist isn't anxious to understand the prophecies, but the precepts, and he isn't concerned about the subtleties of the law, but the commonplace everyday rules of it, which are described as *the way of thy precepts*.

So I shall meditate of thy wondrous works. It is not good to talk about what we don't understand. We must be taught by God until we understand, and then we can hope to communicate our knowledge to others with a hope of benefitting them. Talk without intelligence is mere talk – idle talk – but the words of the instructed are like pearls which adorn the ears of those who hear. When our heart has been opened to understand, our lips should be opened to share that knowledge. We may hope that we have been taught ourselves when we feel a willingness in our hearts to teach the way of the Lord to those among whom we live.

Thy wondrous works. Notice that the clearest understanding does not cause us to stop from wondering at the ways and works of God. The fact is, the more we know about God's doings, the more we admire them, and the more ready we are to speak about them. Half the wonder in the world is born of ignorance, but holy wonder is the child of understanding. When a person understands the way of the divine precepts, he never talks about his own works. As the tongue must have some topic about which to speak, he begins to extol the works of the all-perfect Lord.

In this verse, the word *meditate* is very near to the word *talk*. It is extraordinary that the words are so closely related, and yet it is right that they should be, because only foolish people talk without thinking. If we read the passage in this sense, we take it to mean that in proportion as David understood the Word of God, he would meditate on it more and more. It usually works like this. The thoughtless do not care to know the deep meaning of the Scriptures, while those who know them best are the very people who strive to know them even better, and so they give themselves up to meditating upon them.

Notice the third verse of the last group of eight (verse 19) and see how the sense is similar to this. In that verse he described himself as *a stranger in the earth*, and here he prays to *understand the way*. There he prayed that the Word might not be hidden from him, and here he promises that he will not hide it from others.

28. *My soul melts for heaviness; strengthen me according to thy word.*

My soul melts for heaviness. He was dissolving away in tears. The solid strength of his constitution was turning to liquid, as if melted by the extreme heat of his afflictions. Heaviness of soul kills, and when it abounds, it threatens to turn life into a long death in which a person seems to drop away in a perpetual drip of grief. Tears are the distillation of the heart. When a person weeps, he wastes away his soul. Some of us know what great heaviness means, for we have been brought under its power again and again. We have often felt as if we were being poured out like water, close to being like water spilled on the ground, never to be gathered up again. There is one good point regarding this downcast state, for it is better to be melted with grief than to be hardened by lack of repentance.

Strengthen me according to thy word. He had found an ancient promise that the saints will be strengthened, and here he pleads it. In his state of depression, his hope does not lie in himself, but in his God. If he can be strengthened from on high, he will yet shake off his heaviness and rise to joy again. See how he pleads the promise of the Word, asking for nothing more than to be dealt with according to the manner written in the Scriptures of the Lord of mercy. Did not Hannah sing, *He shall give strength unto his king and exalt the horn of his anointed* (1 Samuel 2:10)?

God strengthens us by infusing grace through His Word. The Word that creates can certainly sustain. Grace can enable us to bear the constant fret of an abiding sorrow. It can repair the decay caused by the perpetual dripping of tears, and it can give *the garment of praise for the spirit of heaviness* (Isaiah 61:3).

Let us always resort to prayer in our despairing times, for it is the surest and shortest way out of the depths. In that prayer, let us plead nothing but the Word of God, for there is no plea like a promise, and no argument like a word from our covenant God.

Note how David records his inner soul-life. In verse 20 he says, *My soul is broken.* In verse 25 he says, *My soul cleaves unto the dust.* Here he says, *My soul melts.* Further on, in verse 81, he cries, *My soul faints*; in verse 109, *My soul is continually in my hand*; in verse 167, *My soul has kept thy testimonies*; and lastly, in verse 175, *Let my soul live.* Some people don't even know that they have a soul, and here is David all soul. What a difference there is between the spiritually living and the spiritually dead!

29. *Remove from me the way of lying, and from thy law grant me mercy.*

Remove from me the way of lying. This is the way of sin, error, idolatry, foolishness, self-righteousness, formalism, and hypocrisy. David did not just want to be kept from that way, but he wanted that way to be kept from him. He cannot bear to have it near him; he wants it swept away from his sight. He desired to be right and upright, true and in the truth, but he feared that a measure of falsehood would cling to him unless the Lord took it away. Therefore, he earnestly cried for its removal.

At times, false motives may sway us, and we may fall into mistaken ideas and views of our own spiritual condition before God. Such erroneous concepts can go on due to a natural bias in our own favor, and so we can be confirmed in a delusion and live under error unless grace comes to the rescue. No true heart can rest in a false view of itself. It finds no anchorage, but is tossed to and fro until it gets into the truth and the truth gets into it. The trueborn child of heaven sighs and cries out against a lie, desiring to have it taken away as much as one desires to be set at a distance from a venomous serpent or a raging lion.

And from thy law grant me mercy. The one who looks on the law itself as a gift of grace is in a gracious state. David wants to have the law opened up to his understanding, engraved on his heart, and carried out in his life. For this, he seeks the Lord and pleads for it as a gracious grant. No doubt he viewed this as the only way of deliverance from the power of falsehood. If the law is not in our hearts, the lie will enter in. David seems to have remembered those times when, according to the ways of the East, he had practiced deceit for his own preservation, and he saw that he had been weak and erring on that point. Therefore, he was bowed down in spirit and begged to be quickened and delivered from sinning in that way anymore. Holy men and women cannot review their sins without tears, nor weep over them without begging to be saved from offending further.

There is evident opposition between falsehood and the

gracious power of God's law. The only way to expel the lie is to accept the truth. Grace also has a clear liking for truth. No sooner do we meet with the sound of the word "graciously" than we hear the footsteps of truth: *I have chosen the way of truth* (verse 30). Grace and truth are forever linked together, and a belief in the doctrines of grace is a grand preservative from deadly error.

In the fifth verse of the preceding octave (verse 21) David cries out against pride, and here he cries out against lying. These are much the same thing. Is not pride the greatest of all lies?

30. *I have chosen the way of truth; I have laid thy judgments before me.*

I have chosen the way of truth. Since he abhorred the way of lying, David chose the way of truth. A person must choose one or the other, for there cannot be any neutrality in this matter. People do not drop into the right way by chance. They must choose it, and continue to choose it, or they will soon wander from it. In due time, those whom God has chosen choose His way.

There is a doctrinal way of truth which we ought to choose. It rejects every dogma devised by man. There is a ceremonial way of truth that we should follow. It detests all the forms that apostate churches have invented. Then there is a practical way of truth, the way of holiness, to which we must adhere, no matter what our temptation may be to forsake it.

Let our election be made and be made irrevocably. Let us answer all who try to entice others to leave the path of righteousness: "I have chosen, and what I have chosen I have chosen." O Lord, by Your grace, lead us with an enthusiastic free will to choose to do Your will; then Your eternal choice of us will bring forth the end that it designs.

I have laid thy judgments before me. What he had chosen he kept in mind, laying it out before his mind's eye. People do not become holy by wishful thinking. There must be study, consideration, deliberation, and sincere inquiry, or the way of truth will be missed. The commands of God must be set before us like the target to aim at, the model to work by, and the road to walk in. If we put God's judgments into the background, we will soon find ourselves going back from them.

> *The commands of God must be set before us like the target to aim at.*

Here again the sixth verses of the third and fourth octaves ring out a similar note. *I have kept thy testimonies* (verse 22), and *I have laid thy judgments before me* (verse 30). This is a cheerful confession, and it is no wonder it is repeated.

> 31. *I have stuck unto thy testimonies; O LORD, put me not to shame.*

I have stuck unto thy testimonies, or, "I have cleaved," because the word is the same as in verse 25. Though he cleaved to the dust of sorrow and death, he still held fast to the divine Word. This was his comfort, and his faith stuck to it. His love and obedience held on to it, and his heart and mind stayed in meditation upon it. His choice was so genuinely and deliberately made that he stuck to it for life and could not be moved from it by the reproaches of those who despised the way of the Lord.

What could he have gained by quitting the sacred testimony? Rather, what would he not have lost if he had ceased to cleave to the divine Word? It is pleasant to look back on past perseverance and to expect grace to continue equally steadfast in the future. He who has enabled us to stick to Him will surely stick to us.

In these days, when so many boast about their "progressive thinking," it may sound unusual to speak about sticking to God's testimonies; but whether unusual or not, let us imitate the man of God. Perseverance in the truth when it is unfashionable is the test of a real believer. The faith of God's elect wears faithfulness as its crown. Others may live it up pursuing the amusement of human opinion, but the trueborn child of God glories in saying to his heavenly Father, *I have stuck unto thy testimonies.*

O LORD, put me not to shame. This would happen if God's promises were unfulfilled and if the heart of God's servant were allowed to fail. We have no reason to fear this since the Lord is faithful to His Word. This might also happen through the believer's inconsistent actions, like David himself once did when he fell into the way of lying and pretended to be a madman. If we are not true to our profession of faith, we may be left to reap the fruit of our foolishness – the bitter fruit called *shame*. It is evident from this that a believer should never be ashamed, but should act bravely, like a person who has nothing to be ashamed of by believing his God. He does not need to take on a cowardly tone in the presence of the Lord's enemies. If we ask the Lord not to put us to shame, then surely we should not be ashamed on our own in the presence of the adversary.

The prayer of this verse is found in the parallel verse of the next section (verse 39): *Turn away my reproach which I have feared.* It is evidently a petition that was often on the psalmist's heart. A brave heart is more wounded by shame than by any weapon a soldier's hand can wield.

32. *I will run the way of thy commandments when thou shalt enlarge my heart.*

I will run the way of thy commandments. With energy, quickness of action, and zeal, David could perform the will of God, but he needed more life and liberty from the hand of God.

When thou shalt enlarge my heart. Yes, the heart is the master;

the feet run quickly when the heart is free and energetic. Let the passions be aroused and eagerly set on divine things, and our actions will be full of vigor, swiftness, and delight. God must work in us first, and then we will desire and act according to His good pleasure. He must change the heart, unite the heart, encourage the heart, strengthen the heart, and enlarge the heart, and then the course of life will be gracious, sincere, happy, and earnest, so that from our lowest to our highest state in grace, we must attribute all to the free favor of our God. We must run, for grace is not an overwhelming force that compels unwilling minds to move contrary to their will. Our running is the spontaneous leaping forward of a mind that has been set free by the hand of God and delights to show its freedom by its bounding speed.

What a change from verse 25 to this present verse – from cleaving to the dust to running in the way! It is the excellence of holy sorrow that it works in us the quickening for which we seek, and then we show the sincerity of our grief and the reality of our revival by being zealous in the ways of the Lord.

For the third time, an octave closes with *I will.* These "I wills" of the Psalms are truly worthy of each one being the subject of study and discussion.

Notice how the heart has been spoken of up to this point: *whole heart* (verse 2), *uprightness of heart* (verse 7), *hid in my heart* (verse 11), and *enlarge my heart* (verse 32). Many more allusions are found further on, and they all show the heartwork of David's faith. It is one of the great deficiencies of our age that heads count for more than hearts, and people are far readier to learn than to love, though they are by no means eager to move in either direction.

Psalm 119:33-40

HE

Teach me, O LORD, the way of thy statutes, and I shall keep it unto the end.

Give me understanding, and I shall keep thy law; yea, I shall observe it with my whole heart.

Make me to go in the path of thy commandments, for therein do I delight.

Incline my heart unto thy testimonies and not to covetousness.

Turn away my eyes from beholding vanity, and cause me to live in thy way.

Confirm thy word unto thy slave, who is devoted to thy fear.

Turn away my reproach which I have feared, for thy judgments are good.

Behold, I have longed after thy precepts; cause me to live in thy righteousness.

A sense of dependence and a consciousness of extreme need permeate this section, which is made up of prayers and pleas. The former eight verses trembled with a sense of sin, quivering with a childlike sense of weakness and foolishness.

This caused the man of God to cry out for the only help by which his soul could be kept from falling back into sin. That cry for help is expressed in this octave in requests for teaching, upholding, favoring, establishing, and quickening.

This section is a honeycomb of prayers. Let us lift up similar petitions while we read, and we can be assured that prayers taught to us by the Lord in this way will be answered by Him.

33. *Teach me, O LORD, the way of thy statutes, and I shall keep it unto the end.*

Teach me, O LORD, the way of thy statutes. These childlike, blessed words are from the lips of an old, experienced believer, who is also a king and a man inspired by God. We can be sad for those who will never be taught. They adore their own wisdom, but their foolishness is apparent to all who rightly judge. The psalmist desires to have the Lord for his teacher, for he feels that his heart will not learn from any less effective instructor.

A sense of great slowness to learn drives us to seek a great teacher. What condescension it is on our great Jehovah's part that He comes down to teach those who seek Him! The lesson desired is thoroughly practical. The holy man did not just want to learn the statutes, but also the way of them, the daily use of them, their meaning, spirit, direction, habit, and objective. He wanted to know that path of holiness that is enclosed by divine law, along which the commands of the Lord stand as signposts of direction and milestones of information, guiding and marking our progress. The very desire to learn this way is in itself an assurance that we will be taught in it, because He who made us desire to learn will be sure to satisfy the desire.

And I shall keep it unto the end. Those who are taught by God never forget their lessons. When divine grace sets someone in the true way, he will be true to it. Mere human intellect and will have no such enduring influence. All perfection of the flesh comes to an end, but there is no end to heavenly grace except its own end, which is the perfecting of holiness in the fear of the Lord (2 Corinthians 7:1).

Perseverance to the end is most certainly to be predicted for those whose beginning is in God and with God and by God; but those who start without the Lord's teaching soon forget what they learn and start departing from the way upon which they professed to have entered. No one can boast that he will hold to his way in his own strength, for that must depend on the continual teaching of the Lord. We will fall like Peter if we presume to depend on our own strength like he did.

If God keeps us, we will keep His way, and it is a great comfort to know that it is God's way to keep the feet of His saints in the right way. Yet we are to watch as if our keeping of the way depended wholly on ourselves, because according to this verse, our perseverance does not rest on any force or compulsion, but on the teaching of the Lord. Certainly teaching, whoever the teacher is, requires learning on the part of the one taught. No one can teach a person who refuses to learn. Earnestly then, let us drink in divine instruction so we can hold fast our integrity and follow the path of uprightness to life's last hour. If we receive the living and incorruptible seed of the Word of God, we must live. Apart from this, we have no life eternal, but only a name to live.

> *Perseverance to the end is most certainly to be predicted for those whose beginning is in God and with God and by God.*

The *end* of which David speaks is the end of life, or the fullness of obedience. He trusted in grace to make him faithful to the utmost, never drawing a line and saying to obedience, "To here you may come, but no farther." The end of our keeping the law will come only when we stop breathing. No good person will think of marking a date on the calendar and saying, "It is enough. I can now relax my watchfulness and live like the rest of the world." As Christ loves us to the end, so we must serve Him to the end. The purpose of divine teaching is that we can persevere to the end.

The segments of eight continue to show a relationship. The *Gimel* section begins with prayer for life, that he may keep the Word (verse 17). The *Daleth* portion cries for more life, according to that Word (verse 25); and now the *He* octave opens with a prayer for teaching, that the man of God can keep the way of God's statutes. If a sharp eye takes a more careful look at these verses, a closer relationship will be discerned.

34. *Give me understanding, and I shall keep thy law;*
yea, I shall observe it with my whole heart.

Give me understanding, and I shall keep thy law. This is the same prayer expanded, or rather it is a supplement which intensifies it. He not only needs teaching, but he also needs the power to learn. He not only needs to understand, but he also needs to obtain *an understanding.* How low sin has brought us, for we even lack the ability to understand spiritual things, and we are quite unable to know them until we are provided with spiritual discernment.

Will God in fact give us understanding? Yes, this is a miracle of grace. It will, however, never be worked upon us until we know of our need for it, and we will not even discover that need until God gives us a measure of understanding to perceive it. We are in a state of complicated ruin, from which nothing but grace can deliver us. Those who feel their foolishness are encouraged by the psalmist's example to pray for understanding. Let each person by faith cry, *Give me understanding.* Others have obtained it, so why can it not come to me? It was a gift to them; will not the Lord also freely bestow it upon me?

We are not to seek this blessing so we can become famous for our wisdom, but that we can be abundant in our love for the law of God. He who has understanding will learn, remember, treasure up, and obey the commandment of the Lord. The gospel gives us grace to keep the law. The free gift leads us to holy service. There is no way of achieving holiness except by accepting the gift of God.

If God gives, we keep; but we never keep the law in order to obtain grace. The sure result of regeneration, or the giving of understanding, is a devout reverence for the law and a determined keeping of it in the heart. The Spirit of God makes us to know the Lord and to understand somewhat of His love, wisdom, holiness, and majesty. The result is that we honor the law and surrender our hearts to the obedience of the faith.

Matthew Henry wisely notes that "an enlightened understanding is that which we are indebted to Christ for; for *the Son of God is come and has given us understanding*" (1 John 5:20). Any writer can give us something to understand, but only the Lord Jesus can give understanding itself to us.

I shall observe it with my whole heart. Understanding operates on the affections. It convinces the heart of the beauty of the law so that the soul loves it with all its powers. Then it reveals the majesty of the lawgiver, and the whole nature bows before His supreme will. An enlightened judgment heals the divisions of the heart and bends the united affections to a strict and watchful observance of the one rule of life. He who can say, "My Lord, I want to serve You with all my heart," obeys God, and no one can truly say this until they have received the inward enlightenment of the Holy Spirit as a free gift. To observe God's law with all our heart at all times is a great grace, and few find it. Yet if we consent to be taught of the Lord, it can be obtained.

Look back and examine the parallels to this verse in verses 2 and 10, where the *whole heart* is spoken of in reference to seeking, and then look forward to the similar parallel in verse 58 in pleading for mercy. These are all second verses in their sections of eight. The frequent repetition of the phrase *whole heart* shows the importance of undivided love. The heart is never whole or holy until it is whole and wholly united in the fear of the Lord. The heart is never one with God until it is one with itself, and it is never one with itself until it is at one with God.

> 35. *Make me to go in the path of thy commandments,*
> *for therein do I delight.*

For I have the desire, but I am not able to perform that which is good (Romans 7:18). You have made me to love the way; now make me to walk in it. It is a clear path that others are treading through Your grace. I see it and admire it; cause me to travel in it.

This is the cry of a child who longs to walk, but is too feeble; of a pilgrim who is exhausted, yet longs to be on the march; of a lame man who longs to be able to run. It is a blessed thing to delight in holiness, and surely He who gave us this delight will work in us the still higher joy of possessing and practicing it. This is our only hope, for we will not go in the narrow path until we are made to do so by the Maker's own power. Oh, You who once made me, I pray for You to make me again. You have made me to know; now make me to go! Certainly I will never be happy until I do, for my sole delight lies in walking according to Your will.

The psalmist does not ask the Lord to do for him what he ought to do for himself. He wishes to go or walk in the path of the command. He doesn't ask to be carried while he lies around, but he asks to be made *to go*. Grace doesn't treat us as sticks and stones to be dragged by horses or engines, but as creatures endowed with life, reason, will, and active powers, who are willing and able to go of themselves if once made to do so. God works in us, but it is so we can both desire and act according to His good pleasure.

The holiness we seek after is not a forced compliance to God's commands, but it is the pleasure of a wholehearted passion for goodness, such as that which will conform our life to the will of the Lord. Can the reader say, *for therein do I delight*? Is practical godliness the very jewel of your soul, the coveted prize of your mind? If so, the outward path of life, however rough, will be clean and will lead the soul upward to delight indescribable. He who delights in the law should not doubt that he will be enabled to run in its ways, for the feet are sure to follow where the heart already finds its joy.

> *Is practical godliness the very jewel of your soul, the coveted prize of your mind?*

Note that the corresponding verse in the former eight verses was, *Make me to understand* (verse 27), and here in verse 35 we have, *Make me to go*. Notice the order: first understanding and then going, because a clear understanding greatly assists in bringing about practical action.

During the last few octaves, the fourth verses have addressed *my soul* or *my heart*. See verses 20, 28, and now 36. In all the preceding fourths, great wholeheartedness is evident. This also indicates the care with which this sacred song was composed.

36. *Incline my heart unto thy testimonies and not to covetousness.*

Incline my heart unto thy testimonies. Doesn't this prayer seem to be unnecessary, since it is evident that the psalmist's heart was set on obedience? We are sure there is never an excess word in Scripture. After asking for active virtue, it was fitting that the man of God would beg that his heart might be in all that he did. What would his "goings" be if his heart wasn't in it?

It could be that David felt a wandering desire, an unreasonable leaning of his soul toward worldly gain. It might possibly have even intruded into his most devout meditations, and when it did, he at once cried out for more grace. The only way to cure a wrong leaning is to have the soul bent in the opposite direction. Holiness of heart is the cure for covetousness.

What a blessing it is that we can ask the Lord even for the right desire! Our wills are free, and yet, without violating their liberty, grace can bring us around in the right direction. This can be done by enlightening the understanding as to the excellence of obedience, by strengthening our habits of virtue, by giving us an experience of the sweetness of piety, and by many other ways. If any specific duty is bothersome to us, it is appropriate for us to offer this prayer with special reference to it. We are to love all the Lord's testimonies, and if we fail in any one point, we must pay double attention to it.

The leaning of the heart is the way in which the life will lean. That is the reason for the force of the petition, *Incline my heart*. We will be happy when we feel habitually inclined to all that is good! A carnal heart never leans this way. All its inclinations are in opposition to the divine testimonies.

And not to covetousness. Covetousness is the inclination of nature, and grace must make it undesirable to us. This sin is as harmful as it is common, and it is as mean as it is miserable. It is idolatry, and so it dethrones God. It is selfishness, and so it is cruel to all in its power. It is shameful greed, and so it would sell the Lord Himself for pieces of silver. It is a degrading, groveling, hardening, and deadening sin that withers everything around it that is lovely and Christlike. He who is covetous is like Judas, and will in all probability turn out to be a son of perdition.

The crime of covetousness is common, but very few will

confess it, for when a man heaps up gold in his heart, the dust of it blows into his eyes and he cannot see his own fault. Our hearts must have some object of desire, and the only way to keep worldly gain out is to put the testimonies of the Lord in its place. If we are inclined or bent one way, we will be turned from the other. The negative virtue is most surely attained by making sure of the positive grace which inevitably produces it.

37. *Turn away my eyes from beholding vanity, and cause me to live in thy way.*

Turn away my eyes from beholding vanity. David prayed about his heart, and one would think the eyes would surely have been influenced by the heart, thus eliminating the need to make them the objects of a special prayer, but the psalmist is resolved to make doubly sure. If the eyes do not see, perhaps the heart might not desire. At any rate, one door of temptation is closed when we do not even look at the painted trinket.

Sin first entered man's mind through the eye, and it is still a favorite gate for Satan's incoming temptations; therefore, there is need of a double watch on that opening. The prayer is not so much that the eyes may be shut as "turned away," for we need to have them open, but directed toward the right objects. For instance, if we are gazing on foolishness, we need to have our eyes turned away, and if we are focusing on heavenly things, we will be wise to beg that our eyes will be kept away from the vanity and emptiness of the world. Why should we look on worthless or futile things? Such things melt away like a vapor. Why not look on things eternal?

Sin is vanity, unjust gain is vanity, self-conceit is vanity, and all that is not of God certainly comes under the same heading. We must turn away from all this. That the psalmist even asks to have his eyes turned for him is proof of the sense of weakness he felt and of his entire dependence upon God. He did not mean to make himself passive, but he intended to set forth his own utter helplessness apart from the grace of God. For fear he might forget himself and gaze with a lingering longing upon forbidden things, he entreats the Lord quickly to make him turn away his eyes, hurrying him away from so dangerous a confrontation with iniquity. If we are kept from looking on vanity, we will be protected from loving iniquity.

And cause me to live in thy way. Give me so much life that dead vanity can have no power over me. Enable me to travel so swiftly on the road to heaven that I will not stop long enough within sight of vanity to be fascinated by it.

The prayer indicates our greatest need – more life in our obedience. It shows the preserving power of increased life to keep us from the evils around us, and it also tells us that increased life must come from the Lord alone. Vitality is the cure for vanity. When the heart is full of grace, the eyes will be cleansed from impurity. On the other hand, if we want to be full of life regarding the things of God, we must keep ourselves apart from sin and foolishness, or the eyes will soon captivate the mind, and like Samson who could slay his thousands, we may be overcome through the lusts which enter through the eye.

This verse is parallel to verses 21 and 29 in the previous segments of eight: *reprehended, remove,* and *turn away;* and *proud, lying,* and *vanity.*

38. *Confirm thy word unto thy slave, who is devoted to thy fear.*

Confirm thy word unto thy slave. Make me sure of Your unerring Word. Make it sure to me, and make me sure of it. If we possess the spirit of service, yet are troubled with skeptical thoughts, we can do nothing better than pray to be established in the truth. Times will arise when every doctrine and promise seems to be shaken, and our mind gets no rest. Then we must appeal to God to establish us in the faith, for He wants all His servants to be well instructed and confirmed in His Word. We must remember that we are the Lord's servants, or else we will not be sound in His truth for long.

Practical holiness is a great help toward doctrinal certainty. If we are God's servants, He will confirm His Word in our experience. *If anyone desires to do his will, he shall know of the doctrine* (John 7:17), and he will know it well enough to be fully assured of it. Atheism in the heart is a horrible plague to a God-fearing person. It brings more torment with it than can be described, and nothing but the visitation of divine grace can settle the soul after it has been violently attacked by it. Vanity or falsehood is bad for the eyes, but it is even worse when it defiles the understanding and casts a doubt on the Word of the living God.

> *Practical holiness is a great help toward doctrinal certainty.*

Who is devoted to thy fear, or simply, *to thy fear.* In other words, make good Your Word wherever godly fear exists. Strengthen the whole body of reverent men. *Confirm thy word*, not only to me, but also to all the godly people under the sun. Or, again, it may mean *Confirm thy word . . . to thy fear*; specifically, that people will be led to fear You, since a sure faith in the divine promise is the fountain and foundation of godly fear.

People will never worship a God in whom they do not believe. More faith will lead to more godly fear. We cannot look for the fulfillment of promises in our experience unless we live under the influence of the fear of the Lord. Establishment in grace is the result of holy watchfulness and prayerful energy. We will never be rooted and grounded in our belief unless we daily practice what we profess to believe. Full assurance is the reward of obedience. Answers to prayer are given to those whose hearts answer to the Lord's commands. If we are devoted to God's fear, we will be delivered from all other fear. The one who is filled with fear of the Author of the Word has no fear as to the truth of the Word. Skepticism is both the parent and the child of impiety, but strong faith both produces piety and is produced by it.

We recommend this whole verse to any devout person whose tendency is toward skepticism, for it is an excellent prayer for use in times of unusually strong misgivings.

There is in this an argumentative element in this prayer. As good Bishop Cowper says, "He who has received of the Lord grace to fear Him, may be bold to seek any necessary good thing from Him; because the fear of God hath annexed to it the promise of all other blessings."

39. Turn away my reproach which I have feared, for thy judgments are good.

Turn away my reproach which I have feared. He feared righteous reproach, trembling for fear that he might cause the enemy to blaspheme through any glaring inconsistency in his life. We also ought to fear this and be vigilant to avoid it.

Persecution in the form of slander can also be prayed against, for it is a severe trial, perhaps the harshest of trials for people of sensitive minds. Many would sooner be burned at the stake than be cruelly mocked. David was quick tempered, and he probably had greater dread of slander because it raised his anger, and he could hardly tell what he might do under great provocation. If God turns away our eyes from falsehood, we can also expect that He will turn away falsehood from injuring our good name. We will be kept from lies if we keep from lies.

The judgments of the wicked are bad, and therefore we can appeal them to the judgment of God. If, however, we have acted in such a way as to come under the just condemnation of men, what cause we have to fear even more just judgments of the Lord!

For thy judgments are good. Consequently, David is concerned about others speaking evil of the ways of God through hearing a bad report about himself. We grieve when we are slandered, for the shame is cast on our Christianity rather than ourselves. If people could be content to attribute evil to us, and go no further, we might bear it, for we are evil; but our sorrow is that they slander the Word and character of God, who is so good that there is none good in comparison with Him.

When people denounce God's governing of the world, it is our duty and privilege to stand up for Him and openly declare before Him, *Thy judgments are good.* We should do the same when people criticize the Bible, the gospel, the law, or the name of our Lord Jesus Christ. But we must take care that they can bring no truthful accusation against us, or our testimony will be nothing but wasted breath.

This prayer against reproach is a parallel to verse 31, and in general to many of the other seventh verses in the octaves, which usually imply hostility or opposition from without and a sacred satisfaction within. Consider the things that are "good": *Thy judgments are good* (verse 39); *Thou art good and doest good* (verse 68); and *good for me that I have been humbled* (verse 71).

40. *Behold, I have longed after thy precepts; cause me to live in thy righteousness.*

Behold, I have longed after thy precepts. The psalmist can at least claim sincerity. He is deeply bowed down by a sense of his weakness and need of grace, but he desires to be conformed to the divine will in all things. Where our longings are, there are we in the sight of God. If we have not yet attained spiritual maturity, it is something notable if we are hungering after it.

He who has given us the desire will also grant us the ability to obtain it. These precepts are grievous to the ungodly, and so when we are changed and long for them, we have clear evidence of conversion and can safely conclude that *he who has begun a good work in you will perfect it* (Philippians 1:6). Any person can long for the promises, but to long after the precepts is the mark of a renewed heart.

Cause me to live in thy righteousness. The psalmist had life enough to long for more life, in order that he might more perfectly know and observe the precepts of the Lord. Give me more life with which to follow Your righteous law, or give me more life because You have promised to hear prayer, and it is according to Your righteousness to keep Your word.

David often pleads for quickening, but never once too often. We need quickening every hour of the day, for we are sadly inclined to become slow and lethargic in the ways of God. It is the Holy Spirit who can pour new life into us. Let us not cease crying to Him. The creation of life is a divine work, and so is the increase of it. Never let us forget to pray for quickening in each and every duty. Even the precepts seem like a dead letter unless we feel life in our obedience to them. Nothing is worse in religion than spiritual death. The living God should be served with living worship.

> *Never let us forget to pray for quickening in each and every duty.*

The last verses of the octaves generally exhibit an onward look of resolve, hope, and prayer. Past fruits of grace should cause us to plea for further blessing. "Onward in the heavenly life!" is the cry of this verse. Oh, for grace to press forward and make daily advances towards heaven!

John Keble thus versifies these eight verses:

PSALM 119:33-40

Lord, shower thy light along my way,
    That I may keep thy laws entire,
Thy precepts teach me to obey,
    And watch with all my heart's desire.

By thine appointed rule and line,
    Guide me, for there I love to be;
My heart to thy decrees incline,
    And not to gold's base witchery.

From sight of ill mine eyes withdraw,
    Give life and gladness in thy road,
And on thy servant bind thy law,
    As best may teach thy fear, O God.

Spare me the shame I deeply fear,
    Most merciful in judgment spare;
Thou seest I hold thy counsels dear,
    Give life, thy righteousness to share.[8]

---

[8] John Keble, *The Psalter, Or, Psalms of David in English Verse* (Oxford: John Henry Parker; J. G. and F. Rivington, London, 1839), 312.

Psalm 119:41-48

VAU

Let thy mercy come unto me, O LORD, even thy salvation, according to thy spoken word.

And I shall answer him that reproaches me, by saying that I trust in thy word.

And take not at any time the word of truth out of my mouth; for I wait for thy judgment.

So shall I keep thy law continually from age to age.

And I will walk at liberty, for I sought thy commandments.

I will speak of thy testimonies also before kings and will not be ashamed.

And I will delight myself in thy commandments, which I have loved.

I will lift up My hands unto thy commandments, which I have loved, and I will meditate in thy statutes.

In these verses, holy fear is apparent and prominent. The man of God trembles for fear that in any way or degree the Lord might remove His favor from him. The eight verses are one continuous pleading for God's grace to abide in his soul, and it is supported by such holy arguments that can only bring to mind a spirit burning with love for God.

41. *Let thy mercy come unto me, O LORD, even thy salvation, according to thy spoken word.*

Let thy mercy come unto me, O LORD. David desired mercy as well as teaching, for he was guilty as well as ignorant. He needed much mercy and wide-ranging mercy, and that is why the request is in the plural (*Let thy mercies*, KJV). He needed mercies from God rather than from man, and so he asks for *thy mercy.* The way of grace appeared to be blocked, and so he begs that the mercies may have their way cleared by God and may come to him.

He who said *Let there be light* (Genesis 1:3) can also say, "Let there be mercy." It may be that under a sense of unworthiness the writer feared that mercy would be given to others, but not to himself. Therefore he cries, "Let them come unto me." *Bless me, even me also, O my father* (Genesis 27:38). The words are synonymous to our well-known verse:

> "Lord, I hear of showers of blessing
> Thou art scattering, full and free;
> Showers, the thirsty land refreshing;
> Let some droppings fall on me,
> Even me."[9]

Lord, Your enemies come to me to reproach me. Let Your mercies come to me to defend me. Trials and troubles abound and great labors and sufferings approach me. Lord, let Your mercies

---
[9] Elizabeth Codner, "Even Me" (1860).

enter by the same gate at the same time and in great number, for are You not *the God of my mercy* (Psalm 59:10)?

Even thy salvation. This is the sum and crown of all mercies – deliverance from all evil, both now and forever. Here we find the first mention of salvation in this psalm, and it is joined with mercy. *By grace are ye saved* (Ephesians 2:8). Salvation is rendered *thy salvation*, and so David ascribes it wholly to the Lord. *He that is our God is the God of salvation* (Psalm 68:20).

What a group of mercies are heaped together in the one salvation of our Lord Jesus! It includes the mercy that spares us until our conversion, and leads to that conversion. We have calling mercy, regenerating mercy, converting mercy, justifying mercy, and pardoning mercy. Nor can we exclude from complete salvation any of those many mercies that conduct the believer safely to glory. Salvation is a collection of mercies, incalculable in number, priceless in value, unending in application, and eternal in endurance. To the God of our mercies be glory, world without end.

According to thy spoken word. The way of salvation is described in the Word. Salvation itself is promised in the Word, and its inward manifestation is worked in us by the Word. So in all respects, the salvation that is in Christ Jesus is in accordance with God's Word. David loved the Scriptures, but he longed to know the salvation contained in them experientially. He wasn't satisfied to just read the Word, but he longed to experience it inwardly. He valued the field of Scripture for the sake of the treasure that he had discovered in it. He was not content with just having chapter and verse, but he also wanted mercies and salvation.

Notice that in the first verse of the section which bears the letter *He* (verse 33), the psalmist prayed to keep God's Word, and here in the *VAU* section, he begs the Lord to keep His Word. In the first case, he longed to come to the God of mercies, and here he wants the Lord's mercies to come to him. There he sought grace to persevere in faith, and here he seeks the goal of his faith – even the salvation of his soul.

42. *And I shall answer him that reproaches me, by saying that I trust in thy word.*

And I shall answer him that reproaches me. This is an unanswerable answer. When God, by granting us salvation, gives an answer of peace to our prayers, we are ready at once to answer the objections of the unbeliever, the quibbles of the skeptical, and the sneers of the contemptuous. It is most desirable that revilers be answered, and so we can expect the Lord to save His people, in order that a weapon with which to rout His adversaries may be put into their hands. When those who reproach us are also reproaching God, we can ask Him to help us to silence them by sure evidence of His mercy and faithfulness.

I trust in thy word. David's faith was seen by his being trustful while under trial, and here he pleads it as a reason why he should be helped to beat back reproaches by a happy experience. Faith is our argument when we seek mercies and salvation – faith in the Lord who has spoken to us in His Word.

I trust in thy word is a declaration more worth making than any other, for he who can truly make this declaration has received power to become a child of God, and so to be the heir of unnumbered mercies. God has more respect for a person's trust than anything else found in him, for the Lord has chosen faith to be the hand into which He places His mercies and salvation. If anyone criticizes us for trusting in God, we reply to them with arguments that are most conclusive when we show that God has kept His promises, heard our prayers, and supplied our needs. Even the most skeptical are forced to bow before the logic of facts.

In this second verse of this octave, the psalmist makes a confession of faith and a declaration of his belief and experience. Note that he does the same thing in the corresponding verses of the sections that follow. See verse 50, *Thy spoken word has caused me to live*; verse 58, *I intreated thy presence with my whole heart*; verse 66, *I have believed thy commandments*; and verse 74, *I have waited on thy word*. A wise preacher might find a valuable series of experiential messages in these verses.

43. And take not at any time the word of truth out of my mouth; for I wait for thy judgment.

And take not at any time the word of truth out of my mouth. Do not prevent my pleading for You by leaving me without deliverance, for how could I continue to proclaim Your Word if I found that it failed me? The Word of truth cannot be a real joy when we speak it unless we have experienced it in our lives, and it might be wise for us to be silent if we cannot support our testimonies by the verdict of our consciousness.

This prayer may also refer to other ways we might be unable to speak in the name of the Lord, including falling into open sin, becoming depressed and hopeless, laboring under sickness or mental abnormalities, or finding no opportunity to speak to or meet with a willing audience. He who has once preached the gospel from his heart is filled with horror at the idea of being put out of the ministry. He will crave a little part in the holy testimony and will count his Sabbaths when he is unable to preach the gospel to be days of banishment and punishment.

For I wait for thy judgment. David had expected God to show up and vindicate his cause, so much so that he could speak with confidence concerning His faithfulness. God is the author of our hopes, and we can most suitably ask Him to fulfill them. The judgments of His providence are the outcome of His Word.

What He says in the Scriptures, He actually performs in His governing. Therefore, we can expect Him to show Himself strong on behalf of His own threatenings and promises, and we will not be watching in vain.

God's ministers are sometimes silenced through the sins of their people, and it is suitable for them to plead against such a judgment. It is much better if they suffer sickness or poverty than to have the candle of the gospel snuffed out among them, and that in this way they would be left to perish without a remedy. May the Lord save those of us who are His ministers from being made the instruments of inflicting such a penalty. Let us exhibit a cheerful hopefulness in God, that we may plead it in prayer with Him when He threatens to close our lips.

At the close of this verse there is a declaration of what the psalmist had done in reference to the Word of the Lord, and in this, the thirds of the octaves are often alike. See verse 35, *therein do I delight*; verse 43, *I wait for thy judgment*; verse 51, *yet I have not deviated from thy law*; verse 59, *I considered my ways and turned my feet unto thy testimonies*; and verses 67, 83, 99, etc. These verses furnish an admirable series of meditations.

44. *So shall I keep thy law continually from age to age.*

Nothing more effectively secures a person to the way of the Lord than an experience of the truth of His Word exemplified in the form of mercies and deliverances. Not only does the Lord's faithfulness open our mouths against His adversaries, but it also knits our hearts to His fear and makes our union with Him more and more intense. Great mercies lead us to feel an inexpressible gratitude, which failing to utter itself in time, promises to engage eternity with praises. To a heart on fire with thankfulness, the *continually from age to age* of the text won't seem to be redundant. The extravagance of Addison in his famous verse will only make solid sense:

> "Through all eternity to thee
> A joyful song I'll raise;
> But oh! eternity's too short
> To utter all thy praise."[10]

God's grace alone can enable us to keep His commandments without interruption and without end. Eternal love must grant us eternal life, and out of this eternal life will come everlasting obedience. There is no other way to ensure our perseverance in holiness except by the Word of truth abiding in us, as David prayed it would remain in him.

The verse begins with *so*, and when God grants His salvation, we are *so* favored that we silence our worst enemy and glorify our best friend. Mercy answers all things. If God just gives us salvation, we can conquer hell and communicate with heaven, answer reproaches, and keep the law, and that *continually from age to age*.

> *God's grace alone can enable us to keep His commandments without interruption and without end.*

We must not overlook another idea suggested here. David prayed that the Word of truth might not be taken out of his mouth, and so he would keep God's law. In other words, by public testimony as well as by his personal life, he would fulfill God's divine will and confirm the bonds which bound him to his Lord forever. Undoubtedly, the grace which enables us to bear witness with the mouth is a great help to ourselves, as well as to others.

We feel that the vows of the Lord are for us, and that we

---

10   Joseph Addison, "When All Thy Mercies, O My God," *The Spectator*, London, issue 453 (August 9, 1712).

can't run back. Our ministry is useful to ourselves first, or else it would not be useful to others. We must so preach and teach the Word of God that we fulfill our lifework and the law of love constantly and consistently. It is a horrible thing when a man's preaching only increases his sin because he preaches something other than what Scripture teaches.

45. *And I will walk at liberty, for I sought thy commandments.*

Believers find no bondage in holiness. The Spirit of holiness is a free spirit. He sets men free and enables them to resist every effort to bring them under subjection. The way of holiness is not a path for slaves, but it is the King's highway for freemen who are joyfully journeying from the Egypt of bondage to the Canaan of rest. God's mercies and salvation, by teaching us to love the precepts of the Word, set us at a happy rest. The more we seek after the perfection of our obedience, the more we will enjoy complete freedom from every form of spiritual slavery.

At one time in his life, David was in great bondage as he followed a crooked tactic. He deceived Achish so persistently that he was driven to acts of ferocity to conceal it, and he must have felt very unhappy in his unnatural position as an ally of the Philistines and captain of the bodyguard of their king. He must have feared that falling into the crooked ways of falsehood would lead to the truth no longer being on his tongue. Therefore, he prayed that God would work his deliverance in some way and set him free from such slavery. In righteousness, the Lord answered him by terrible things at Ziklag, and the snare was broken and David escaped.

This verse is linked to what comes before it, for it begins with the word *and*, which acts like a hook to attach it to the preceding verses. It mentions another benefit expected from the coming mercies of God. The man of God had mentioned the silencing of his enemies (verse 42), power to proceed in testimony (verse 43), and perseverance in holiness (verse 44). Now in this verse, he concentrates on liberty, which, next to life, is dearest to all brave men. He says, *I will walk*, indicating his daily progress through life, *at liberty*, like someone who is out of prison without hindrance of adversaries, unencumbered by burdens, unshackled, and allowed a wide range of freedom to roam without fear. Such liberty would be dangerous if a man were seeking what he wanted or pursuing his own lusts, but when the one objective is to seek after the will of God, there is no need to restrain the searcher.

We do not need to restrict or confine the man who says, *I sought thy commandments*. Notice that in the preceding verse he said he would keep the law, but here he speaks of seeking it. Does not this mean that he will obey what he knows and endeavor to know more? Is not this the way to the highest form of liberty – to be always at work to know the mind of God and to be conformed to it? Those who *keep* the law are sure to *seek* it and to stir themselves up to keep it more and more.

46. *I will speak of thy testimonies also before kings and will not be ashamed.*

This is part of his liberty. He is free from fear of the greatest, proudest, and most tyrannical of men. David was called to stand before kings when he was an exile, and afterwards, when he was himself a monarch, he knew the tendency of men to sacrifice their religion to a show of ceremony and political maneuvering; but David's resolve was to do nothing of the kind. He wanted to sanctify politics and make cabinets know that the Lord alone is governor among the nations. As a king, he wanted to speak to kings concerning the King of Kings. He says, *I will speak*.

Wisdom might have suggested that his life and conduct would be enough, and that it would be better not to mention religion in the presence of royal dignitaries who worshipped other gods and claimed to be right in doing so. David already had preceded this resolve most suitably by the declaration, *I will walk*, but he doesn't make his personal conduct an excuse for sinful silence, for he adds, *I will speak*. David claimed religious liberty and was careful to use it, for he spoke out about what he believed, even when he was in the most important company.

He was careful to keep to God's Word in what he said, for he says, *I will speak of thy testimonies*. No topic is like this, and there is no way of handling this subject other than keeping close to the Bible and using its thought and language. The great hindrance to our speaking about holy topics in all company is shame, but the psalmist said he *will not be ashamed*. In fact, there is nothing to be ashamed of and there is no excuse for being ashamed, yet many believers are as quiet as the dead for fear that some person like themselves should be offended. When God gives grace, cowardice quickly vanishes. He who speaks for God in God's power will not be ashamed when beginning to speak, while speaking, or after speaking, because his topic is one which is proper, needful, and beneficial for kings. If kings object, we may rightly be ashamed of them, but never of our Master who sent us, or of His message, or of His plan in sending it.

47. *And I will delight myself in thy commandments, which I have loved.*

Next to liberty and courage comes delight. When we have done our duty, we find great reward in it. If David hadn't spoken for his Master before kings, he would have been afraid to think about the law he had neglected; but after speaking up for his

Lord, he felt a sweet serenity of heart when reflecting upon the Word. Obey the command, and you will love it; carry the yoke, and it will be easy, and rest will come by it.

After speaking about the law, the psalmist wasn't tired of his topic, but rather he retired to meditate on it. He discussed it and then he delighted in it. He preached it, and then went to his study to renew his strength by feeding on the precious truth yet again. Whether he delighted others or not when he was speaking, he never failed to delight himself when he was meditating on the Word of the Lord.

David declares that he loved the Lord's commands, and by his own admission, he unveils the reason for his delight in them: where our love is, there is our delight. David did not delight in the courts of kings, for there he found much that might tempt him and result in his being ashamed of himself. His heart was in them, and they gave him supreme pleasure. No wonder he spoke about keeping the law, which he loved. Jesus says, *He who loves me will keep my words* (John 14:23). No wonder he spoke about walking in liberty and speaking boldly, for true love is forever free and fearless. Love is the fulfilling of the law, and where love of the law of God reigns in the heart, the life must be full of blessedness. Lord, let Your mercies come to us, that we may love Your Word and way and find our entire delight in them.

> *Obey the command, and you will love it; carry the yoke, and it will be easy, and rest will come by it.*

Verse 47 is in the future, and consequently, it sets forth not only what David had done, but also what he would do. In time, he would come to delight in his Lord's commands. He knew they would neither change nor fail to provide him joy. He also knew that grace would keep the condition of his heart the same toward the precepts of the Lord, so that he could take supreme delight in holiness throughout his whole life. His heart was so fixed in love toward God's will that he was sure that grace would always keep him under its delightful influence.

This entire psalm is fragrant with love for the Word, but here, for the first time, love is expressly spoken of. Here it is paired with delight, and in verse 165 with *great peace*. All the verses in which love declares itself in so many words are worthy of note. See verses 47, 97, 113, 119, 127, 140, 159, 163, 165, and 167.

48. *I will lift up My hands unto thy commandments, which I have loved, and I will meditate in thy statutes.*

I will lift up My hands unto thy commandments, which I have loved. David stretches toward perfection as much as he possibly can, hoping to reach it one day. When his hands hang down, he cheers himself out of sluggishness with the expectation of glorifying God through obedience. He offers a sincere sign of his wholehearted agreement and consent to all that his God commands.

The phrase *lift up My hands* is very full of meaning, and without a doubt the sweet singer meant all we can see in it and a great deal more. Again, he declares his love, for a true heart loves to express itself. It is a kind of fire which must send forth its flames. It was natural that he would reach out toward a law in which he delighted, just like a child holds out its hand to receive a gift it desires. When such a lovely object as holiness is set before us, we are bound to rise toward it with our whole nature, and until it is fully accomplished, we should at least lift up our hands in prayer toward it. Where holy hands and holy hearts go, the whole person will one day follow.

And I will meditate in thy statutes. David can never have enough of meditation. Loving subjects wish to be familiar with their sovereign's laws, for fear they might offend through ignorance. Prayer with lifted hands and meditation with upward-glancing eyes work in joyful harmony for the best inward results. The prayer of verse 41 is already fulfilled in the man who is struggling upward and intensely studying. The entirety of this verse is in the future, and it can be viewed not only as a determination of David's mind, but also as a result which he knew would follow from the Lord's sending him His mercies and His salvation. When mercy comes down, our hands will be lifted up. When we enjoy the realization that God thinks of us with special love, we are sure to think of Him.

Psalm 119:49-56

ZAIN

Remember the word unto thy slave, in which thou hast caused me to wait.

This is my comfort in my affliction; for thy spoken word has caused me to live.

The proud have had me greatly in derision; yet I have not deviated from thy law.

I remembered thy judgments of old, O LORD, and have consoled myself.

Horror has taken hold upon me because of the wicked that forsake thy law.

Thy statutes have been my songs in the house of my pilgrimage.

I have remembered thy name, O LORD, in the night, and have kept thy law.

This I had, because I kept thy precepts.

This group of eight verses deals with the comfort of the Word. It begins by seeking the main consolation, which is the Lord's fulfillment of His promise. It then shows how the Word sustains us under affliction and makes us so impervious to ridicule that we are moved by the harsh conduct of the wicked and shudder at their sin, rather than submit to any of their temptations. We are then shown how the Scripture furnishes songs for pilgrims and memories for those who watch in the night. Finally, this portion concludes with the general statement that all of this happiness and comfort arises out of keeping the statutes of the Lord.

49. Remember the word unto thy slave, in which thou hast caused me to wait.

Remember the word unto thy slave. David doesn't ask for a new promise, but he asks to have the old Word fulfilled. He is grateful that he has received such a good Word, and he embraces it with all his heart. He now entreats the Lord to deal with him according to it. He doesn't say, "remember my service to thee," but *remember the word unto thy slave.* The words of masters to servants are not always those that servants want their lords to say as they think of their servants, because they usually take note of the faults and failings of the work done, showing that it doesn't agree with the word of command.

We who serve the best of masters are not worried that even one of His words will fall to the ground, since the Lord so kindly remembers His Word of command as to give us grace by which we can obey, and He will combine it with a remembrance of His word of promise so that our hearts will be comforted. If God's Word to us as His servants is so precious, what will we say about His Word to us as His sons?

The psalmist doesn't fear that the Lord will fail to remember, but he makes use of the promise as a plea, and in this way he speaks in the same manner as people when they plead with one another. When the Lord remembers the sins of His servant and brings them before his conscience, the repentant person cries, "Lord, remember Your word of pardon, and therefore remember my sins and iniquities no more." There is a world of meaning in that word *remember*, as it is addressed to God. It is used in Scripture in the most tender sense, and it suits those who are sorrowing and depressed.

The psalmist cried, *LORD, remember David and all his afflictions* (Psalm 132:1). Job also prayed that the Lord would appoint him a set time and remember him (Job 14:13). In the present instance with David, the prayer is as personal as the *remember me* of the thief on the cross beside Jesus, for its essence lies in the words *unto thy slave*. It would all be in vain for us if the promise were remembered by everyone if it didn't come true for us, but there is no fear of failure, for the Lord has never forgotten a single promise to a single believer.

In which thou hast caused me to wait. The argument is that God, having given grace to hope in the promise, will never disappoint that hope. He cannot have caused us to hope without reason. If our hope is based on His Word, we have a sure basis to build upon. Our gracious Lord will never mock us by exciting false hopes. *Hope deferred makes the heart sick* (Proverbs 13:12); that is the reason for the petition for immediate remembrance of the cheering word. Even more than that, it is the hope of a servant, and it is not possible that a great and good master would disappoint his dependent. If such a master's word were not kept, it would only be through an oversight. This is the reason for the anxious cry, *Remember.* Our great Master will not forget His own servants or disappoint the expectation He Himself has raised. Because we are the Lord's and we attempt to remember His Word by obeying it, we can be sure that He will think about His servants and remember His own promise by making it good.

> Our gracious Lord will never mock us by exciting false hopes.

This verse is the prayer of love fearing to be forgotten, of humility conscious of insignificance and anxious not to be overlooked, of repentance trembling for fear that the evil of its sin would overshadow the promise, of eager desire longing for the blessing, and of holy confidence feeling that all that is needed is understood in the Word. Just let the Lord remember His promise, and the promised act is as good as done.

50. This is my comfort in my affliction; for thy spoken word has caused me to live.

David means that God's Word is his comfort, or the fact that God's Word has brought life to him is his comfort. He means that the hope that God had given him was his comfort, for God had quickened him by this. Whatever the exact sense may be, it is clear that the psalmist experienced affliction – affliction unique to himself – which he calls *my affliction*, and that he had comfort in it – comfort especially his own – for he describes it as *my comfort*. He knew what the comfort was and where it came from, for he exclaims, *This is my comfort*.

The worldly person clutches his wallet and says, "This is my comfort." The squanderer points to his high spirits and shouts, "This is my comfort," and the drunkard lifts his glass and sings, "This is my comfort." However, the man whose hope comes from God feels the life-giving power of the Word of the Lord, and he testifies, *This is my comfort*. Paul said, *I know whom I have believed* (2 Timothy 1:12).

Comfort is desirable at all times, but comfort in affliction is like a lamp in a dark place. Some people are unable to find comfort in tribulation, but that is not the case with believers, for their Savior has said to them, *I will not leave you orphans* (John 14:18). Some have comfort and no affliction, and others have affliction and no comfort, but the saints have comfort in their affliction.

The Word frequently comforts us by increasing the force of our inner life: *This is my comfort in my affliction; for thy spoken word has caused me to live.* To quicken the heart cheers the whole man. Often the immediate way to consolation is through sanctification and being refreshed. If we cannot clear away the fog, it might be better to rise to a higher level and get above it.

Troubles that weigh us down while we are half dead become mere trivialities when we are full of life. In this way, our spirits are often raised by quickening grace, and the same thing happens again, for the Comforter is still with us, the Consolation of Israel lives forever, and the very God of peace is our Father forevermore. On looking back on our past life, there is one area of comfort in regard to our condition: the Word of God has made us alive and kept us so. We were dead, but we are dead no longer. From this, we gladly conclude that if the Lord had meant to destroy us, He would not have quickened us. If we were only hypocrites worthy of contempt, like proud people say, He wouldn't have revived us by His grace. An experience of quickening by the Word of God is a fountain of good cheer.

See how the experience of this verse is turned into a prayer in verse 107: *Cause me to live, O LORD, according to thy word.* Experience teaches us how to pray, and it furnishes arguments in prayer.

> 51. *The proud have had me greatly in derision; yet I have not deviated from thy law.*

Proud people never love gracious people, and since they fear them, they veil their fear under a pretended contempt. In this case, their hatred revealed itself in ridicule, and that ridicule was loud and long. When they wanted to ridicule someone, they ridiculed David because he was God's servant. People do not see clearly who can ridicule true faith in God and who laugh at holiness, yet it is sadly the case that people who are short on wisdom can generally make fun of those who follow Jesus.

Conceited sinners like to kick godly people around. They call it fun to mock those who seek holiness and who want to fully follow Jesus. These arrogant sinners love to joke about those with biblical morals and principles and who do not follow the ways of the world. These proud fools love to mock and ridicule those who hate sin and speak against it, calling them puritanical and strait-laced hypocrites. If David was greatly ridiculed, we cannot expect to escape the scorn of the ungodly. Multitudes of proud people are still on the face of the earth, and if they find a believer suffering hardship, they will be mean enough and cruel enough to make jokes at his expense. It is the nature of the son of the bondwoman to mock the child of the promise (Genesis 21:9).

Yet I have not deviated from thy law. Those who mocked missed their target. They laughed, but they didn't win. The godly man, so far from turning aside from the right way, did not even slacken his pace or fall away from his holy habits in any sense. Many would have fallen away from God if ridiculed, but David didn't. It pays too much honor to fools to yield even half a point to them. Their unholy humor won't harm us if we pay no attention to it, just as the moon doesn't suffer anything from the dogs that howl at it. God's law is our highway of peace and safety, and those who want to laugh us out of it wish us no good.

From verse 61 we note that David was not overcome by the taking of his possessions any more than by these cruel mockings. See also verse 157, where the multitude of persecutors and enemies were baffled in their attempts to make David fall away from God's ways.

52. I remembered thy judgments of old, O LORD, and have consoled myself.

David had asked the Lord to remember, and here he remembers God and His judgments. When we see no present demonstration of the divine power, it is wise to fall back on the records of former ages, since they are just as available to us as if God's actions occurred yesterday, since the Lord is always the same. Our true comfort must be found in what our God works on behalf of truth and right, and since the histories of the former times are full of divine interventions, it is good to be thoroughly acquainted with them. Additionally, if we are advanced in years, we have the examples of God working in our lives and on our behalf from our earlier days to review. These should by no means be forgotten or left out of our thoughts.

> *When he was greatly ridiculed, the psalmist did not sit in despair, but he rallied his spirits.*

The argument is good and solid. He who has shown Himself strong on behalf of His believing people is the unchanging God, and therefore we can expect deliverance at His hands. The grinning of the proud will not trouble us when we remember how the Lord dealt with their predecessors in former times. He destroyed them in the flood, He confounded them at Babel, He drowned them in the Red Sea, and He drove them out of Canaan. In all ages, He has bared His arm against the arrogant and broken them like potters' vessels.

While we humbly drink of the mercy of God in the stillness of our own hearts, we are not without comfort in times of turmoil and ridicule, for then we turn to God's justice and remember how He scoffs at the scoffers. *He that sits in the heavens shall laugh: the Lord shall have them in derision* (Psalm 2:4).

When he was greatly ridiculed, the psalmist did not sit in despair, but he rallied his spirits. He knew that comfort was needed for strength in service and for endurance of persecution, and so he comforted himself. In doing this, he resorted not so much to the sweet side, but to the stern side of the Lord's dealings. He meditated on His judgments. If we can find sweetness in divine justice, how much more will we perceive it in divine love and grace! How thoroughly must that one be at peace with God who can find comfort, not only in His promises, but also in His judgments. Even the dreadful things of God provide cheer for believers. They know that nothing is more advantageous to all God's creatures than to be ruled by a strong hand that deals out justice.

The righteous man has no fear of the ruler's sword, which is only a terror to evildoers (Romans 13:3). When a godly person is unjustly treated, he finds comfort in the fact that there is a Judge of all the earth who will avenge His own elect and set right the troubles of these disordered times.

53. *Horror has taken hold upon me because of the wicked that forsake thy law.*

David was horrified at their action, at the pride which led them to it, and at the punishment which would be sure to befall them for it. When he meditated on the ancient judgments of God, he was filled with terror at the fate of the godless, as he well should be.

Their laughter had not distressed him, but he was distressed by a foresight of their overthrow. Truths that were amusing to them caused amazement to him. He saw them utterly turning away from the law of God and leaving it as a path forsaken and overgrown from lack of traffic. This forsaking of the law filled him with the most painful emotions. He was astonished at their wickedness, stunned by their presumption, alarmed by the expectation of their sudden overthrow, and amazed by the terror of their certain doom.

See verses 106 and 158, and note the tenderness related to all this. Those who are the firmest believers in the eternal punishment of the wicked are the most distressed at their doom. Shutting one's eyes to the awful doom of the ungodly is no proof of tenderness. Compassion is shown far better by trying to save sinners than in attempting to make things seem pleasant for all. Oh, that we were all more distressed as we think about the punishment of the ungodly in hell. The usual plan is to shut your eyes to it or try to doubt it, but the faithful servant of God can say, "I did not close my eyes to it, because of the fear of God."

54. *Thy statutes have been my songs in the house of my pilgrimage.*

Like other servants of God, David knew he wasn't at home in this world, but rather was a pilgrim traveling through, seeking a better country. He did not, however, mourn over this fact, but he sang about it. He tells us nothing about his pilgrim laments, but he speaks of his pilgrim songs. Even the palace in which he lived was only *the house of my pilgrimage*, the inn at which he rested, the station at which he paused for a little while. When men come to their inn, they usually sing, and this godly sojourner did the same. He sang the songs of Zion, the statutes of the great King. The commands of God were as well known to him as the ballads of his country, and they were pleasant to his taste and musical to his ear.

Happy is the heart that finds its joy in the commands of God and makes obedience its recreation. When religion is set to music, it goes well. When we sing in the ways of the Lord, it shows that our hearts are in them. Our songs are pilgrim psalms or Songs of Degrees, but they are the kind that we can sing throughout eternity, for the statutes of the Lord are sacred songs of the highest heaven.

Saints are horrified by sin and find harmony in holiness. The wicked shun the law, but the righteous sing about it. In the past, we have sung the Lord's statutes, and in this we can find comfort during affliction. Since our songs are so very different from those of the proud, in the end we can expect to join a very different choir from that in which they sing, and to make music in a place far removed from their dwelling place.

Note how in the sixth verses of their respective octaves we often find resolutions to bless God, or records of testimony. In verse 46 it says, *I will speak*, and in verse 62, *I will rise to give thanks*, while here in verse 54, David speaks of songs.

55. *I have remembered thy name, O LORD, in the night, and have kept thy law.*

I have remembered thy name, O LORD, in the night. David is saying that while others slept, he woke to think of the Lord: His person, His actions, His covenant, His name. In God's name, David comprehends the divine character as far as it is revealed. He was so earnest in seeking after the living God that he woke up in the dead of night to think about Him.

These were David's night thoughts. If they weren't sunny memories, they were memories of the Sun of Righteousness. It is good when our memory furnishes us with consolation, so that we can say with the psalmist, "Having been taught to know You early in life, I had only to remember the lessons of Your grace, and my heart was comforted."

This verse not only shows that the man of God had remembered, but also that he still remembered the Lord his God. We are to hallow the name of God, and we cannot do so if it slips from our memory.

And have kept thy law. He found sanctification through meditation. By his thoughts in the night, he governed his actions during the day. In the same way that the actions of the day often create dreams of the night, so do the thoughts of the night produce the deeds of the day. If we don't keep the name of God in our memory, we won't keep the law of God in our conduct. Forgetfulness in mind leads to forgetfulness in life.

When we hear the night songs of revelers, we have clear evidence in them that they don't keep God's law; but the quiet reflections of gracious men are proof positive that the name of the Lord is dear to them. We may judge nations by their songs, and we can do the same with people. In the case of the righteous, their singing and their thinking are both indications of their love for God. Whether they lift up their voices or sit in silence, they are still the Lord's. Blessed are the people whose night thoughts are memories of the eternal light. They will be remembered by their Lord when the night of death arrives.

Dear reader, as you lie in the dark, are your thoughts full of light because they are full of God? Is His name the natural subject of your evening reflections? If so, it will provide a mood to your morning and noonday hours. Or do you give your whole mind to the fleeting cares and pleasures of this world? If so, it is little wonder that you do not live as you should. No one is holy by chance. If we have no memory for the name of Jehovah, we aren't likely to remember His commandments. If we don't think about Him privately, we will not obey Him openly.

56. *This I had, because I kept thy precepts.*

He had this comfort, this remembrance of God, this power to sing, this courage to face the enemy, and this hope in the promise, because he had earnestly observed the commands of God and desired to walk in them. We are not rewarded for our works, but there is a reward in them. Many comforts are obtainable only through careful living, and we can surely say of such consolations, "I had comfort, because I kept Your precepts." How can we defy ridicule if we are living inconsistently? How can we comfortably remember the name of the Lord if we live carelessly?

It might be that David means he had been able to keep the law because he had focused on the separate precepts. He had taken the commands in detail, and so had reached toward holiness of life. He who is not careful in observing the individual parts of the law cannot keep it as a whole. Or he might mean that by keeping certain precepts he had gained spiritual strength to keep others, for God gives more grace to those who have some measure of it, and those who improve their talents will find themselves improving (Matthew 25:15-19). It is probably best to leave the passage open, so we can say of a thousand priceless blessings, "These came to us in the way of obedience."

All our possessions are gifts of grace, and yet it is unquestionably true that certain ones come in the shape of reward. Even when good things come to us in this way, the reward is not because of debt, but of grace. God first works good works in us, and then He rewards us for them. This is a complex condescension and a mixed work of goodness.

In this verse, we have a suitable conclusion to this section of the psalm, since it contains a strong argument for the prayer with which the section began. If we have been helped to remember our Lord's commands, we may be sure that He will remember our true needs. The sweet singer had evidence of having kept God's precepts, and therefore he could more properly beg the Lord to keep His promises. All through the passage we can find pleas, especially in the three forms of *remember*: *Remember the word unto thy slave*, *I remembered thy judgments*, and *I have remembered thy name*.

Psalm 119:57-64

CHETH

My portion, O LORD, I have said, will be to keep thy words.

I intreated thy presence with my whole heart; be merciful unto me according to thy word.

I considered my ways and turned my feet unto thy testimonies.

I made haste and did not delay to keep thy commandments.

The company of the wicked have robbed me, but I have not forgotten thy law.

At midnight I will rise to give thanks unto thee because of the judgments of thy righteousness.

I am a companion of all those that fear thee and of those that keep thy precepts.

The earth, O LORD, is full of thy mercy and teaches me thy statutes.

In this section, the psalmist seems to take firm hold of God Himself: appropriating Him (verse 57), crying out for Him (verse 58), returning to Him (verse 59), comforting himself in Him (verses 61 and 62), associating with His people (verse

63), and longing for His personal instruction (verse 64). Note how the first verse of this octave is linked to the last verse of the former one and works as an expansion. *This I had, because I kept thy precepts. My portion, O LORD, I have said, will be to keep thy words.* Though they are many, these verses are still but one bread.

57. *My portion, O LORD, I have said, will be to keep thy words.*

My portion, O Lord. This is a broken expression. Some translators have amended it with insertions, but it might be better to have left it alone to read as an exclamation: *My portion, O Lord!* The poet is lost in wonder as he realizes that the great and glorious God is all his own! This is quite understandable, for there is no possession like Jehovah Himself.

The form of the sentence expresses joyous recognition and expresses personal use: *My portion, O Lord.* David had often seen prey divided and heard victors shouting over it. In this verse he rejoices as one who seizes his share of the spoil. He chooses the Lord to be his portion of the treasure. Like the Levites, he took God to be his portion, and left other matters to those who coveted them. This is a large and lasting inheritance, for it includes everything, and more than everything, and it outlasts everything, yet no one chooses it for himself until God has chosen and renewed him.

What truly wise person would hesitate for a moment when the infinitely blessed God is set before him to be the object of his choice? David leaped at the opportunity and grasped the priceless blessing. The psalmist here dares to reveal the title deeds of his portion before the eyes of the Lord Himself, for he addresses his joyful utterance directly to God, whom he boldly calls his own. Because David was a king, he was a man of great resources with many other things to choose from, but he deliberately turned from all the treasures of the world and declared that the Lord, Jehovah, is his portion.

To keep thy words. We can't always look back on what we have said with comfort, but in this instance David spoke wisely and well. He had declared his choice: he preferred the Word of God to the wealth of the world. It was his firm resolve to keep – to treasure up and observe – the words of his God; as he had solemnly expressed it earlier in the presence of the Lord Himself, so now he confesses the binding obligation of his former vow.

Jesus said, *He who loves me will keep my words* (John 14:23), and this is a case which He might have quoted as an illustration, for the psalmist's love for God as his portion led to his keeping the words of God. David took God to be his Prince as well as his Portion. He was confident in regard to his interest in God, and therefore he was resolute in his obedience to Him. Full assurance is a powerful source of holiness.

> *He who knows God to be his God will seek His face and long for His presence.*

The very words of God are to be stored up, for whether they relate to doctrine, promise, or command, they are most precious. When the heart is determined to keep these words and has registered its purpose in the court of heaven, it is prepared for all the temptations and trials that may take place, for with God as its heritage, it is always in good standing.

58. *I intreated thy presence with my whole heart; be merciful unto me according to thy word.*

I intreated thy presence with my whole heart. A fully assured possession of God does not set prayer aside, but rather urges us to practice it. He who knows God to be his God will seek His face and long for His presence. In fact, the idea of seeking

God's presence is conveyed by the Hebrew language that has the idea of seeking God's face. The presence of God is the highest form of his favor, and therefore it is the most urgent desire of gracious souls. The light of His countenance gives us a foretaste of heaven. May we always enjoy it!

The good psalmist entreated God's smile as one begging for his life, and he placed the entire strength of his desire with his entreaty. Such eager pleadings are sure to succeed, for that which comes from our heart will certainly go to God's heart. All of God's favors are ready for those who seek them with their whole heart.

Be merciful unto me according to thy word. He has begged for favor in the form which he needs most – that of mercy – because he is a sinner more than anything else. He asks nothing beyond the promise. He only begs for such mercy as the Word reveals, and what more could he want or wish for? God has revealed such limitless mercy in His Word that it would be impossible to conceive of more. See how the psalmist meditates on favor and mercy. He never dreams of his own merit. He doesn't demand, but he asks, for he feels his own unworthiness.

Note how he continues to petition God, even though he knows that he has all things in his God. God is his portion, and yet he begs for a look at His face. The idea of any other position before God than that of an undeserving one, though favored, never entered his head. Here we have his *be merciful unto me* rising with as much intensity of humble pleading as if he still remained among the most trembling of remorseful sinners. The confidence of faith makes us bold in prayer, but it never teaches us to live without prayer, and it never justifies us in being anything other than humble beggars at mercy's gate.

59. I considered my ways and turned my feet unto thy testimonies.

While studying the Word, David was led to study his own life, and this caused a mighty transformation. He came to the Word and then he came to himself, and this made him rise and go to his Father. Consideration is the beginning of conversion: first we think, and then we turn. When the mind repents of wicked ways, the feet are soon led into good ways, but repenting will not take place until there is deep, sincere thought.

Many people are opposed to thought of any kind, and when it comes to thoughts about their own ways, they can't tolerate it, for they do not want to have to think about their own ways. David's ways had not been as good as he would have wanted them to be, so his thoughts were full of sincere regret in many ways. However, he did not end with idle lamentations, but he set about to correct and improve his ways. He turned and returned; he sought the testimonies of the Lord and hurried to enjoy the conscious favor of his heavenly Friend once more. Action without thought is foolishness, and thought without action is laziness. To think carefully and then to act promptly is a happy combination. David had prayed for renewed fellowship, and now he proved the genuineness of his desire by renewed obedience.

If we are in the dark and mourn because God seems absent, our wisest approach will not be so much to think about our sorrows, but rather to focus on our ways. While we cannot turn the course of providence, we can turn the way in which we walk, and this will soon mend matters. If we can get our feet going in the right direction in regard to holy walking, we will soon get our hearts right as to happy living. God will turn to His saints when they turn to Him. He has already favored them with the light of His face when they began to think and turn.

60. *I made haste and did not delay to keep thy commandments.*

David hurried to get back onto the royal road from which he had wandered, and to run on that road in the King's errands. Speed in repentance and speed in obedience are two excellent things. We are too often in a hurry to sin. May we be in a greater hurry to obey! Delay in repentance is increase of sin. To be slow to keep the commands is to break them. Much evil is found in a lagging pace when God's commands are to be followed. A holy eagerness in service should be readily cultivated. This is worked in us by the Spirit of God, and the preceding verses describe the process. We are made to recognize and mourn our wayward ways, we are led to return to the right path, and then we are eager to make up for lost time by dashing forward to fulfill God's commands.

Whatever the mistakes and wanderings of an honest heart may be, there remains enough true life in it to produce fervent piety once it is quickened by the visitations of God. The psalmist earnestly asked for mercy, and when he received it, he became eager and vigorous in the Lord's ways. He had always loved them, and so when he was enriched with grace he displayed great eagerness and delight in them. He made quick progress, for he positively *made haste* and refused to yield to any motive that suggested procrastination; he *did not delay*. As a consequence, he rapidly advanced and accomplished much service, fulfilling the vow recorded in verse 57: *My portion, O LORD, I have said, will be to keep thy words.* The commands that he was so eager to obey were not rules of man, but were precepts of the Most High.

Many are eager to obey custom and society, yet they are

slow in serving God. It is a crying shame that people would be served quickly, while God's work would be ignored or performed with vague negligence.

61. *The company of the wicked have robbed me, but I have not forgotten thy law.*

The company of the wicked have robbed me. In the past, the wicked derided David, and now they have defrauded him. Ungodly people grow worse and become more and more daring, so that they go from ridicule to robbery. Much of this bold opposition arose from their being bound together. People in a group will dare to do things that they would not even think of doing when alone. When pieces of burning wood are laid together, there is no telling what a flame they will create.

It seems that whole groups of men attacked this one child of God. They were cowardly enough for anything. While they couldn't kill him, they robbed him. The dogs of Satan will trouble saints if they cannot devour them. David's enemies did their utmost; first, the serpents hissed, and then they stung. Since words didn't accomplish their goal, the wicked resorted to force. How much the ungodly have plundered the saints in all ages, and how often the righteous have gladly tolerated the plundering of their belongings.

But I have not forgotten thy law. This was good. David's sense of injustice, his sorrow about his losses, and his attempts at defending himself did not divert him from the ways of God. He would not do wrong in order to prevent suffering wrong nor to avenge wrong that had been done to him. He carried the law in his heart, and therefore no disturbing thoughts could prevent him from following it. He might have forgotten himself if he had forgotten the law. As it was, he was ready to forgive and forget the injuries done to him, for his heart was taken up with the Word of God. The wicked had not robbed him of his most-prized treasure, for they had left him his holiness and his happiness.

Some read this passage as "The company of the wicked surround me." They hemmed him in, cut him off from help, and shut up every avenue of escape; but the man of God had his protector with him. A clear conscience relied upon the promise, and a brave resolve held fast to the precept. He could not be bribed or bullied into sin. The barricades of the ungodly could not keep God from him, nor him from God, for God was his portion, and no one could deprive him of it, either by force or fraud. True grace can withstand the test. Some people are barely gracious among their circle of friends, but this man was holy amid a ring of enemies.

62. At midnight I will rise to give thanks unto thee because of the judgments of thy righteousness.

David was not afraid of the robbers. He rose up at midnight, not to watch his house, but to praise his God. Midnight is the hour for burglars, and entire groups of them surrounded David, but they didn't occupy his thoughts. Instead, his thoughts were all focused upward on the Lord his God. He did not think about thieves, but about thanks; not about what they would steal, but of what he would give to his God. A thankful heart is such a blessing that it drives out fear and makes room for praise. Thanksgiving turns night into day and consecrates every hour to the worship of God. For a Christian, every hour is to be lived according to God's Word.

The psalmist paid attention to posture; he did not lie in bed and praise. While there isn't much in the position of the body, there is still something about it that ought to be observed whenever it is helpful to devotion and meaningful for our diligence or humility. Many kneel without praying, and some pray without kneeling; but the best posture is to kneel and pray. Here in verse 62, it would have added no virtue to rise without giving thanks, and it wouldn't have been a sin to give thanks without rising; but to both rise and give thanks is a happy combination.

As for the season, it was quiet and lonely, and also proved his zeal. At midnight he would be unobserved and undisturbed. It was his own time which he kept from his sleep so he would have time free from the responsibilities of public duties to devote to private devotions. Midnight ends one day and begins another. Therefore, it was suitable to use these solemn moments in communion with the Lord. At the turn of the night, he turned to his God. He had thanks to give for mercies which God had given. He had his mind on the truth of verse 57, that God is his portion, and if anything can make someone sing in the middle of the night, that is it.

The righteous activities of the great Judge gladdened the heart of this godly man. While His judgments reveal the side of God that may cause terror and dread in the hearts of the wicked, they offer no terror to the righteous. The righteous admire them and adore the Lord for them. They rise at night to bless God so He will vindicate his elect. Some hate the very notion of divine justice, and in this they are as far away from the understanding of man of God as the north is from the south, for David was filled with joyful gratitude at the memory of the sentences of the Judge of all the earth.

Without a doubt, in the expression *judgments of thy righteousness*, David refers also to the written judgments of God upon various points of moral conduct. Indeed, all the divine precepts can be viewed in that light. They are all the legal decisions of the Supreme Arbiter of right and wrong. David delighted in these judgments. Like Paul, he could say, *For I delight with the law of God with the inward man* (Romans 7:22). He could not find enough time during the day to study the words of divine wisdom or to bless God for them, so he gave up his sleep that he might express his gratitude for such a law and such a Lawgiver.

This verse is an expansion on the wisdom of verse 52, and also includes the principle of verse 55. Our author never repeats himself. Even though he runs up and down the same scale, his music has infinite variety. The variations and combinations that can be formed in connection with a few vital truths are innumerable.

63. *I am a companion of all those that fear thee and of those that keep thy precepts.*

I am a companion of all those that fear thee. The last verse said, *I will*, and this verse says, *I am.* We can hardly hope to be right in the future unless we are right now. The holy man spent his nights with God and his days with God's people. Those who fear God love those who fear Him, and they make little choice as to the rank of their companions as long as they are truly God-fearing people. David was a king, and yet he consorted with all who feared the Lord, whether they were obscure or famous, poor or rich. He was a fellow commoner of the College of All-Saints.

He didn't select a few especially distinguished saints and leave ordinary believers alone. No, he was glad for the company of those who only had the beginning of wisdom in the form of the *fear of the Lord*. He was pleased to sit with them and discuss the basic lessons of the school of faith. He looked for inward godly fear, but he also expected to see outward piety in those with whom he associated. For this reason, he adds *and of those that keep thy precepts*. If they kept the Lord's commands, the Lord's servant would keep their company.

David was known to be on the godly side. He was always

of the Puritan party, desiring to follow God strictly and in all things. The wicked men of Belial hated him for this, and no doubt despised him for keeping such unfashionable company as that of humble men and women who held to godly manners, morals, and opinions. The man of God is by no means ashamed of his associates. So far was he from this that he even found it honorable to declare his union with them and let his enemies make what they could of it. He found both pleasure and benefit in keeping godly company. He became a better person by associating with the good, and he derived honor from keeping proper honorable company.

What do you say, dear reader? Do you love holy company? Are you at home among virtuous people? If so, you can derive comfort from that fact. Birds of a feather flock together. A man is known by his company. Those who have no fear of God seldom desire the company of true believers. It is too slow and too dull for them. Let this be our comfort: when death lets us go, we will be go to our own company, and those who loved the saints on earth will be numbered with them in heaven.

> *He found both pleasure and benefit in keeping godly company.*

There is a measure of parallelism between this seventh verse of its octave and the seventh of *Teth* (verse 71) and of *Jod* (verse 79), but as a rule, the similarities that were so clearly manifested in earlier verses are now becoming dim. As the sense deepens, the artificial form of expression is less regarded.

> 64. *The earth, O LORD, is full of thy mercy and teaches me thy statutes.*

The earth, O LORD, is full of thy mercy. David had been exiled, but he had never been driven beyond the range of mercy, for he found the world to be filled with it everywhere. He had wandered in deserts and hidden in caves, and there, too, he had seen and felt the lovingkindness of the Lord. He had learned that the love of Jehovah extended far beyond the boundaries of the land of promise and the people of Israel, and in this verse he expressed that large-hearted idea of God that is so seldom seen in the modern Jew.

How sweet it is to us to know that not only is there mercy all over the world, but there is such an abundance of it that the earth is full of it. It is little wonder that since the psalmist knew the Lord to be his portion, he hoped to obtain a degree of his mercy for himself. He desired to know more about one so good; and as the Lord has so freely revealed Himself in nature, he felt encouraged to pray, "Teach me Your statutes."

It was the greatest standard of excellence to David to be taught of God and to be taught in God's own law. He could not think of a greater mercy than this. Surely, He who fills the universe with His grace will grant such a request as this to His own child. Let us breathe this desire to the All-merciful Jehovah, and we may be assured of its fulfillment.

The first verse of this group of eight is fragrant with full assurance and strong resolve, and this last verse overflows with a sense of the divine fullness and the psalmist's personal dependence. This is an illustration of the fact that full assurance neither stifles prayer nor hinders humility. It would not be wrong to say that it creates humility and suggests supplication. "You are *my portion, O LORD*" is good to be followed by "teach me," because the heir of a great estate should be thoroughly educated so his behavior can agree with his fortune. What manner of disciples ought we to be whose inheritance is the Lord of hosts!

Those who have God for their portion long to have Him for their teacher. Moreover, those who have resolved to obey are the most eager to be taught. "I have said that I would keep thy words" is beautifully succeeded by *teach me thy statutes*. Those who wish to keep a law are anxious to know all its clauses and provisions, for fear they might inadvertently offend by not keeping the whole law. He who does not care to be instructed by the Lord has never honestly resolved to be holy.

Psalm 119:65-72

TETH

Thou hast dealt well with thy slave, O LORD, according unto thy word,

which teaches me discernment and knowledge, for I have believed thy commandments.

Before I was humbled, I went into error, but now I keep thy spoken word.

Thou art good and doest good; teach me thy statutes.

The proud have forged a lie against me, but I will keep thy precepts with my whole heart.

Their heart became fat like grease, but I delight in thy law.

It was good for me that I have been humbled, that I might learn thy statutes.

The law of thy mouth is better unto me than thousands of gold and silver.

In this ninth section, the verses in Hebrew all begin with the letter *Teth*. In our own version, they all begin with the letter T, except verses 66, 67, and 71, and these can easily be made to do so by moving "which" from the start of verse 66 to the end of verse 65 to read, *teaches me discernment and knowledge.* Verse 67 can be read, "Till I was humbled," and verse 71 read, "Tis good for me."

These verses are tributes of experience, testifying to the goodness of God, the graciousness of His dealings, and the preciousness of His Word. The psalmist especially proclaims the excellent purposes of adversity and the goodness of God in afflicting him. The sixty-fifth verse summarizes the entire octave.

65. *Thou hast dealt well with thy slave, O LORD, according unto thy word.*

This is the summary of David's life, and it is also most assuredly the sum of ours. The psalmist tells the Lord the verdict of his heart; he cannot be silent, but must speak his gratitude in the presence of Jehovah, his God. From the universal goodness of God in nature, seen in verse 64, it is an easy and pleasant step to confess the Lord's uniform goodness to ourselves personally.

It is amazing that God has dealt at all with such insignificant and undeserving beings as we are, and it is far more amazing that He has dealt well with us, and so wondrously well. He has done all things well; this rule has no exception. In providence and grace, in giving prosperity and in sending adversity, in everything, Jehovah has *dealt well* with us. It is dealing well on our part to tell the Lord that we feel that He has *dealt well* with us, for praise of this kind is especially fitting and pleasant.

However, this kindness of the Lord is not by chance. He promised to do so, and He has done it according to His Word. It is very precious to see the Word of the Lord fulfilled in our happy experience. It endears the Scripture to us and makes us love the Lord of the Scripture. The book of providence corresponds with the book of promise. What we read in the pages of inspiration we encounter again in the leaves of our life-story.

We may not have thought it would be like this, but now that we have repented of our unbelief, we see the Lord's mercy to us and His faithfulness to His Word. From now on, we are bound to display a firmer faith both in God and in His promise. He has spoken well, and He has dealt well. He is the best of masters, for it is to very unworthy and incapable servants that He has acted so graciously. Does this not cause us to delight to serve Him more and more?

We cannot say that we have dealt well with our Master, for when we have done everything we can, we are only unprofitable servants (Luke 17:10); but as for our Lord, He has given us light work, large support, loving encouragement, and generous wages. It is a wonder He did not dismiss us long ago, or at least reduce our support or treat us harshly; yet we have not been dealt with in that way, but everything has been orderly and done with as much consideration as if we had submitted in perfect obedience. We have had enough bread to eat and some to spare, our clothing has been supplied as expected, and serving Him has dignified us and made us happy as kings. We have no complaints. We lose ourselves in loving gratitude, and we find ourselves again in careful thanks-living.

> *He has given us light work, large support, loving encouragement, and generous wages.*

66. *Which teaches me discernment and knowledge, for I have believed thy commandments.*

Which teaches me discernment and knowledge. Again, David begs for teaching, like he did in verse 64, and again he uses God's mercy as an argument. Since God had dealt well with him in the past, David is encouraged to pray for judgment to appreciate the Lord's goodness. The gift of good judgment is a form of goodness that the godly man needs and most desires, and it is one that the Lord is most ready to grant.

David felt that he had frequently failed in judgment in the matter of the Lord's dealings with him. From lack of knowledge, he had misjudged the chastening hand of the heavenly Father, and therefore he now asks to be better instructed, since he recognizes the injustice he had done toward the Lord by his hasty conclusions. He means to say, "Lord, You dealt well with me when I thought you were hard and stern. Please give me more understanding so I may not think so unfavorably of You again."

Recognizing our errors and sensing our ignorance should make us teachable. We are not able to correctly judge, for our knowledge is sadly inaccurate and imperfect. If the Lord teaches us knowledge, we will acquire good judgment, but not in any other way. The Holy Spirit alone can fill us with light and give our understanding proper balance. Since it is most desirable that we no longer be mere children in knowledge and understanding, let us fervently long for His teachings.

For I have believed thy commandments. His heart was right, and therefore he hoped his head would be made right. He had faith, and therefore he hoped to receive wisdom. His mind had been settled that the precepts of the Word were from the Lord, and so he understood that they were just, wise, kind, and profitable. He believed in holiness, and as that belief is no little work of grace upon the soul, he looked for still further acts of divine grace.

He who believes the commands of God is the one who will know and understand His doctrines and promises. If in looking back upon our mistakes and ignorance we can yet see that we wholeheartedly love the principles of His divine will, then we have good reason to hope that we are Christ's disciples and that He will teach us and make us people of good judgment and sound knowledge. Someone who has learned discernment by experience, and in this way has become a person of sound judgment, is a valuable member of the church and the means of much edification to others. Let all who desire to be greatly useful offer the prayer of this verse: "Teach me good judgment and knowledge."

67. Before I was humbled, I went into error, but now I keep thy spoken word.

Before I was humbled, I went into error. This is likely in part due to the lack of difficulty. Often our difficulties act like a thorny hedge to keep us in the good pasture, while our prosperity is a gap through which we go astray. If we remember a time during which we faced no trouble, we also probably recollect that grace was low and temptation was strong at that time.

Some believers may cry, "Oh, if only it could be like those summer days before I was afflicted!" Such a complaint is most unwise and arises from a fleshly love of ease. The spiritual person who values growth in grace will praise God that those dangerous days of complaining are over, realizing that if the weather is stormier, it is also healthier.

It is good when the mind is open and candid, like in this instance. Perhaps David would never have known and confessed his own strayings if he had not been corrected with the rod. Let us join in his humble acknowledgments, for we have no doubt imitated him in his straying. Why is it that a little ease works so much disease in us? Can we never rest without rusting? Can we never be filled without growing fat? What weak creatures we are to be unable to bear a little pleasure! What corrupt hearts are those that turn the abundance of God's goodness into an occasion for sin!

But now I keep thy spoken word. Grace is in that heart that profits by its chastening. It is no use to plow barren soil. When there is no spiritual life, affliction works no spiritual benefit; but where the heart is sound, trouble awakens conscience, wandering from God's path is confessed, and the soul becomes obedient to the commands again and continues to be so.

Whipping will not turn a rebel into a child of God, but for the true child, a touch of the rod is a sure means of correction. In the psalmist's case, the medicine of affliction worked a change: *but*; an immediate change: *now*; a lasting, inward change: *I keep*; and a change Godward: *thy spoken word*. Before his trouble, he wandered; but after his trouble he kept within the hedge of the Word and found good pasture for his soul. The trial secured him to his proper place. It kept him, and then he kept God's Word. The uses of adversity are sweet, and this is one of them: it puts a bridle upon transgression and furnishes a spur for holiness.

68. *Thou art good and doest good; teach me thy statutes.*

Thou art good and doest good. Even in affliction, God is good and does good. This is the confession of experience. In Himself, God is essential goodness, and in every attribute of His nature, He is good in the fullest sense of the term. Indeed, He has a monopoly on goodness, for *there is none good but one, that is, God* (Mark 10:18). His acts are according to His nature; from a pure source flow pure streams.

God's goodness is not dormant or inactive. He displays Himself by His actions. He is actively benevolent. He does good. How much good He does, no tongue can tell. How good He is, no heart can conceive. It is good to worship the Lord like the poet does here – by describing Him. Facts about God are the best praise of God. All the glory we can give to God is to reflect His own glory back on Himself. We can say no more good about God than God is and God does. We believe in His goodness, and so we honor Him by our faith. We admire that goodness, and so we glorify Him by our love. We declare that goodness, and so we magnify Him by our testimony.

Teach me thy statutes. This is the same prayer as before, backed with the same argument. David prays, "Lord be good and do good to me, that I may both be good and do good through Your teaching." The man of God was a learner and delighted to learn. He credited this to the goodness of the Lord, and he hoped that for the same reason he would be allowed to remain in the school and continue learning until he could perform every lesson perfectly. His chosen textbook was the royal statutes, and he wanted no other book.

His chosen textbook was the royal statutes, and he wanted no other book.

He knew the sad result of breaking those statutes, and through a painful experience he had been led back to the way of righteousness. Therefore he begged, as the greatest possible instance of the divine goodness, that he might be taught a perfect knowledge of the law and complete conformity to it. He who grieves because he has not kept the Word longs to be taught it, and he who rejoices that by grace he has been taught to keep it is no less eager for the same instruction to be continued.

In verse 12, which is the fourth verse of *Beth*, we have much the same sense as in this fourth verse of *Teth*.

69. *The proud have forged a lie against me, but I will keep thy precepts with my whole heart.*

The proud have forged a lie against me. They first derided him (verse 51), then defrauded him (verse 61), and now they have slandered him. To harm his character they resorted to falsehood, for they could not find anything against him if they spoke the truth. They forged a lie as a blacksmith pounds out a weapon of iron. They counterfeited the truth as people make counterfeit coins. The original language may suggest a common expression: "They have patched up a lie against me."

They were not too proud to lie. Pride is a lie, and when a proud man *speaks a lie, he speaks of his own* (John 8:44). Proud people are usually the bitterest opponents of the righteous. They are envious of their good fame and are eager to ruin it. Slander is a cheap and handy weapon if the objective is the destruction of a virtuous reputation. When many proud people come together and conspire to create, exaggerate, and spread a malicious falsehood, they generally succeed in wounding their victim, and it is no fault of theirs if they do not altogether destroy him. Oh, the venom which lies under the tongue of a liar! Many happy lives have been embittered by it, and many good reputations have been poisoned as with the deadliest drug.

It is incredibly painful to hear unprincipled men hammering away on the devil's anvil, forging a new slander. The only help against it is the sweet promise, *No weapon that is formed against thee shall prosper; and every tongue that shall rise against thee in judgment thou shalt condemn* (Isaiah 54:17).

But I will keep thy precepts with my whole heart. My one concern will be to mind my own business and stick to the commandments of the Lord. If the mud that is thrown at us doesn't blind our eyes or bruise our integrity, it will do us little harm. If we keep the precepts, the precepts will keep us in the day of insult and slander.

David renews his resolve: *I will keep*; he takes a new look at the commands and sees them to really be the Lord's: *thy precepts*; and he stirs up his entire nature to the work: *with my whole heart*. When slander and lies drive us to more unwavering and careful obedience, they work our lasting good. Falsehood hurled against us may be used to promote our faithfulness to the truth, and the malice of men may increase our love to God. If we try to answer lies with our own words, we may be beaten in the battle, but a holy life is an unanswerable refutation of all slander, libel, and smears. Malice hesitates if we persevere in holiness despite all opposition.

70. *Their heart became fat like grease, but I delight in thy law.*

Their heart became fat like grease. They delight in overindulgence, but I delight in You, Lord. Through carnal indulgence, their hearts have grown unfeeling and coarse, but You have saved me from such a fate through Your correcting hand. Proud men become puffed up through fleshly luxuries, and this makes them prouder still. They revel in their prosperity and fill their hearts with the indulgences of the flesh until they become numb, effeminate, and self-indulgent. A greasy heart is hard and insensitive. It is a fatness that makes a person weak and foolish. It is a fatty degeneration of the heart that leads to feebleness and death. The fat in such men is killing the life in them. John Dryden wrote:

> "O souls! In whom no heavenly fire is found,
> Fat minds, and ever grovelling on the ground!"

In this condition, people have no heart except for indulgence. Their very being seems to swim and stew in the fat of food preparation and banqueting. Living on the fat of the land, their nature is overcome by what they have fed upon. The muscle of their nature has gone soft and fat.

But I delight in thy law. How much better is it to delight in the law of the Lord than in carnal indulgences! This makes the heart healthy and keeps the mind humble. No one who loves holiness has the slightest cause to envy the prosperity of those who are worldly. Delight in the law elevates and dignifies, while fleshly, carnal pleasures clog the intellect and degrade the passions. There is and always should be a clear contrast between the believer and the one who places his principal happiness in fleshly pleasures. That contrast is seen in the affections of the heart as much as in the actions of the life. *Their heart became fat like grease*, and our heart is delighted with the law of the Lord. Our delights are a better test of our character than anything else: As a man *thinks in his soul, so is he* (Proverbs 23:7).

David oiled the wheels of life with his delight in God's law, and not with the fat of sensuality. He had his delights and things he was fond of, his festivals and amusements, and he found all these in doing the will of the Lord his God. When law becomes delight, obedience is bliss. Holiness in the heart causes the soul to eat the fat of the land. To have the law for our delight will breed in our hearts the very opposite effects of pride. Deadness, sensuality, and stubbornness will be cured, and we will become teachable, sensitive, and spiritual. How careful we should be to live under the influence of the divine law so that we do not fall under *the law of sin and death* (Romans 8:2)!

71. *It was good for me that I have been humbled, that I might learn thy statutes.*

It was good for me that I have been humbled. Even though the humbling came from bad men, it was used for good results. Even though it was bad in that it came from them, it was good for David. It benefited him in many ways, and he knew it. Whatever he might have thought while enduring the trial, he recognized that he was better for it when it was over. It wasn't good for the proud to be prosperous, for their hearts grew sensual and senseless; but affliction was good for the psalmist. Our worst is better for us than the sinner's best. It is bad for sinners to rejoice and good for saints to sorrow. A thousand benefits have come to us through pain and grief, and among the rest is that we have been taught in the law.

That I might learn thy statutes. We have come to know and to keep these statutes by feeling the sting of the rod. We prayed for the Lord to teach us (verse 66), and now we see how He has already been doing it. Truly He has dealt well with us, for He has dealt wisely with us. We have been kept from the ignorance of the hard-hearted by our trials, and this, if nothing else, is good cause for constant gratitude. To be fattened by prosperity is not good for the proud, but to have the truth learned through adversity is good for the humble. Very little is to be learned without affliction. If we want to be scholars, we must be sufferers. As the Latins say, *Experientia docet,* or experience teaches. There is no royal road to learning the royal statutes. God's commands are best read by eyes wet with tears.

> *God's commands are best read by eyes wet with tears.*

72. *The law of thy mouth is better unto me than thousands of gold and silver.*

The law of thy mouth. This is a sweetly expressive name for the Word of God. It comes from God's own mouth with freshness and power to our souls. Written things are like dried herbs, but speech has a liveliness and freshness about it. It is good for us to look on the Word of the Lord as though it were newly spoken into our ear, for it is not decayed due to its age, but is as powerful and sure as though newly spoken.

Its precepts are valued when it is seen that they come from the lips of our Father who is in heaven. The same lips which spoke us into existence have spoken the law by which we are to govern that existence. From where could a law so sweetly proceed as from the mouth of our covenant God? We may rightly value beyond all price that which comes from such a source.

It *is better unto me than thousands of gold and silver.* If a poor man had said this, the people of the world without much understanding would have hinted that the author was jealous and that those without wealth are the first to despise it. However, this is the verdict of a man who owned thousands and could judge the value of money and the value of truth by actual experience.

David speaks about great riches; he heaps it up by thousands and mentions the varieties of its forms – *gold and silver.* Then he sets the Word of God above it all as better to him, even if others did not think that it was better for them. Wealth is good in some respects, but obedience is better in all respects. It is good to keep the treasures of this life, but it is far more commendable to keep the law of the Lord. The law is better than gold and silver, for these can be stolen from us, but the Word cannot be. These take flight, but the Word of God remains. These are useless in the hour of death, but that is the time the promise of God is most dear.

Instructed Christians recognize the value of God's Word, and they warmly express it, not only in their testimony to other people, but also in their devotion to God. It is a sure sign of a heart that has learned God's statutes when it values God's Word above all earthly possessions. It is an equally certain indication of grace when the precepts of Scripture are as precious as its promises. May the Lord cause us to prize the law of His mouth in this way.

See how this portion of the psalm is flavored with goodness. God's dealings are good (verse 65), holy judgment is good (verse 66), affliction is good (verse 67), God is good (verse 68), and here the law is not only good, but also better than the best treasure. Lord, make us good, through Your good Word! Amen.

Psalm 119:73-80

JOD

Thy hands have made me and fashioned me; give me understanding, and I shall learn thy commandments.

Those that fear thee will be glad when they see me because I have waited on thy word.

I know, O LORD, that thy judgments are right and that thou in faithfulness hast afflicted me.

Let, I pray thee, thy mercy be for my comfort, according to thy spoken word unto thy slave.

Let thy mercy come unto me, that I may live, for thy law is my delight.

Let the proud be ashamed, for they dealt perversely with me without a cause, but I will meditate in thy precepts.

Let those that fear thee turn unto me and those that have known thy testimonies.

Let my heart be perfect in thy statutes that I not be ashamed.

We have now come to the tenth portion of eight verses. In this group, each stanza begins with *Jod*, but it certainly doesn't talk about jots and tittles and other trivialities.

Its subject seems to be personal experience and its pleasing influence on others. The prophet is in deep sorrow, but he looks to be delivered and made a blessing. Attempting to teach, the psalmist first seeks to be taught (verse 73), persuades himself that he will be well received (verse 74), and then repeats the testimony that he intends to bring forth (verse 75). He prays for more experience (verses 76 and 77), for the confusing of the proud (verse 78), for the gathering together of the godly to him (verse 79), and again for himself, that he would be fully equipped for bearing witness and being strengthened in it (verse 80). This is the anxious yet hopeful cry of one who is heavily afflicted by cruel adversaries, and therefore makes his appeal to God as his only friend.

> 73. *Thy hands have made me and fashioned me;*
> *give me understanding, and I shall learn thy*
> *commandments.*

Thy hands have made me and fashioned me. It is beneficial for us to remember our creation. It is pleasant to see that the divine hand has had much to do with us, for it never makes a move apart from divine thought. It inspires reverence, gratitude, and affection toward God when we view Him as our Maker, who with careful skill and the power of His hands formed us and made us. He took a personal interest in us, making us with His own hands. He was doubly thoughtful, for He is represented as both making us and forming us. In both giving existence and arranging existence, the Lord manifested love and wisdom. Therefore, we find reasons for praise, confidence, and expectation in our being and well-being.

Give me understanding, and I shall learn thy commandments. As You have made me, teach me. Here I am, the vessel which You have made; Lord, fill it! You have given me both soul and body. Grant me now Your grace that my soul may know Your will, and my body can join in performing it. The plea is very forcible and magnifies the cry, *Forsake not the works of thine own hands* (Psalm 138:8).

Without understanding the divine law and obediently submitting to it, we are imperfect and useless; but we can reasonably hope that the great Potter will complete His work and give the finishing touch to it by imparting to us sacred knowledge and holy character. If God had made us without precision and hadn't elaborately fashioned us, this argument would lose much of its force; but certainly from the delicate art and marvelous skill that the Lord has shown in the formation of the human body, we may conclude that He is prepared to take equal pains with the soul until it will perfectly bear His image.

A man without a mind is an idiot – the mere mockery of a man, and a mind without grace is wicked – the sad perversion of a mind. We pray that we will not be left without spiritual judgment or understanding. This is what the psalmist sought in verse 66, and here in verse 73 he pleads for it again. There is no true knowing and keeping of the commandments without it. Fools can sin, but only those who are taught of God can be holy. We often speak about gifted men, but he whom God has given a sanctified understanding has the best gifts with which to know and value the ways of the Lord. Note that David's prayer for understanding is not for the sake of speculative knowledge or the gratification of his curiosity. He desires an enlightened judgment so he can learn God's commandments and become obedient and holy. This is the best of learning.

A man can live at this school where this understanding of truth is taught all his days, and yet cry out for the ability to learn more. The commandment of God is exceedingly broad, and so it provides opportunity for the most vigorous and instructed mind to continue to learn. In fact, no one by nature has an understanding capable of taking in such a wide field. It is because of this that we have the prayer, *Give me understanding* – as much as to say I can learn other things with the mind I have, but Your law is so pure, perfect, spiritual, and sublime, that I need to have my mind enlarged before I can become proficient in it.

David appeals to his Maker to do this, as if he felt that no power short of that which made him could make him wise unto holiness. We need to become a new creation, and who can grant us this but the Creator Himself? He who made us live must make us learn. He who gave us power to stand must give us grace to understand. Let each one of us breathe to heaven the prayer of this verse before we take one more step, for we will be lost in these petitions unless we pray our way through them and cry to God for understanding.

74. *Those that fear thee will be glad when they see me because I have waited on thy word.*

When a man of God obtains grace for himself, he becomes a blessing to others – especially if that grace has made him a man of sound understanding and holy knowledge. God-fearing people are encouraged when they meet with experienced believers. A hopeful man is a gift sent by God when things are going downhill or when he is in danger. When the hopes of one believer are fulfilled, his companions are made glad, strengthened, and led to hope also. It is good for the eyes to see a person whose witness is that the Lord is true. It is one of the joys of Christians to hold conversations with more spiritually mature brothers and sisters.

The fear of God is not a left-handed grace, as some have called it; it is quite consistent with gladness, for if even the sight of a friend in Christ gladdens the God-fearing, how glad must they be in the presence of the Lord Himself! We do not only meet to share each other's burdens, but we also meet to partake in each other's joys. People filled with God's grace contribute much to the mutual gladness of other Christians. People full of hope bring gladness with them. Despondent spirits spread the infection of depression, and so few are glad to see them; but those whose hopes are grounded upon God's Word carry sunshine in their faces and are welcomed by their companions. When those who profess to know Christ chill all hearts by their freezing words, the godly avoid their company. May this never be our character!

> *We do not only meet to share each other's burdens, but we also meet to partake in each other's joys.*

> 75. *I know, O LORD, that thy judgments are right and that thou in faithfulness hast afflicted me.*

I know, O LORD, that thy judgments are right. He who desires to learn more must be thankful for what he already knows, and he must be willing to confess it to the glory of God. The psalmist had been severely tested, but he continued to hope in God under his trial, and now, in this verse, he affirms his conviction that he had been justly and wisely disciplined. He did not only think this, but he knew it to be true, and was so sure of it that he spoke it without a moment's hesitation. True Christians are sure about the rightness of their troubles, even when they cannot see the intent of them. It made the godly glad to hear David say, *Thou in faithfulness hast afflicted me.*

Because love required severity, the Lord exercised it. It was not because God was unfaithful that the believer found himself in severe difficulty, but for just the opposite reason. It was the faithfulness of God to His covenant that brought the chosen one under the rod. It might not be necessary that others should be tried just then, but it was necessary for the psalmist, and so the Lord did not withhold the blessing. Our heavenly Father is no Eli. He will not allow His children to sin without discipline. His love is too intense for that. The person who makes the confession found in this verse is already progressing in the school of grace and is learning the commandments. This third verse of the section corresponds to the third of *Teth* (verse 67), and to a degree, to several other verses which make the thirds in their octaves.

*76. Let, I pray thee, thy mercy be for my comfort,
according to thy spoken word unto thy slave.*

Having confessed the righteousness of the Lord, David now appeals to God's mercy, and while he does not ask that the rod be removed, he earnestly begs for comfort under it. Righteousness and faithfulness provide us no consolation if we cannot also enjoy mercy, and blessed be God, we can expect this, for this is promised us in the Word. The words *mercy be for my comfort* are a pleasing combination and express exactly what we need during times of affliction. We need mercy to forgive the sin and kindness to sustain us during the time of sorrow. With these, we can be comfortable on the cloudy and dark day, and without them we are miserable indeed. Therefore, let us pray for these to the Lord, whom we have grieved by our sin, and let us plead the word of His grace as our sole reason for expecting His favor.

Blessed be His name, for despite our faults we are still His servants, and we serve a compassionate Master. Some read the last clause, *according to thy spoken word unto thy slave*, and say that when David wrote this he was remembering and pleading some special saying of the Lord. Can't we remember some such "faithful saying," and make it the foundation of our requests to God? That phrase, *according to thy spoken word*, is one that is greatly loved. It shows the motive for mercy and the manner of mercy. Our prayers are according to the mind of God when they are according to the Word of God.

77. Let thy mercy come unto me, that I may live, for thy law is my delight.

Let thy mercy come unto me, that I may live. David was so hard-pressed that if God did not comfort him, he would be at death's door. He did not just need mercy, but mercies, and these had to be of a very gracious and considerate kind, even tender mercies, for he was severely afflicted with his wounds. These gentle favors must be the Lord's giving, for nothing less would be enough.

These mercies must reach all the way to the sufferer's heart, for he was not able to journey after them. All he could do was to breathe out, "Oh, that they would come!" If deliverance did not come soon, he felt ready to die; yet just a verse or so ago he told us that he hoped in God's Word. How true it is that hope lives on when death seems written all around us!

An unbeliever says, *dum spiro spero* (while I breathe, I hope), but the Christian can say, *dum expiro spero* (even when I die, I still expect the blessing). Yet no true child of God can live without the tender mercy of the Lord. To be under God's displeasure is death to him. Notice again the delightful combination of the words – tender mercies – used in most English versions. Was there ever a sweeter sound than this – tender mercies? The one who has been grievously afflicted, and yet tenderly comforted, is the only one who knows the meaning of such fine language.

How truly we live when tender mercy comes to us! Then we do not merely exist, but we live. We are lively, full of life, vibrant, and vigorous. We do not know what life is until we know God. Some are said to die by the visitation of God, but we live by it.

For thy law is my delight. Oh, blessed faith! He is a noble believer who rejoices in the law even when its broken precepts cause him to suffer. To delight in the Word when it rebukes us is proof that we are profiting under it. Surely, this is a plea that will prevail with God, however bitter our griefs might be. If we still delight in the law of the Lord, He cannot let us die. He must and will cast a tender look upon us and comfort our hearts.

78. *Let the proud be ashamed, for they dealt perversely with me without a cause, but I will meditate in thy precepts.*

Let the proud be ashamed. David begged that the judgments of God might no longer fall on himself, but rather upon his cruel adversaries. God will not allow those who hope in His Word to be put to shame, for He reserves that reward for those who are arrogant. They will yet be overtaken with confusion and become the subjects of contempt, while God's afflicted ones will lift up their heads again. Shame is for the proud, for it is a shameful thing to be proud. Shame is not for the holy, for there is nothing in holiness to be ashamed of.

For they dealt perversely with me without a cause. Their desire to do evil to David was unprovoked. Lies were invented to forge an accusation against him. They had to bend his actions out of their true shape before they could assail his character. Evidently, the psalmist strongly felt the hatred of his enemies. His awareness of his innocence regarding them created a burning sense of injustice, and he appealed to the righteous Lord to take his part and clothe his false accusers with shame. He probably mentioned them as *the proud* because he knew that the Lord always takes vengeance on those who are proud, and He vindicates the cause of those whom they oppress. Sometimes David mentions the proud, and sometimes the wicked, but he always means the same people. The words are interchangeable. The person who is proud is sure to be wicked, and proud persecutors are the worst of the wicked.

But I will meditate in thy precepts. David left the proud in God's hands and gave himself up to holy studies and contemplations. In order to obey the divine precepts, we have to know them and think much about them; that is why this persecuted saint felt that meditation must be the main use of his time. He would study the law of God and not the law of retaliation. The proud are not worth a thought. The worst harm they can do us is to take us away from our devotions. Let us confuse them by keeping all the closer to our God when they are most malicious in their onslaughts.

In a similar position to this, we have met with the proud in other octaves, and we will meet with them again. They are evidently a great plague to the psalmist, but he rises above them.

79. *Let those that fear thee turn unto me and those that have known thy testimonies.*

Perhaps the tongue of slander had alienated some of the godly, and probably the actual faults of David had grieved many more. He begs God to turn to him, and then to turn His people toward him. Those who are right with God are also anxious to be right with His children. David craved the love and sympathy of gracious men of all classes – those who were beginners in grace and those mature in piety – *those that fear thee* and *those that have known thy testimonies.*

We cannot afford to lose the love of the least of the saints, and if we have lost their respect, we may most properly pray to have it restored. David was the leader of the godly party in the nation, and it wounded him to the heart when he perceived that those who feared God were not as glad to see him as they had been in the past. He did not rant and say that if they could do without him, then he could very well do without them. Rather, he so deeply felt the value of their sympathy that he made it a matter of prayer that the Lord would turn their hearts to him again. Those who are dear to God and are instructed in His Word should be very precious in our eyes, and we should do our utmost to be on good terms with them.

David has two descriptions for the saints: they are God-fearing and God-knowing. They possess both devotion and instruction. They have both the spirit and the knowledge of true faith. We know some believers who are gracious, but not intelligent; on the other hand, we know certain professors of Christianity who have all head knowledge and no heart conviction. David, however, is a man who combines devotion with intelligence. We want neither devout dunces nor intellectual icebergs. When fearing and knowing walk hand in hand, they cause people to be *thoroughly furnished unto all good works* (2 Timothy 3:17).

If those select people who both love God and learn of God are my favorite companions, I may hope that I am one of their group. Grant, O Lord, that such people always turn to me because they find me to be pleasant company.

80. *Let my heart be perfect in thy statutes that I not be ashamed.*

This is even more important than to be held in esteem by good people. This is the root of the matter. If the heart is firm in obedience to God, all is well, or will be well. If the heart is right, then we are generally right. If we are not spiritually healthy before God, calling ourselves pious is nothing more than an empty sound. Mere profession of faith will fail, and undeserved esteem will disappear like a bubble when it bursts. Only sincerity and truth will endure in the evil day. He who is right at heart has no reason for shame, and he will never have any. Hypocrites should be ashamed now, and one day they will be put to shame without end. Their hearts are rotten, and their names will rot.

This eightieth verse is a variation of the prayer of the seventy-third verse. There the psalmist sought sound understanding. Here he goes deeper and begs for a sound heart. Those who have learned their own frailty through sad experience are led to dive beneath the surface and cry to the Lord for truth in the inward parts. In closing the consideration of these eight verses, let us join with the writer in the prayer, *Let my heart be perfect in thy statutes.*

Psalm 119:81-88

CAPH

My soul faints with desire for thy salvation as I await thy word.

Mine eyes fail for thy spoken word, saying, When wilt thou comfort me?

For I am become like a wine skin in the smoke; yet I have not forgotten thy statutes.

How many are the days of thy slave? When wilt thou execute judgment on those that persecute me?

The proud have dug pits for me, but they do not proceed according to thy law.

All thy commandments are of the same truth; they persecute me wrongfully; help me.

They have almost consumed me upon earth, but I have not forsaken thy precepts.

Cause me to live according to thy mercy, so I shall keep the testimony of thy mouth.

This portion of this gigantic psalm sees the psalmist *in extremis* (in extreme difficulty). His enemies have brought him to the lowest condition of anguish and depression, yet he is faithful to the law and trustful in his God. This octave is the midnight of the psalm and is very dark and dreary. However, stars shine out, and the last verse gives promise of the dawn. After this, the tone will become more cheerful, but meanwhile it should comfort us to see such an eminent servant of God so harshly abused by the ungodly, because it shows us that evidently, in our own persecutions, nothing out of the ordinary has happened to us.

81. *My soul faints with desire for thy salvation as I await thy word.*

My soul faints with desire for thy salvation. David wanted no deliverance except that which came from God. His one desire was for *thy salvation*; but for that divine deliverance, he was eager to the last degree – up to the full measure of his strength and even beyond it, until he fainted. His desire was so strong that his spirit was exhausted. He grew weary while waiting, weak with watching, and sick with urgent need. As a result, the sincerity and eagerness of his desires were proved. Nothing else could satisfy him except deliverance brought about by the hand of God. His inmost nature yearned and hungered for salvation from the God of all grace, that he must have it or utterly fail.

As I await thy word. David felt that salvation would come, for God cannot break His promise nor disappoint the hope which His Word has excited. Truly the fulfillment of His Word is near at hand when our hope is firm and our desire fervent. Hope alone can keep the soul from losing strength or courage by using the smelling salts of the promise. Yet hope does not extinguish the desire for a speedy answer to prayer. It increases our persistence, for it both stimulates zeal and sustains the heart burdened with delays. To faint for salvation and to be kept from utterly failing in the hope of it is the frequent experience of the Christian. We are *faint from the pursuit* (Judges 8:4). Hope sustains when desire exhausts. While the grace of desire throws us down, the grace of hope lifts us up again.

82. *Mine eyes fail for thy spoken word, saying, When wilt thou comfort me?*

His eyes gave out from eagerly gazing for the compassionate appearance of the Lord, while his heart, in weariness, cried out for speedy comfort. To read the Word until the eyes can no longer see is only a small thing compared with watching for the fulfillment of the promise until the inner eyes of expectancy begin to grow dim with hope delayed.

We cannot set timetables for God, for this would be to limit the Holy One of Israel. However, we can earnestly petition and make fervent requests as to why the promise is delayed. David did not seek comfort other than that which comes from God. His question is, *When wilt thou comfort me?* If help doesn't come from heaven, it will never come at all. All the good man's hopes look in that direction, and he doesn't cast a glance any other way.

If help doesn't come from heaven, it will never come at all.

This experience of waiting and growing weak is well known by mature Christians, and it teaches them many precious lessons which they would never learn any other way. Among the best results is that the body rises into sympathy with the soul, both heart and flesh cry out for the living God, and even the eyes find a tongue, *saying, When wilt thou comfort me?* It must be an intense longing that is not satisfied to express itself by the lips, but speaks with the eyes – eyes failing through intense watching. Eyes can speak quite eloquently; they can be both silent and flowing, and can sometimes say more than tongues.

David says in another place, *The LORD has heard the voice of my weeping* (Psalm 6:8). Our eyes are especially eloquent when they begin to fail with weariness and sorrow. A humble eye lifted up to heaven in silent prayer can flash a flame hot enough to melt the bolts that block the entrance of vocal prayer, and so heaven will be taken by storm with the artillery of tears. Blessed are the eyes that are strained in looking after God. The eyes of the Lord will see to it that such eyes do not fail. How much better to watch for the Lord with aching eyes than to have them sparkling at the glitter of empty desires!

> 83. *For I am become like a wine skin in the smoke; yet I have not forgotten thy statutes.*

For I am become like a wine skin in the smoke. The skins used for containing wine, when emptied, were hung up in the tent, and when the place reeked with smoke the skins grew black and sooty, and in the heat they became wrinkled and worn. Through sorrow, the psalmist's face had become dark and dismal, furrowed and lined. His whole body so sympathized with his sorrowing mind that it lost its natural moisture and became like a skin dried and tanned. His character had been smoked with slander, and his mind parched with persecution. He was half afraid that he would become useless and incapable through so much mental suffering, and that people would look at him like an old worn-out wineskin that could hold nothing and serve no purpose. What a metaphor for a man to use who was certainly a poet, a theologian, and a leader in Israel, if not a king, and a man after God's own heart!

It is little wonder if we common people think very little of ourselves and are filled with distress of mind. Some of us know the inner meaning of this comparison, for we, too, have felt dingy, low, and worthless, only suitable to be cast away. The smoke which has engulfed us has been very black and hot. It seems not only to have come from the Egyptian furnace, but also from the bottomless pit; it has a clinging power which makes soot cling to us and darken us with miserable thoughts.

Yet I have not forgotten thy statutes. Here is the patience of the saints and the victory of faith. The man of God might be stained by falsehood, but the truth was still in him, and he never gave it up. He was faithful to his King even when he felt deserted and left to the vilest treatment. The promises of God came to his mind, and what was still better evidence of his loyalty was that the statutes were there, too. He held to his duties as well as to his comforts.

The worst circumstances cannot destroy the true believer's hold on his God. Grace is a living power that survives situations that would suffocate all other forms of life. Fire cannot consume it and smoke cannot smother it. A man may be reduced to skin and bone and all his comfort may be dried out of him, yet he may hold fast his integrity and glorify his God. It is, however, no surprise that in such a case the eyes that are tormented by the smoke cry out for the Lord's delivering hand, and the heart, exasperated and weak, longs for the divine salvation.

> 84. *How many are the days of thy slave? When wilt thou execute judgment on those that persecute me?*

How many are the days of thy slave? I cannot hope to live long in such a condition. You must come quickly to my rescue or I will die. Will my short life be consumed in such crushing sorrows? The brevity of life is a good argument against the length of an affliction. Lord, since I am to live so short a time, be pleased to shorten my sorrow also.

Perhaps the psalmist means that his days seemed too many since they were spent in such distress. He half wished that they were ended, and therefore, feeling troubled he asked, *How many are the days of thy slave?* Long life now seemed like a calamity rather than a blessing. Like a hired servant, he had a certain term to serve, and he would not complain about what he had to bear; but still the time seemed long because his griefs were so heavy.

No one knows the appointed number of our days except the Lord, and therefore the appeal is made to Him that He would not prolong them beyond His servant's strength. It cannot be the Lord's mind that His own servant would always be treated so unjustly. There must be an end to it. When will it be?

When wilt thou execute judgment on those that persecute me? He had placed his case in the Lord's hands, and he prayed that a sentence might be given and executed. He desired nothing but justice – that his character might be cleared and his persecutors silenced. He knew that God would certainly avenge His own people, but the day of rescue did not come. The hours dragged along heavily, and the persecuted one cried day and night for deliverance.

85. *The proud have dug pits for me, but they do not proceed according to thy law.*

As men who hunt wild beasts are accustomed to make pitfalls and snares, so David's enemies endeavored to entrap him. They painstakingly and cleverly worked to ruin him. *The proud have dug pits* – not one pit, but many. If one pit did not take him down, perhaps another would, and so they dug again and again.

One would think that such proud people would not have wanted to get their hands dirty by digging, but they swallowed their pride in hopes of swallowing their victim. Although they should have been ashamed of such nastiness and malice, they were conscious of no shame. On the contrary, they were proud of their cleverness. They were proud of setting a trap for a godly man.

They do not proceed according to thy law. Neither the men nor their pits were according to the divine law. These people were cruel and crafty deceivers, and their pits were contrary to the Levitical law and contrary to the command which tells us to love our neighbor. If people kept the statutes of the Lord, they would lift the fallen out of the pit, or they would fill it up so no one would ever stumble into it. However, when such people become proud, they are sure to despise others, and for this reason, they seek to outwit them so they can later hold them up to ridicule.

> *He believed that in the end, God's command would turn out to his advantage, and that he would not be on the losing end by obeying it.*

It was good for David that his enemies were God's enemies, and that their attacks upon him had no approval from the Lord. It was also much to his advantage that he wasn't ignorant of their schemes, because it prepared him to put up his guard, and he watched his ways for fear he might fall into their pits. While he kept to the law of the Lord, he was safe, though even then it was an uncomfortable thing to have his path made dangerous by the work of willful malice.

86. *All thy commandments are of the same truth; they persecute me wrongfully; help me.*

All thy commandments are of the same truth. He found no fault with God's law, even though he had fallen into sad trouble through obedience to it. Whatever the command might cost him, it was worth it. He felt that God's way might be rough, but it was right. It might make him enemies, but still it was his best friend. He believed that in the end, God's command would turn out to his advantage, and that he would not be on the losing end by obeying it.

They persecute me wrongfully. The fault lay with his persecutors and not with his God or with himself. He had done no harm to anyone, nor had he acted any other way than according to truth and justice. Therefore, he confidently appeals to his God and cries, *Help me.* This is a golden prayer, as precious as it is short. The words are few, but the meaning is full. Help was needed so the persecuted one might avoid the snare, might bear up under reproach, and might act so wisely as to confuse his enemies. God's help is our hope. It doesn't matter who might hurt us as long as the Lord helps us, for if the Lord truly helps us, no one can really hurt us.

Many times these words have been groaned out by troubled saints, for these are the kind of words that fit a thousand situations of need, pain, distress, weakness, and sin. "Help, Lord," is a fitting prayer for young and old, for struggles and suffering, for life and death. No other help is sufficient, but God's help is all-sufficient, and we cast ourselves on it without fear.

87. *They have almost consumed me upon earth, but I have not forsaken thy precepts.*

They have almost consumed me upon earth. David's enemies had almost destroyed him so as to make him fail completely. If they could, they would have eaten him or burned him alive – anything to bring a full end to the good man. Evidently he had fallen under their power to a large extent, and they used that power in a way that nearly consumed him. His enemies almost had him, but almost is not good enough, and so he escaped by the skin of his teeth.

The lions are chained. They can roam no further than our God permits. The psalmist perceives the limit of their power. At most, they could only consume him *upon earth.* They could touch his earthly life and earthly goods. *Upon earth* they almost ate him up, but he had an eternal inheritance that they could not even nibble at.

But I have not forsaken thy precepts. Neither fear, pain, nor loss could make David turn from the clear way of God's command. Nothing could drive him from obeying the Lord. If we stick to the precepts, we will be rescued by the promises. If hostile treatment could have driven the oppressed saint from the right way, the purpose of the wicked would have been answered, and we would have heard nothing more about David; but through divine grace, he was not overcome by evil. If we are determined to die rather than forsake the Lord, we can be certain that we will not die, but will live to see the overthrow of those who hate us.

88. *Cause me to live according to thy mercy, so I shall keep the testimony of thy mouth.*

Cause me to live according to thy mercy. This is a most-wise, most-blessed prayer! If we are revived in our own personal piety, we will be out of reach of our assailants. Our best protection from tempters and persecutors is more life. Lovingkindness itself cannot do any greater service for us than to cause us to have life more abundantly. When we are quickened, we are able to bear affliction, to confound those of the world who think they are wise, and to conquer sin. We look to the lovingkindness of God as the source of spiritual revival, and we entreat the Lord to quicken us, not according to what we deserve, but out of the boundless energy of His grace. What a blessed word is this *mercy*! Dissect its meaning and admire its double force of love.

So I shall keep the testimony of thy mouth. If quickened by the Holy Spirit, we will keep God's testimony by a holy character. We will also be faithful to sound doctrine when the Spirit visits us and makes us faithful. No one keeps the word of the Lord's mouth unless the word of the Lord's mouth quickens them.

We should greatly admire the spiritual wisdom of the psalmist, who does not so much pray for freedom from trials as for renewed life so he can be sustained while under those trials. When the inner life is robust, all is well.

In the closing verse of the last octave, David prayed for a sound heart, and here he seeks a revived heart. This goes to the root of the matter by seeking what is the most needful of all things. Lord, let it be heart-work with us, and let our hearts be right with You.

Psalm 119:89-96

LAMED

For ever, O LORD, thy word is settled in the heavens.

Thy truth is from generation to generation; thou hast established the earth, and it perseveres.

They persevere unto this day by thy ordinance; for they are all thy slaves.

Unless thy law had been my delight, I should have perished in my affliction.

I will never forget thy precepts; for with them thou hast caused me to live.

I am thine, keep me; for I have sought thy precepts.

The wicked have waited for me to destroy me, but I will consider thy testimonies.

I have seen an end of all perfection, but thy commandment is exceeding broad.

The tone is now more joyful, for experience has given the sweet singer a comfortable knowledge of the Word of the Lord, and this creates a glad theme. After tossing about on a sea of trouble, the psalmist here leaps to shore and stands upon a rock. Jehovah's Word is not fickle or uncertain; it is settled, determined, fixed, sure, and immovable. Man's teachings change so often that there is never time for them to be settled, but the Lord's Word remains the same from days of old, and it will remain unchanged eternally.

> 89. *For ever, O LORD, thy word is settled in the heavens.*

Some people are never happier than when they are unsettling everything and everybody, but God's view is not the same as theirs. The power and glory of heaven confirms each sentence that the mouth of the Lord has spoken, and so confirmed it that to all eternity it must stay the same – settled in heaven, where nothing can reach it. In the former section, David's soul grew weak, but here the good man looks beyond himself and recognizes that the Lord *does not faint, nor is he weary* (Isaiah 40:28), and neither is there any failure in His Word.

Verse 89 takes the form of attributing praise. The faithfulness and unchangeableness of God are proper themes for holy songs, and when we are tired of looking upon the shifting scene of this life, the thought of the unchanging promise fills our mouth with singing. God's purposes, promises, and precepts are all settled in His mind, and none of them will be changed. Covenant agreements are settled and will not be removed, no matter how unsettled the thoughts of people may become. Therefore, let us settle it in our minds that we will abide in the faith of our Jehovah as long as we live.

> 90. *Thy truth is from generation to generation; thou hast established the earth, and it perseveres.*

Thy truth is from generation to generation. This is an additional note of praise. God is not affected by the lapse of time. Not only is He faithful to one man throughout his lifetime, but also to his children's children after him, and to all generations as long as they keep His covenant and remember and obey His commandments. The promises are ancient, yet they are not worn out by centuries of use, for divine faithfulness endures forever. He who helped His servants thousands of years ago still confirms Himself strong on behalf of all those who trust in Him.

Thou hast established the earth, and it perseveres. Nature is governed by fixed laws; the globe keeps its course by divine command and displays no irregular movements. The seasons keep to their predestined order, the sea obeys the rule of ebb and flow, and everything else is arranged in its appointed order.

There is a similarity between the Word of God and the works of God, in that they are both constant, fixed, and unchangeable. God's spoken word that established the world is the same as that which He has embodied in the Scriptures. By the word of the Lord the heavens were made, and especially by Him who is without doubt THE WORD. When we see the world keeping its place in the universe, and all its laws remaining the same, we have assurance that the Lord will be faithful to His covenant and will not allow the faith of His people to be put to shame. If the earth continues, the spiritual creation will continue. If God's word is sufficient to establish the world, surely it is enough for the establishment of the individual believer. The time will come when the earth will pass away, but even then the Word of the Lord will stand. *Therefore, my beloved brothers, be ye steadfast, unmovable* (1 Corinthians 15:58).

> *The time will come when the earth will pass away, but even then the Word of the Lord will stand.*

91. *They persevere unto this day by thy ordinance; for they are all thy slaves.*

They persevere unto this day by thy ordinance. Because the Lord has told the universe to continue, it remains, and all its laws continue to operate with precision and power. Because the might of God is ever present to maintain them, all things continue. The word which spoke all things into existence has supported them until now, and still supports them both in being and in well-being. God's decree is the reason for the continued existence of creation. What important forces these decrees are! How much all the decrees of God are to be held in reverence!

For they are all thy slaves. Created at first by God's word, they then obey that word, thus answering the purpose of their existence and working out the design of their Creator. Both great and small things pay homage to the Lord. No atom escapes His rule, and no world avoids His government. Will we wish to be free of the Lord's influence and become lords to ourselves? If that were possible, we would be dreadful exceptions to a law that secures the well-being of the universe. Rather, while we read that everything else continues and serves, let us continue to serve, and to serve more perfectly as our lives continue. By that word that is settled (Psalm 119:89), may we be settled. By the voice that establishes the earth, may we be established. By the command that all created things obey, may we be made the servants of the Lord God Almighty.

92. *Unless thy law had been my delight, I should have perished in my affliction.*

The word that has preserved the heavens and the earth also preserves the people of God in their time of trial. We are enamored with that word; it is a mine of delight to us. We take double and triple delight in it and derive a multiplied pleasure from it. This places us in good standing when all other delights are taken from us.

If the spiritual comforts of God's Word didn't uplift us, we would feel ready to lie down and die from our grief, but the sustaining influence of the Word carries us above all that depression and despair that naturally grow out of severe affliction. Some of us can definitely confirm this statement, for if it had not been for divine grace, our affliction would have crushed us out of existence, and we would have perished.

In our darkest times, nothing has kept us from desperation except for the promise of the Lord. At times, nothing has stood between us and self-destruction except for faith in the eternal Word of God. When worn with pain until the brain becomes dazed and our understanding is nearly extinguished, a sweet Scripture passage has whispered its heart-cheering assurance to us, and our poor, struggling mind has rested upon the bosom of God. That which was our delight in good times has been our light in adversity. That which kept us from presuming in the day has kept us from perishing in the night. This verse contains a sad uncertainty – *unless*. This verse also describes a horrible condition – *I should have perished in my affliction*; but this verse also implies a glorious deliverance, for he did not die, but he lived to proclaim the honors of the Word of God.

> 93. *I will never forget thy precepts; for with them thou hast caused me to live.*

When we feel the quickening power of a precept, we can never forget it. We may read it, learn it, repeat it, and think we have it, yet it can slip out of our minds; but once it has given us life or renewed our life, there is no fear of it slipping from our recollection. Experience teaches, and it teaches effectively.

How blessed it is to have God's decrees written on the heart with the golden pen of experience, and engraved on the memory with the divine stylus of grace! Forgetfulness is a great evil in regard to holy things. Here we see the man of God fighting against it and feeling sure of victory because he knew the life-giving energy of the Word in his own soul. That which quickens the heart is sure to quicken the memory.

It seems remarkable that he would credit the precepts with invigorating him, and yet this quickening lies in them and in all the words of the Lord. It is to be noted that when the Lord raised the dead, He spoke to them the word of command. He said, *Lazarus, come forth* (John 11:43), or *Maid, arise* (Luke 8:54). We may preach gospel precepts to spiritually dead sinners, since through divine truth, the Spirit gives them life.

The psalmist does not say that the precepts quickened him, but that the Lord quickened him through those precepts. So, he traces the life from the channel to the source, and he places the glory where it is due. At the same time, he valued the instruments of the blessing and resolved never to forget them. He had already remembered them when he compared himself to a wineskin in the smoke, and now he feels that whether in the smoke or in the fire, the memory of the Lord's precepts will never depart from him.

> *How blessed it is to have God's decrees written on the heart with the golden pen of experience, and engraved on the memory with the divine stylus of grace!*

94. *I am thine, keep me; for I have sought thy precepts.*

I am thine, keep me. This is a comprehensive prayer with a prevailing argument. Consecration is a good plea for preservation. If we are conscious that we are the Lord's, we can be confident that He will save us. We are the Lord's by creation, election, redemption, surrender, and acceptance, and so we have a firm hope and assured belief that He will save us. A man will surely save his own child: Lord, save me. The need of salvation is better seen by the Lord's people than by others, and so the prayer of each one of them is "save me." They know that only God can save them, and so they cry to Him alone. They know that no merit can be found in themselves, and so they need a reason drawn from the grace of God: *I am thine.*

For I have sought thy precepts. David proved that he was the Lord's. He had not achieved the level of holiness he desired, but he had intensely aimed at being obedient, and for this reason he begged to be saved even to the end. A person can seek biblical doctrines and promises, and yet be unrenewed in heart; but to seek the precepts is a sure sign of grace. No one ever heard of a rebel or a hypocrite seeking the precepts.

The Lord had evidently worked a great work in the heart of the psalmist, and so David implored Him to complete it. Saving is linked with seeking – *keep me; for I have sought*; when the Lord sets us seeking, He will grant us the saving. He who seeks holiness is already saved. If we have sought the Lord, we can be sure that the Lord has sought us and will certainly save us.

95. *The wicked have waited for me to destroy me, but I will consider thy testimonies.*

They were like wild beasts crouching along the way, or like robbers ambushing a defenseless traveler; but the psalmist went on his way without considering them, for his mind was focused on something better – namely, the witness or testimony God gave to the sons of men. He didn't allow the malice of the wicked to injure others without cause to take him away from his holy study of the divine Word. He was so calm that he was able to *consider*, so holy that he loved to *consider* the Lord's *testimonies*, and so victorious over all their plots that he did not allow them to drive him from his pious contemplations.

If the Enemy cannot cause us to withdraw our thoughts from holy study, our feet from holy walking, or our hearts from holy desires, he has not had much success in his attack. The wicked are natural enemies of holy people and holy thoughts. If they could, they would not just harm us, but they would destroy us, and if they cannot do this today, they will wait for further opportunities, always hoping that their evil goals can be accomplished. Until now, they have waited in vain, and they will have to wait much longer, for if we are so unmoved that we do not even give them a thought, their hope of destroying us must be a very poor one.

Note the waiting on both sides: the patience of the wicked who watch long and carefully for an opportunity to destroy the godly, and then the patience of the saint who won't quit his meditations, even to quiet his foes. See how the serpent's seed lie in wait like *an adder in the path, that bites the horse heels* (Genesis 49:17); but see how the chosen of the Lord live above their venom, taking no more notice of them than if they did not exist.

96. *I have seen an end of all perfection, but thy commandment is exceeding broad.*

I have seen an end of all perfection. David had seen perfection's limit, for it was only good up to a certain extent. He had witnessed its evaporation under the trials of life, its detection under the searching glance of truth, and its uncovering by the confession of the repentant. He realized that there is no perfection under the moon. Perfect people, in the absolute sense of the word, live only in a perfect world. Some people see no end to their own perfection, but this is because they are perfectly blind. The experienced believer knows that there is no true perfection in himself, in his brothers, or in the best person's best works.

It would be good if some who profess to be perfect could see even the beginning of perfection in their lives, for we fear they could not have begun right, or they would not talk so exceeding proudly. Is it not the beginning of perfection to lament your imperfection? There is no such thing as perfection in anything that comes from man.

But thy commandment is exceeding broad. When the exceeding breadth of the law is known, the notion of perfection in the flesh vanishes, for that law touches every act, word, and thought, and is of such a spiritual nature that it judges the motives, desires, and emotions of the soul. It reveals a perfection that convicts us of shortcomings as well as of sins, and it does not allow us to make up for deficiencies in one direction by being extra careful in others. The divine ideal of holiness is far too broad for us to hope to cover all its wide area, yet it is no broader than it should be. Who would want an imperfect law? No, its perfection is its glory; but it is the death of all boasting in our own perfection.

There is a breadth about the commandment that has never been fully met by a corresponding breadth of holiness in any mere person while here on earth. Only in Jesus do we see it fully embodied. The law of God is in all respects a perfect law, with each separate commandment far-reaching in its sacred meaning. All ten commandments cover everything, leaving us no room to please our passions. We may well adore the infinity of divine holiness, measure ourselves by its standard, and bow before the Lord in all humility, acknowledging how far we fall short of it.

Psalm 119:97-104

MEM

O how I love thy law! it is my meditation all the day.

Thou through thy commandments hast made me wiser than mine enemies, for they are eternal unto me.

I have more understanding than all my teachers, for thy testimonies have been my meditation.

I understand more than the elders because I keep thy precepts.

I have refrained my feet from every evil way, that I might keep thy word.

I have not departed from thy judgments, for thou hast taught me.

How sweet have been thy spoken words unto my taste! yea, sweeter than honey to my mouth!

Through thy precepts I have obtained understanding; therefore I have hated every false way.

Those who know the power of the gospel perceive an infinite loveliness in the law as they see it fulfilled and embodied in Christ Jesus.

97. *O how I love thy law! it is my meditation all the day.*

O how I love thy law! This is a note of exclamation. He loves so much that he must express his love, and he must express it to God in rapturous devotion. In making the attempt, he perceives that his emotion is inexpressible; therefore he cries, *O how I love!*

We not only reverence the law, but we love the law. We obey it out of love, and even when it reprimands us for disobedience, we love it nonetheless. The law is God's law, and therefore it is our love. We love it for its holiness, and we long to be holy. We love it for its wisdom, and we study to be wise. We love it for its perfection, and we yearn to be perfect.

It is my meditation all the day. Meditating upon the Word of God was both the cause and the effect of his love for God's law. He meditated on God's Word because he loved it, and he loved it more because he meditated on it. He so passionately loved it that he couldn't get enough of it; all day long was not too long for him to read and meditate upon it. His morning prayer, his noonday thought, and his evening song were all out of Holy Scripture.

In his worldly business he still kept his mind saturated with the law of the Lord. It is said of some men that the more you know them the less you admire them, but the reverse is true of God's Word. Familiarity with the Word of God breeds affection, and affection seeks still greater familiarity. When *thy law* and *my meditation* are together all day, the day grows holy, devout, and happy, and the heart lives with God in love to His Word and delighting in it. David turned away from everything but the Word and will of the Lord, for in the preceding verse he tells us that he had seen the end of all perfection, but he turned to the law and tarried there the whole time of his life on earth, growing wiser and holier.

98. *Thou through thy commandments hast made me wiser than mine enemies, for they are eternal unto me.*

Thou through thy commandments hast made me wiser than mine enemies. The commandments were David's book, but God was his teacher. The letter of the law gives us knowledge, but only the divine Spirit can make us wise. Wisdom is knowledge put to practical use. Wisdom comes to us through obedience. *If anyone desires to do his will, he shall know of the doctrine* (John 7:17). We learn not only from God's promises, doctrine, and sacred history, but also from His precepts and commands. In fact, from the commandments we gather the most practical wisdom and that which enables us to best cope with our adversaries.

A holy life is the highest wisdom and the surest defense. Our enemies are renowned for subtlety, from the first father of them – the old serpent, Satan – down to the last adder hatched from the egg. It would be pointless for us to try to match them in the craft and mystery of cunning, for the children of this world are wiser than the children of light in their generation (Luke 16:8). We must go to another school and learn from a different instructor; then by uprightness we will confound fraud, with simple truth we will vanquish secret scheming, and by open honesty we will defeat slander.

> *The letter of the law gives us knowledge, but only the divine Spirit can make us wise.*

A thoroughly straightforward man, devoid of all cunning, is a dreadful puzzle to diplomats. They suspect him of a subtle deceit through which they cannot see. He is indifferent to their suspicions, keeps on in his even tone, and confuses all their plans. Yes, honesty is the best policy. He who is taught of God has a practical wisdom that things like malice cannot supply to the crafty. While harmless as a dove, he also exhibits more than the serpent's wisdom.

For they are eternal unto me. David was always studying or obeying the commandments. They were his best and constant companions. If we wish to become proficient, we must be relentless. If we always keep the wise law near us, we will become wise, and when our adversaries attack us, we will be prepared for them with that ready knowledge that comes from having the Word of God at our fingertips. Just as a soldier in battle must never lay aside his weapon, we must never have the Word of God out of our minds; it must always be with us.

99. I have more understanding than all my teachers, for thy testimonies have been my meditation.

I have more understanding than all my teachers. What the Lord had taught David has been useful in the camp, and now he finds it equally valuable in the schools. Our teachers of God's Word are not always to be trusted. In fact, we should not follow any of them unconditionally, for God will call us to account for the use of our understanding. When even our pilot errs, it is necessary for us to follow the chart of the Word of God closely, so we might be able to save the vessel.

If our teachers are sound and safe in all things that they teach, they will be truly happy for us to surpass them, and they will be the first to admit that the teaching of the Lord is better than any teaching they can give us. Disciples of Christ who sit at His feet are often better skilled in divine things than doctors of divinity.

For thy testimonies have been my meditation. Meditating on Scripture itself is the best way to acquire understanding. We may hear the wisest teachers and yet remain fools, but if we meditate on the sacred Word, we must become wise. There is more wisdom in the testimonies of the Lord than in all the teachings of men if they were all gathered into one vast library. The Book of books outweighs all the rest.

In this verse, David does not hesitate to speak the truth concerning himself, even though it is to his own honor, for he is quite innocent of self-consciousness. In speaking of his *understanding*, he intends to commend the law and the Lord, and not himself. Not a grain of boasting is found in these bold expressions, but only a childlike desire to set forth the excellence of the Lord's Word. He who knows the truths taught in the Bible will not be guilty of egotism if he believes himself to be possessed of more important truth than all who profess to be agnostic.

100. *I understand more than the elders because I keep thy precepts.*

The men of antiquity and the men of old age were outdone by the holier and more youthful learner. The learner had been taught to observe the precepts of the Lord in heart and life, and this was more than the most distinguished sinner had ever learned, and more than the philosopher of antiquity had so much as even hoped to know. David had the Word with him, and so surpassed his foes. He meditated on it, and so outran his friends. He practiced it, and so outshone his elders.

Instruction derived from Holy Scripture is useful in many ways, is superior from many points of view, and is unrivaled everywhere and in every way. Just as our soul can make her boast in the Lord, so we can boast in His Word. *There is none like that; give it to me* (1 Samuel 21:9), David said about Goliath's sword, and we can say the same regarding the Word of the Lord. If people value antiquity, they have it here. The ancient men were held in high esteem, but what did they know compared with what we discern in the divine precepts? "The old is better," someone says, but the oldest of all is the best of all, and that is none other than the Word of the Ancient of Days.

101. *I have refrained my feet from every evil way, that I might keep thy word.*

We cannot treasure the Holy Word unless we cast out all unholiness. If we keep the good Word, we must let go of the evil. David had zealously watched his steps and put a check on his conduct; he had refrained his feet. Not one evil way could entice him, for he knew that if he went astray in one road, then he had practically left the way of righteousness. With this in mind, he avoided every sinful way. The bypaths were smooth and flowery, but he knew very well that they were evil, and so he turned away and plodded along the narrow and thorny pathway that leads to God.

It is a pleasure to look back on self-conquests – *I have refrained*. It is still a greater delight to know we did not do this merely out of a desire to be in good standing with our companions, but with the one motive of keeping the law of the Lord. The essence of this verse is that sin is avoided so obedience can be perfected; or maybe the psalmist wanted to teach us that we do not really revere the Scripture if we are not careful to avoid every transgression of its precepts. How can we as servants of the Lord keep His Word if we do not keep our own works and words from bringing dishonor upon it?

102. *I have not departed from thy judgments, for thou hast taught me.*

Those whom God teaches are well taught. What we learn from the Lord we never forget. God's instruction has a practical effect – we follow His way when He teaches us, and it has a continuing effect – we do not depart from holiness. Read this verse in connection with the preceding verse, and you get the believer's *I have* and his *I have not*; he is good both positively and negatively.

What he did in refraining his feet preserved him from doing something other than what he might have done, which would be to "depart from thy judgments." He who is careful not to step an inch to the side will not leave the road. He who never touches the intoxicating cup will never be drunk. He who never utters an idle word will never be profane. If we begin to depart a little, we can never tell where we will end up. The Lord leads us to persevere in holiness by abstaining from even the beginning of sin, but whatever the method, He is the worker of our perseverance, and to Him be all the glory.

> *He who is careful not to step an inch to the side will not leave the road.*

God's Word pronounces *judgments* regarding moral actions, and we will do well to maintain those judgments as our infallible rule of thought and life.

103. *How sweet have been thy spoken words unto my taste! yea, sweeter than honey to my mouth!*

How sweet have been thy spoken words unto my taste! He had not only heard the words of God, but he had also fed upon them. They influenced his palate as well as his ear. They had an inward effect on his taste, as well as an outward effect on his hearing. God's words are many and varied, and the entirety of them make up what we call "the Word."

David loved each one of them individually and all of them as a whole, and therefore he tasted an indescribable sweetness in them. He expresses the fact of their sweetness, but since he cannot express the degree of their sweetness, he cries, *How sweet!*

Being God's words, they were divinely sweet to God's servant. He who put the sweetness into them had prepared the taste of his servant to discern and enjoy it. David makes no distinction between promises and precepts or between doctrines and threatenings. They are all included in God's words, and all are precious to him. Oh, for a deep love for all that the Lord has revealed, whatever form it may take!

Yea, sweeter than honey to my mouth! When he didn't just eat the Word but also spoke it by instructing others, he felt an increased delight in it. The sweetest of all worldly things falls short of the infinite deliciousness of the eternal Word. Honey itself is surpassed in sweetness by the Word of the Lord. When the psalmist fed on it he found it sweet, but when he bore witness of it, it became sweeter still. How wise it will be on our part to keep the Word on our palate by meditation and on our tongue by confessing the truths of God's Word! It must be sweet to our taste when we think about it, or it won't be sweet to our mouth when we talk about it. We must taste in the study what we preach in the pulpit. We must first spiritually become men of taste, and then we will have true enjoyment in setting forth the beauty and sweetness of the truth of God.

104. *Through thy precepts I have obtained understanding; therefore I have hated every false way.*

Through thy precepts I have obtained understanding. God's direction is our instruction. Obedience to the divine will produces wisdom of mind and action. Since God's way is always best, those who follow it are sure to be justified by the result. If the Lawgiver were foolish, His law would be the same, and obedience to such a law would involve us in a thousand mistakes; but since the reverse is the case, we may consider ourselves happy to have such a wise, prudent, and beneficial law to be the standard of our lives. We are wise if we obey, and we grow wise by obeying.

Therefore I have hated every false way. Because he had understanding, and because of the divine precepts, he detested sin and falsehood. Every sin is a falsehood. We commit sin because we believe a lie, and in the end the flattering evil becomes a liar to us and we find ourselves betrayed. True hearts are not indifferent to falsehood, but they grow warm with indignation. Just as they love the truth, so they hate the lie. True Christians have a universal revulsion of everything that is untrue. They tolerate no falsehood or foolishness, and they set themselves against all error of doctrine or wickedness of life.

A person who loves one sin is in league with the whole army of sins. We must have neither truce nor conference with even one of these enemies, because the Lord wars with them from generation to generation, and so must we. It is good to be a good hater. What do I mean by that? It is not to be a hater of any living being, but a hater of *every false way*. The way of self-will, of self-righteousness, of self-seeking, of worldliness, of pride, of unbelief, of hypocrisy, of lustfulness – these are all false ways, and therefore they are not only to be shunned, but they also ought to be abhorred.

This final verse of the stanza marks great progress in character and shows that the man of God is growing stronger, bolder, and happier than before. He has been taught of the Lord, so he discerns between the precious and the vile, and while he loves the truth fervently, he hates falsehood intensely. May all of us reach this status of discrimination and determination so we can greatly glorify God!

Psalm 119:105-112

NUN

Thy word is a lamp unto my feet and a light unto my way.

I have sworn, and I will perform it, that I will keep the judgments of thy righteousness.

I am afflicted very much; cause me to live, O LORD, according to thy word.

Accept, I beseech thee, the freewill offerings of my mouth, O LORD, and teach me thy judgments.

My soul is continually in my hand; yet I do not forget thy law.

The wicked have laid a snare for me; yet did not I err from thy precepts.

I have taken thy testimonies as a heritage for ever; for they are the rejoicing of my heart.

I have inclined my heart to perform thy statutes always, even unto the end.

One of the most practical benefits of Holy Scripture is guidance in the actions of daily life. God did not send it to astound us with its brilliant light, but to guide us by its instruction.

105. *Thy word is a lamp unto my feet and a light unto my way.*

Thy word is a lamp unto my feet. We walk through this world and are often called to go out into its darkness. Let us never venture there without the light-giving Word, so that our feet will not slip. Everyone should use the Word of God personally, practically, and habitually, so he can see his way and what lies in it. When darkness settles all around me, the Word of the Lord reveals my way like a flaming torch.

In olden times, some towns had no fixed lamps, and each passenger carried a lantern with him so he wouldn't fall into the open sewer or stumble over the heaps of excrement that defiled the road. This is a true picture of our path through this dark world. We would not know the way or how to walk in it unless Scripture, like a blazing torch, revealed it.

It is true that the head needs illumination, but the feet need direction even more, or else the head and feet might both fall into a ditch. Happy is the person who personally appropriates God's Word and practically uses it as his comfort and counselor – a lamp to his feet.

A light unto my way. It is a lamp by night, a light by day, and a delight at all times. David guided his own steps by it, and he also saw the difficulties of his road by its beams of light. He who walks in darkness is sure to stumble sooner or later, but he who walks by the light of day or by the lamp of night stumbles not, but stays upright. Ignorance is painful regarding practical subjects. It breeds indecision and suspense, which are uncomfortable. By imparting heavenly knowledge, the Word of God leads to decision, and when that is followed by determination, as in this case, it brings with it great restfulness of heart.

This verse converses with God in adoring yet familiar tones. Do we have a similar tone when we address our heavenly

Father? Note how much this verse is like the first verse of the first octave, and the first of the second and other octaves. The second verses are also often in unison.

> 106. *I have sworn, and I will perform it, that I will keep the judgments of thy righteousness.*

Under the influence of the clear light of knowledge, David had firmly made up his mind and had solemnly declared his resolve in the sight of God. Perhaps because he mistrusted his own changing mind, he had pledged himself in sacred form to abide faithful to the purposes and decisions of his God. Whatever path might open before him, he was determined to only follow the way upon which the lamp of the Word shone. The Scriptures are God's judgments, or verdicts, upon great moral questions. They are all righteous, and that is why righteous people should be resolved to keep them at all costs, since it is always right to do right.

The Scriptures are God's judgments, or verdicts, upon great moral questions.

Experience shows that the less covenants and promises people make to do the right thing, the better, and the brilliance of our Savior's teaching is against all unnecessary pledging and promising. Yet under the gospel, we should feel as obligated to obey the Word of the Lord as if we had taken an oath to do so. The bonds of love are not less sacred than the chains of law. When a person has made a vow, he must be careful to *perform it*, and when a person has not specifically vowed to keep the Lord's judgments, he is just as much bound to do so by obligations that exist apart from any promise on our part – obligations established in the eternal fitness of things and confirmed by the abounding goodness of the Lord our God.

Will not every believer realize that he is under bonds to the redeeming Lord to follow His example and to keep His words? Yes, the vows of the Lord are upon us, especially upon those who have professed discipleship, have been baptized into the holy name of the Trinity, have eaten of the Lord's Supper, and have spoken in the name of the Lord Jesus. We are enlisted and sworn in and bound to be loyal soldiers all through the war. So, having taken the Word into our hearts with a firm resolve to obey it, we have a lamp within our souls as well as in the Book, and our way will be light to the end.

107. *I am afflicted very much; cause me to live, O LORD, according to thy word.*

I am afflicted very much. According to the last verse, David had been sworn in as a soldier of the Lord, and in this verse he is called to suffer hardship in that capacity. Our service to the Lord does not shield us from trial, but rather secures it for us. The psalmist was a man consecrated to God, and yet he was a man who was chastened by God. His chastisements were not light, either, for it seemed as if the more he was obedient the more he was afflicted. He evidently felt the rod to be severely bruising him, and he pleads before the Lord the severity of his affliction as a reason why he needed to be sustained under it by an increase of his inner life. He doesn't complain, but he speaks by way of pleading. He pleads for much quickening due to his severe afflictions.

Cause me to live, O LORD, according to thy word. This is the best remedy for tribulation. The soul is raised above the thought of present distress and is filled with that holy joy that accompanies all vigorous spiritual life, and as a result, the affliction grows light. Jehovah alone can give life, for He has life in Himself, and therefore can impart it readily. He can give us life at any moment; yes, even at this very instant, for it is of the nature of quickening to be swift in its operation. The Lord has promised, prepared, and provided this blessing of renewed life for all His waiting servants. It is a covenant blessing, and it is as obtainable as it is needful. Frequently, the affliction is used as the means of bringing in the renewed life, just like the stirring of a fire promotes the heat of the flame.

In their affliction, some desire death; let us pray for life. Our forebodings under trial are often very gloomy, so let's plead with the Lord to deal with us not according to our fears, but according to His own Word. David did not have a lot of promises to quote, and many of these promises had been recorded in his own psalms, yet he pleads the Word of the Lord. How much more should we do so, since so many holy men have spoken to us by the Spirit of the Lord in that wonderful library that is now our Bible. Seeing we have more promises, let us offer more prayers, and let us exhibit more of the quickening power of the Word.

108. *Accept, I beseech thee, the freewill offerings of my mouth, O LORD, and teach me thy judgments.*

Accept, I beseech thee, the freewill offerings of my mouth, O LORD. Those who are living praise the living God, and therefore the one who is made alive spiritually presents his sacrifice. He offers prayer, praise, confession, and testimony. These, presented with his voice in the presence of an audience, were the tribute of his mouth to Jehovah. He trembles for fear that these might be so poorly uttered as to displease the Lord, and therefore he pleads for acceptance. He pleads in a way that the honor and praise of his mouth are cheerfully and spontaneously offered. All his words are freewill offerings.

There can be no value in forced confessions. God's revenue is not derived from forced taxation, but from freewill donation. There can be no acceptance where there is no willingness.

There is no work of free grace where there is no fruit of free will. Acceptance is a favor to be sought from the Lord with all earnestness, for without it our offerings are worse than useless. What a wonder of grace that the Lord will accept anything from such unworthy people as we are!

And teach me thy judgments. When we give the Lord our best, we become all the more concerned with doing better. When we know that the Lord has accepted us, we then desire to be instructed further so we can become even more acceptable. After being quickened, we need teaching, because life without light or zeal without knowledge would be only half a blessing.

David's repeated cries for teaching show the humility of the man of God, and also reveal to us our own need of similar instruction. Our judgment needs educating until it knows, agrees with, and acts upon the judgments of the Lord. Those judgments are not always so clear as to be understood instantly. We need to be taught in them as soon as we become aware of them until we admire their wisdom and adore their goodness.

109. *My soul is continually in my hand; yet I do not forget thy law.*

My soul is continually in my hand. David lived in the midst of danger. He always had to be fighting for existence – hiding in caves or contending in battles. This is a very uncomfortable and difficult state of affairs, and people are apt to think any means justifiable to end such a condition. However, David did not turn aside to find safety in sin, for he says, *yet I do not forget thy law.*

People say "All is fair in love and war," but David did not think this way. While he carried his life in his hand, he also carried the law in his heart. No danger to our body should make us endanger our soul by forgetting what is right. Trouble makes many people forget their duty, and it would have had the same effect on the psalmist if he had not been caused to live (verse 107) and received teaching (verse 108). His safety lay in his memory of the Lord's law. He certainly was not forgotten by his God, for his God was not forgotten by him. It is a special confirmation of grace when nothing can drive truth from our thoughts or holiness out of our lives. If we remember the law even when death stares us in the face, we may be well assured that the Lord is remembering us.

> 110. *The wicked have laid a snare for me; yet did not I err from thy precepts.*

The wicked have laid a snare for me. Spiritual life is the scene of constant danger. The believer lives with his life in his hand, and in the meantime, everyone seems to plot to take it from him, by deceit, if not by violence. We won't find it an easy thing to live the life of the faithful. Wicked spirits and wicked people will leave no stone unturned for our destruction. When all other strategies fail, and even hidden pits don't succeed, the wicked still persevere in their treacherous endeavors, and becoming craftier still, they set snares for the victim of their hate.

Smaller species of game are usually taken by this method, by snare, trap, net, or noose. Wicked people are quite indifferent as to the manner in which they can destroy a good person. They think no more of him than if he were a rabbit or a rat. Cunning and treachery are always the allies of malice, and anything like a generous or considerate feeling is unknown among the graceless, who treat the godly like vermin to be exterminated. When a person knows he is attacked in this way, he is too apt to become fearful or nervous and to rush upon some hasty and possibly sinful strategy for deliverance. But David calmly kept his way on the Lord's path and was able to write, *Yet did not I err from thy precepts.*

David was not snared, for he kept his eyes open and stayed near his God. He was not trapped and robbed, for he followed the King's highway of holiness, where God secures safety for every traveler. He didn't go astray from the right way, and he was not deterred from following it, because he consulted the Lord for guidance and obtained it. If we err or go astray from God's precepts, we part with the promises. If we get away from God's presence, we wander into the wilds where the fowlers freely spread their nets.

Let us learn from this verse to be on our guard, for we, too, have enemies who are crafty and wicked. Hunters set their traps in places animals usually visit, and our worst snares are laid in our own ways. By keeping to the ways of the Lord, we will escape the snares of our adversaries, for the Lord's ways are safe and free from treachery.

111. *I have taken thy testimonies as a heritage for ever; for they are the rejoicing of my heart.*

I have taken thy testimonies as a heritage for ever. David chose the Lord's testimonies as his lot, his portion, and his estate, and what is more, he took hold of them and made them so by taking them into his possession and enjoyment. David's choice is our choice. If we could have our desire, we would desire to keep the commands of God perfectly. To know the doctrine, to enjoy the promise, to practice the command – this is a kingdom large enough for us. Here we have an inheritance that cannot fade and cannot be divided. It is forever, and it is ours forever, if we have so taken it.

Sometimes, like Israel at their first coming into Canaan, we have to take hold of our heritage by difficult fighting, and if so, it is worthy of all our hard work and suffering. But it always has to be taken by a deliberate choice of the heart and will. God's election must be our election. What God gives by grace we must take by faith.

For they are the rejoicing of my heart. The gladness that had come to him through the Word of the Lord had caused him to make an unalterable choice of it. All the parts of Scripture had been pleasing to David and were still pleasing to him, and therefore he stuck to them and intended to stick to them forever. That which rejoices the heart is sure to be chosen and treasured. It isn't the head-knowledge, but the heart-experience that brings the joy.

In this verse – the seventh of its octave – we have reached the same sweetness as in the seventh verse of the last group of eight (verse 103). It is worthy to note that in several of the adjoining sevenths, delight is also evident. How good a thing it is when experience ripens into joy, passing through sorrow, prayer, conflict, hope, decision, and holy content into rejoicing! Joy fixes the spirit. Once a man's heart rejoices in the divine Word, he greatly values it and is therefore forever united to it.

112. *I have inclined my heart to perform thy statutes always, even unto the end.*

David was active and energetic in ruling his own heart. Not only could he say, "I am inclined," but also, *I have inclined*. He wasn't just half inclined toward righteousness, but was wholeheartedly inclined to it. His whole heart was bent on practical, persevering godliness. He was determined to keep all the statutes of the Lord with all his heart, throughout all his life, without straying or stopping. He made it his objective to always keep the law to the fullest. By prayer, meditation, and resolution, he leaned his whole being towards God's commands; or, the grace of God had inclined him to incline his heart in a sanctified direction.

Many people are inclined to preach, but the psalmist was inclined to practice. Many are inclined to perform ceremonies, but he was inclined to perform God's statutes. Many are inclined to obey occasionally, but David was inclined to always obey. Unfortunately, many are inclined to practice temporary religion, but this godly man was so inclined that he felt bound to all eternity to perform the statutes of his Lord and King. Lord, send us such a heavenly desire of heart as this, and then we will show that You have quickened and taught us. To this end, create in us a clean heart and renew a right spirit within us daily (Psalm 51:10), because only in that way will we be inclined in the right direction.

Many who once seemed inclined to better things have declined. May the Lord so rule our hearts that we will never lose our wholehearted inclination toward holy living.

Psalm 119:113-120

SAMECH

I hate vain thoughts; but I love thy law.

Thou art my hiding place and my shield; I have waited for thy word.

Depart from me, ye evildoers; for I will keep the commandments of my God.

Uphold me according unto thy word, and I shall live; and let me not be ashamed of my hope.

Hold me up, and I shall be saved, and I shall delight in thy statutes continually.

Thou hast trodden down all those that err from thy statutes; for their deceit is falsehood.

Thou dost cause all the wicked of the earth to come undone like dross; therefore I have loved thy testimonies.

My flesh trembles for fear of thee, and I am afraid of thy judgments.

This octave, whose initial letter is *Samech*, or *S*, has been compared to Samson at his death, when he took hold of the pillars of the house and pulled it down on the Philistines. Note how the psalmist grips the pillars of divine power with

Uphold me and *Hold me up*, and see how the house falls down in judgment on the unholy. *Thou dost cause all the wicked of the earth to come undone like dross.* This section carries the war into the enemy's country and reveals the believer as militant against falsehood and iniquity.

113. *I hate vain thoughts; but I love thy law.*

In this paragraph, the psalmist deals with thoughts, things, and people that are the opposite of God's holy thoughts and ways. He is evidently moved with great indignation against the powers of darkness and their allies, and his whole soul is stirred to stand against them with a determined opposition.

Just as he began the *Mem* octave with *O how I love thy law!* (verse 97), so he begins here with a declaration of intense love, but he prefaces it with an equally fervent declaration of hatred against that which breaks the law. The opposite of the fixed and infallible testimony of God is the wavering, changing thoughts of people. David had an out-and-out contempt and abhorrence for the vain opinions of man's conceited wisdom. All his reverence and respect went to the sure Word of divine truth. In proportion to his love for the law was his hatred of man's made-up beliefs and opinions.

The word *vain* is very properly supplied by the translators, for the original word denotes "halting between two opinions," and so it includes skeptical doubts. The thoughts of men are vanity, but the thoughts of God are truth. These days we hear a lot about "men of thought," "thoughtful preachers," and "modern thought." What is this except the old pride of the human heart? Vain man wants to appear wise, but the psalmist did not glory in his own thoughts. What was called "thought" in his day was something he detested. Even when a person thinks his best, his greatest thoughts are as far below those of divine revelation as the earth is beneath the heavens.

Some thoughts are especially vain in the sense of glorying in oneself, pride, conceit, and self-trust; others are vain in the sense of bringing disappointment, such as foolish ambition, unfounded hope, and forbidden confidence in man. Many thoughts are vain in the sense of emptiness and lightheartedness, such as the idle dreams and empty delusions in which many indulge. Many thoughts are vain in the sense of being sinful, evil, and foolish. The psalmist is not indifferent to evil thoughts like the careless are, but he looks on them with a hate as real as the love was with which he clung to the pure thoughts of God.

> *When we love the law, it becomes a law of love, and we cleave to it with our whole heart.*

The last octave was practical; this one is thoughtful. In the last one, the man of God paid attention to his feet; here he pays attention to his heart. The emotions of the soul are as important as the acts of the life, for they are the fountain and spring from which our actions proceed. When we love the law, it becomes a law of love, and we cleave to it with our whole heart.

114. *Thou art my hiding place and my shield; I have waited for thy word.*

Thou art my hiding place and my shield. God was David's shelter and shield. He ran to God for refuge from vain thoughts. There he hid from their tormenting intrusion, and in solemn silence of the soul he found God to be his place of sanctuary. When moving about the world, if David could not be alone with God as in a hiding place, the man of God could have the Lord with him as his shield, and in this way he could ward off the poisoned arrows of evil suggestion.

This is an experiential verse, and it testifies to what the writer knew of his own personal knowledge. He couldn't fight with his own thoughts or escape from them until he fled to his God, and then he found deliverance. Notice that he doesn't talk about God's Word as being his double defense, but he ascribes his safeguard to God Himself. *Thou art my hiding place and my shield.* When we are afflicted by subtle spiritual assaults, like those that arise from vain thoughts, we will do well to flee directly to the real presence of our Lord and to throw ourselves upon His power and love. The true God truly realized is the death of falsehood.

Happy is he who truly can say to the Triune God, *Thou art my hiding place*! He has witnessed God under that glorious covenant aspect that ensures the strongest comfort and support to the one who sees.

I have waited for thy word. David hoped in and waited on the Word of God, as well he should, since he had tried and proved it. That which has been true in the past can be trusted for the future. The psalmist looked to the Lord who had been the tower of his defense on previous occasions for protection from all danger and for preservation from all temptation. It is easy to exercise hope where we have experienced help. Sometimes, when gloomy thoughts afflict us, the only thing we can do is hope. Happily, the Word of God always sets before us objects of hope, reasons for hope, and invitations to hope, in such abundance that it becomes the very sphere and support of hope, and thus fearful and tempting thoughts are overcome. Amid fret and worry, a hope from heaven is effective in quieting such thoughts.

115. *Depart from me, ye evildoers; for I will keep the commandments of my God.*

Depart from me, ye evildoers. Those who govern their thoughts according to conscience are not likely to tolerate evil company. If we flee to God from vain thoughts, much more will we avoid vain men. Kings are all too apt to be surrounded by a class of men who flatter them, and at the same time take liberty to break the laws of God. David purged his palace of such parasites and wouldn't shelter them under his roof. No doubt such men would have damaged his reputation, for their actions would have been blamed on him, since the acts of courtiers are generally considered to be acts of the court itself. Therefore the king sent them packing, bag and baggage, saying, *Depart from me.*

Here he anticipated the sentence of the last great day, when the Son of David will say, *Depart from me, ye that work iniquity* (Matthew 7:23). We cannot send all evildoers out of our houses in this manner, but on occasion we may be bound by duty to do so. The standard of truth and reason requires that we not be frequently troubled with unrepentant servants or reprehensible tenants. A house is all the better for being rid of liars, thieves, filthy talkers, and slanderers.

In places where we have our choice of the company we keep, we are bound at all times to keep ourselves clear of doubtful associates. As soon as we have reason to believe that someone's character is unkind or cruel, it is better for us to have their room than their company. Evildoers make evil counselors, and therefore we must not sit with them. Those who say to God, "Depart from us," ought to hear the immediate echo of their words from the mouths of God's children, who should say to them, "Depart from us." We cannot eat bread with traitors, for fear that we also will become corrupted with high treason.

For I will keep the commandments of my God. Since David found it hard to keep the Lord's commandments in the company of the ungodly, he gave them their marching orders. He must keep the commandments, but he didn't need to keep the company of evildoers.

What a beautiful title this verse contains for the Lord! *My God*. The word *God* only occurs in this one place throughout this long psalm, and then it is accompanied by the personal word "my" – *my God*.

> "My God! How cheerful is the sound!
> How pleasant to repeat!
> Well may that heart with pleasure bound,
> Where God hath fix'd his seat."
> – Philip Doddridge

Because Jehovah is our God, we determine to obey Him and to chase out of our sight those who want to hinder us in His service. It is a wonderful thing for the mind to have come to a decision and to be steadfastly focused in holy determination – *I will keep the commandments of my God*. God's law is our delight when the God of the law is our God.

116. *Uphold me according unto thy word, and I shall live; and let me not be ashamed of my hope.*

Uphold me according unto thy word, and I shall live. It was so necessary that the Lord should hold up His servant that he couldn't even live without it. If the Lord would withdraw His sustaining hand, our soul would die, and every grace of spiritual life would die also. It is a sweet comfort that this great need for support is provided for in the Word, and we don't have to ask for it as if it isn't promised by the covenant of mercy. We must simply plead for the fulfillment of a promise, saying, *Uphold me according unto thy word*.

He who has given us eternal life has secured for us all that is essential to it, and since gracious support to keep us from falling is one of the necessary things, we can be sure we will have it. Note that when David chased away the evildoers, he did not feel safe when alone. He knew he needed to be preserved from his own weakness as well as from other men's evil examples, and so he prayed for upholding grace.

And let me not be ashamed of my hope. In verse 114, David had spoken about his hope as founded on the Word of the Lord, and now he begs for the fulfillment of the promise so his hope will be justified in the sight of men. A man will soon be ashamed of his hope if it is not based upon a sure foundation; but this can never happen in our case, since we trust a faithful God. We may be ashamed of our thoughts, our words, and our deeds, for they spring from ourselves, but we will never be ashamed of our hope, for that springs from the Lord.

> *We will never be ashamed of our hope, for that springs from the Lord.*

We may well be ashamed of our doubt, but we never need to be ashamed of our hope. Our frail nature is such that unless we are continually sustained by grace, we will fall so disgracefully as to be ashamed of ourselves and ashamed of all those glorious hopes that are now the crown and glory of our life. This can be the case even in solitude, for when evildoers are gone, we can still fall victim to our foolish fears. The man of God had voiced firm resolutions, but he couldn't trust in his own resolutions, no matter how solemnly they had been made. That is why he offered these prayers. It is not wrong to make resolutions, but it is useless to do so unless we season them well with believing cries to God. David intended to keep the law of the Lord, but first he needed the Lord of the law to keep him.

117. *Hold me up, and I shall be saved, and I shall delight in thy statutes continually.*

Hold me up – as a nurse holds up a little child. *And I shall be saved,* and not otherwise, for unless You hold me up, I will fall like an infant that is weak on its legs. We have been saved by past grace, but we are still not safe unless we receive present grace. Our English version first translates the word *uphold,* and then *hold up,* and we truly need this blessing in every form in which it can come, for our adversaries seek to throw us down in all sorts of ways. To be safe is a happy condition, and there is only one way to it, and that is by divine upholding. Thank God, for that way is open to the least among us.

Hold me up can also be a plea for elevation of mind. "Nearer, my God, to thee," is the same prayer. We want to be held *up* above self and sin, and everything else that would abase us, for then we are surely safe.

And I shall delight in thy statutes continually. In this manner of being held up and sustained, we obey; and in obeying, we are safe. No one will outwardly keep the Lord's statutes for long unless he has an inward respect for them, and this will never happen unless the hand of the Lord perpetually sustains the heart in holy love. Perseverance to the end, or continual obedience, comes only through divine power, and unless we are kept right by Him who first gave us grace, we will start going off course.

Happy is the man who realizes this verse in his life. Upheld through his whole life in a course of unswerving integrity, he becomes a "saved" man, a trusted man. Such a man demonstrates a sacred sensitivity of conscience that is unknown to others. He feels a tender respect for the statutes of the Lord, which keeps him clear of those inconsistencies and conformities to the world that are so common among others. Consequently, he becomes a pillar in the house of the Lord. Regrettably, we know some who profess faith in Christ who are not living uprightly, and so they lean toward sin until they fall over. Even when they are restored and set up again, they are never safe or reliable, nor do they have that sweet purity of soul that is the beauty of those who have been kept from falling into the mire.

118. *Thou hast trodden down all those that err from thy statutes; for their deceit is falsehood.*

Thou hast trodden down all those that err from thy statutes. There is no holding up those who are thrown down and then trodden down, for they choose to go into the wandering ways of sin. Sooner or later, God will set His foot on those who turn their foot from His commands. It has always been so, and it will always be so to the end. *If the salt has lost its savour,* what is it fit for but *to be trodden under foot?* (Matthew 5:13). God puts away the wicked like dross, which is only fit to be cast out like road-metal to be trodden down.

For their deceit is falsehood. They call it shrewd judgment, but it is absolute falsehood and will be treated as such. Ordinary people call it clever diplomacy, but the man of God calls a spade a spade and declares it to be falsehood, and nothing less, for he knows that is what it is in the sight of God. People who go astray from the right road invent nice excuses with which to deceive themselves and others, and so attempt to quiet their conscience and maintain their respect; but their mask of falsehood is too transparent. God treads down falsehoods. They are only fit to be trampled by His feet and crushed into the dust. How horrified will those be who have spent all their lives in fabricating a made-up religion when they see it all trodden on by God as a sham which He cannot endure!

119. *Thou dost cause all the wicked of the earth to come undone like dross; therefore I have loved thy testimonies.*

Thou dost cause all the wicked of the earth to come undone like dross. God doesn't mess around with them or handle them with kid gloves. No, He judges them to be the scum of the earth, and He treats them accordingly by putting them away. He puts them away from His Church, away from their honors, away from the earth, and finally, away from Himself. He says, *Depart from me, ye cursed* (Matthew 25:41).

If even a good man feels forced to put away the evildoers from him, how much more must the thrice-holy God put away the wicked! They looked like precious metal because they were intimately mixed up with it and laid up in the same heap, but the Lord is a refiner, and every day He removes some of the wicked from among His people, either by making a shameful discovery of their hypocrisy or by consuming them from off the earth. They are cast away like dross, never to be brought back. As the metal is better for losing its alloy, so the Church is better for having the wicked removed.

These wicked ones are *of the earth* and are called *the wicked of the earth.* They have no right to be with those who are *not of the world* (John 17:16). The Lord perceives them to be out of place and harmful, and therefore He puts them away, all of them, leaving none of them to deteriorate His people. The process will one day be perfected; no dross will be spared, and no gold will be left impure. Where will we be when that great work is finished? Will we be treasured with the gold or trampled with the dross?

Therefore I have loved thy testimonies. Even the Lord's stern punishment excites the love of His people. If He allowed people to sin without punishment or penalty, He would not be so fully the object of our loving admiration. He is glorious in holiness because He thus rids His kingdom of rebels and rids His temple of those who defile it.

In these evil days, when God's punishment of sinners has become the object of arrogant skepticism, we can consider it a mark of the true man of God that he does not love the Lord any less, but a great deal more, because of His appropriate judgment of the ungodly. We greatly value those passages of Scripture that are most dreadful in their condemnation of sin and sinners. We love those testimonies that foretell the overthrow of evil and the destruction of the enemies of God. A God more lenient would be a God less loving and less loved. Holy hearts love best a perfectly righteous God.

> *We love those testimonies that foretell the overthrow of evil and the destruction of the enemies of God.*

120. *My flesh trembles for fear of thee, and I am afraid of thy judgments.*

My flesh trembles for fear of thee. He did not rejoice over the punishment of others, but he trembled on his own account. Such was his awe in the presence of the Judge of all the earth, whose judgment he had just been considering, that he exceedingly feared and trembled. Familiarity with God breeds a holy awe of Him. Even the viler part of David's being – his flesh – felt a solemn dread at the thought of offending One so good and great, who would so effectively sever the wicked from among the just. Oh, poor flesh, this is the highest thing to which you can attain! Yet this is far better than your pride when you exalt yourself against your Maker.

And I am afraid of thy judgments. God's words of judgment are solemn, and His deeds of judgment are dreadful. They may well make us afraid. At the thought of the Judge of all – His piercing eye, His books of record, His day of examination, His fearful sentence, and the execution of His justice – we may well cry for cleansed thoughts, hearts, and ways, lest His judgments should fall upon us.

When we see the great Refiner separating the precious from the vile, we may well feel a godly fear, lest we could be cast away by Him and left to be trampled under His feet. Even His judgments, as we find them written in the Word, fill us with trembling, and this becomes a sign of grace to us. But what will the judgments themselves be when carried into effect? Oh, the trembling and fear that will be the eternal portion of those who run up against Jehovah's shield and defy His wrath!

Love in the previous verse is quite consistent with fear in this verse. The fear that contains torment is cast out, but not the fear that a child has for one's father that leads to reverence and obedience.

Psalm 119:121-128

AIN

I have complied with judgment and righteousness; do not leave me to my oppressors.

Be surety for thy slave for good; do not let the proud do violence unto me.

Mine eyes fail for thy saving health and for the spoken word of thy righteousness.

Deal with thy slave according to thy mercy, and teach me thy statutes.

I am thy slave; give me understanding, that I may know thy testimonies.

It is time for thee, O LORD, to act; for they have dissipated thy law.

Therefore I have loved thy commandments above gold, yea, above fine gold.

Therefore I have esteemed all thy precepts concerning all things to be right and I have hated every false way.

In this octave, the psalmist first entreats the Lord to intervene on his behalf. He asks for judgment from the great King, just like David had dealt out justice to his own people. He then declares his genuine and unreserved satisfaction with all the

Lord's commands and precepts and begs Him to defend His own law. He writes from the standpoint of his official experience. In our public as well as our private position, the Word is precious.

> 121. *I have complied with judgment and righteousness; do not leave me to my oppressors.*

I have complied with judgment and righteousness. This was a huge thing for an Eastern ruler to say at any time, for these tyrannical rulers mostly cared more for gain than justice. Some of them entirely neglected their duty and wouldn't even make judgments at all, preferring their pleasures to their duties. Many more of them sold their judgments to the highest bidders by taking bribes or being partial toward certain people. Some rulers gave neither judgment nor justice, while others offered judgment without justice. David gave both judgment and justice, and he saw that his sentences were carried out. He could claim before the Lord that he had dealt out evenhanded justice and was doing so still. On this fact, he founded a plea with which he backed the prayer: *Do not leave me to my oppressors.*

He who has been doing right, as far as his ability allows, can hope to be delivered from his oppressors when they make attempts to do him wrong. If I will not oppress others, I can pray that others won't be permitted to oppress me. A course of upright conduct is one that gives us boldness in appealing to the Great Judge for deliverance from the injustice of wicked men. This kind of pleading is not to be criticized as self-righteous, for it is most fit and acceptable.

When we are dealing with God regarding our shortcomings, we use a very different tone from that with which we face the criticisms of our fellow men. When untruthful accusers are involved and we are guiltless towards them, we are justified in pleading our innocence. Moral integrity is a great helper of spiritual comfort. If we are right in our conduct, we can be sure that the Lord will not leave us at all, and certainly will not leave us to our enemies.

122. *Be surety for thy slave for good; do not let the proud do violence unto me.*

Be surety for thy slave for good. This was the cry of Job and of Hezekiah, and it is the cry of every soul who believes in the great Intercessor and Mediator. Answer for me. Do not leave Your poor servant to die by the hand of his enemy and Yours. Take up my interests, weave them with Your own, and stand for me. As my Master, undertake Your servant's cause and represent me before the faces of arrogant men until they see what an imposing ally I have in the Lord my God.

Our greatest salvation comes from the divine guarantee. The Son of God as our guarantee has hurt for us, and in doing so He has brought good to us and saved us from our proud oppressor, the archenemy of souls. In this verse, we don't have the law mentioned under any of its many names, and this is the only instance in the whole psalm in which a verse omits mention of the Word of the Lord. Yet this is no exception to the spirit

> *When the proud see that You are my advocate, they will hide their heads.*

of the rule, for here we find mention of our Guarantee, who is the fulfillment of the law. Where the law fails we have Christ, the guarantee of a better covenant. This guarantee is always for good, but how much good no tongue can tell.

Do not let the proud do violence unto me. Your intervention will answer the purpose of my rescue. When the proud see that You are my advocate, they will hide their heads. We would have been crushed beneath our proud adversary the devil if our Lord Jesus had not stood between us and the accuser to become a guarantee for us. It is by His guarantee that we escape like a bird from the snare of the fowler. What a blessing to be able to leave our matters in His hands, knowing that all will be well, since He has an answer for every accuser and a rebuke for everyone who reviles us!

Good people dread oppression, for it makes even a wise person senseless, and they send up their cries to heaven for deliverance. That cry will not be in vain, for the Lord will undertake the cause of His servants and fight their battles against the proud. The word *slave* is wisely used as a plea for favor for David himself, and the word *proud* as an argument against his enemies. It seems to be inevitable that proud men would become oppressors and would take much delight in oppressing the true servants of God. Their oppressions will soon be put down, because they *are* oppressions, because their works are *proud*, and because the objects of these works are the Lord's *slaves*.

123. *Mine eyes fail for thy saving health and for the spoken word of thy righteousness.*

Mine eyes fail for thy saving health. He wept, waited, and watched for God's saving hand, and these exercises tried the eyes of his faith until they were almost ready to give out. He looked to God alone, he looked eagerly, he looked long, and he looked until his eyes ached. The kindness of this is that if our eyes fail, God does not fail, nor do His eyes fail. Eyes are tender things, and so are our faith, hope, and expectation. The Lord will not test them above what they are able to bear (1 Corinthians 10:13).

And for the spoken word of thy righteousness. This is a word that would silence the unrighteous words of David's oppressors. His eyes as well as his ears waited for the Lord's Word. He looked to see the divine Word come forth as an order for his deliverance. He was waiting for the verdict – the verdict of righteousness itself. How happy are we if we have righteousness on our side, for then the very thing that is the sinners' terror is our hope, and that which the proud dread is our expectation and desire.

David left his reputation entirely in the Lord's hand and was eager to be cleared by the word of the Judge rather than by any defense of his own. He knew that he had done right, and therefore, instead of avoiding the supreme court, he begged for the sentence that he knew would work out his deliverance. He even watched eagerly for the judgment and the deliverance, the word of righteousness from God which meant salvation to himself.

124. *Deal with thy slave according to thy mercy, and teach me thy statutes.*

Deal with thy slave according to thy mercy. Here David recollects himself. Although he was so free from doubt before men regarding the Word of righteousness, before the Lord, as His servant, he felt that he must appeal to mercy. We feel safest here. Our heart has more rest in the cry, "God be merciful to me," than in appealing to justice. It is good to be able to say, "I have executed judgment and justice," and then to add, in all lowliness, yet *deal with thy slave according to thy mercy.*

The title of *slave* includes a plea; a master should clear the character of his servant if he is falsely accused, and he should rescue him from those who want to oppress him. Besides, the master would show mercy to a servant, even if he deals severely with a stranger. The Lord lowers Himself to deal with and communicate with His servants. He does not reject His servants, but communes with them in a loving and tender way, for in any other way we would be crushed into the dust.

And teach me thy statutes. This is one way of dealing with us in mercy. We can expect a master to teach his servant the meaning of his orders, but since our ignorance frequently arises from our sinful stupidity, it is great mercy on God's part that He humbles Himself to instruct us in His commands. For our ruler to become our teacher is an act of great grace for which we cannot be too grateful. Among our mercies, this is one of the best.

125. *I am thy slave; give me understanding, that I may know thy testimonies.*

I am thy slave. This is the third time he has repeated this title in this section. He is evidently fond of the name and considers it to be a very effective plea. We who rejoice that we are sons of God are by no means less delighted to be His servants. Did not the firstborn Son assume the servant's form and fulfill the servant's work completely? What higher honor can the younger brothers desire than to be made like the Heir of all things?

Give me understanding, that I may know thy testimonies. In the previous verse, David sought teaching, but here he goes much further and craves understanding. Usually if the instructor supplies the teaching, the pupil finds the understanding; but in our case, we are far more dependent and must beg for understanding as well as for teaching. The ordinary teacher cannot provide this, and we are very happy that our Divine Tutor can furnish us with it.

We must confess ourselves to be fools, and then our Lord will make us wise, as well as give us knowledge. The best understanding is that which enables us to render perfect obedience and to exhibit intelligent faith, and it is this that David desires – *understanding, that I may know thy testimonies.* Some people would rather not know these things. They prefer to be at ease in the dark rather than possess the light which leads to repentance and diligence.

The servant of God desires to know in an understanding manner all that the Lord reveals about mankind and to mankind. He wants to be so instructed that he can apprehend and comprehend what he is taught. A servant should not be ignorant concerning his master or his master's business. He should study the mind, will, purpose, and aim of him whom he serves, for only in this way can he fulfill his service. Since no one knows these things as well as his master himself, he should often go to him for instructions, lest his very zeal would cause him to make more unnecessary mistakes.

It is remarkable that the psalmist does not pray for understanding through acquiring knowledge, but begs of the Lord first that he may have the gracious gift of understanding, and then obtain the desired instruction. All that we know before we have understanding is apt to spoil us and breed pride in us, but if there is an understanding heart first, then the stores of knowledge enrich the soul and bring neither sin nor sorrow with it. Likewise, this gift of understanding also acts in the form of discernment, and in this way the good man is preserved from hoarding up that which is false and dangerous. He knows what are and what are not the testimonies of the Lord.

126. *It is time for thee, O LORD, to act; for they have dissipated thy law.*

David was a servant, and therefore it was always his time to work; but in being oppressed by the sight of people's ungodly behavior, he feels his Master's hand is needed, and so he appeals to God to work against the workings of evil.

People make void the law of God by denying it to be God's

law, by spreading commands and doctrines in opposition to it, by setting up tradition in its place, or by utterly disregarding and scorning the authority of the lawgiver. Then sin becomes fashionable, a holy walk is regarded as contemptible puritanism, sin is seen as pleasure, and vanity leads the way. Then the saints sigh for the presence and power of their God.

Oh, for an hour of the King upon the throne with the rod of iron in His hand! Oh, for another Pentecost with all its wonders, to reveal the energy of God to opposers and make them see there is a God in Israel! Man's extremity, whether of need or of sin, is God's opportunity. When *the earth was without order, and empty; . . . the Spirit of God moved upon the face of the waters* (Genesis 1:2). Should He not come when society is returning to a similar chaos?

When Israel was brought to its lowest point in Egypt and it seemed that the covenant would be void, then Moses appeared and worked mighty miracles. So too, when the church of God is trampled down and her message is derided, we can expect to see the hand of the Lord stretched out for the revival of religion, the defense of the truth, and the glorifying of the divine name. The Lord can work either through judgments which hurl down the fortifications of the enemy, or by revivals which build up the walls of His own Jerusalem.

How wholeheartedly we can pray for the Lord to raise up new evangelists, to quicken those we already have, to set His whole church on fire, and to bring the world to His feet! God's work is forever honorable and glorious, and as for our work, it is as nothing apart from Him.

127. *Therefore I have loved thy commandments above gold, yea, above fine gold.*

Just as it was God's time to work, so it was David's time to love.

He was so far from being swayed by the example of evil men as to join them in slighting the Scriptures, he was instead led into a stronger love of those divine revelations. He not only loved the doctrines, but also the commandments. As he saw the commandments looked down upon by the ungodly, David's heart was in sympathy with God, and he felt a burning love for His holy precepts. It is a sign of a true believer that he does not depend upon others for his religion, but drinks water out of his own well that springs up even when the cisterns of earth are all dried. In the midst of a general depreciation of the law, our holy poet felt his own respect for that law rising so high that gold and silver sank in comparison.

Wealth brings with it so many conveniences that people naturally hold it in high regard, and gold is often used as the symbol of wealth; yet, in the judgment of the wise, God's laws are more enriching and bring with them more comfort than all the highest-quality treasures. The psalmist could not boast that he always kept the commands, but he could declare that he loved them. He was perfect in heart, and he would gladly have been perfect in life. He judged God's holy commands to be better than the best earthly thing – gold. Yes, David knew that God's Word was better than the best of the best earthly thing – fine gold – and this esteem was confirmed when forced to express it by those very oppositions of the world that drive hypocrites to forsake the Lord and His ways.

A miser watches his treasure all the more eagerly when he hears there are thieves out there plotting to deprive him of it. The more that people hate the eternal truths, the more we treasure them. We can truly say:

> "The dearer, for their rage,
> Thy words I love and own–

A wealthier heritage
   Than gold and precious stone."
   – John Keble

128. Therefore I have esteemed all thy precepts concerning all things to be right and I have hated every false way.

Therefore I have esteemed all thy precepts concerning all things to be right. Because the ungodly found fault with the precepts of God, David was all the more certain that God's precepts were right. Criticism from the wicked is a certificate of worth. That which they sanction we may justly suspect, but that which they detest we may fervently admire. The good man's delight in God's law is unreserved; he believes in all God's precepts concerning all things. We state our faith all the more broadly in proportion to the opposition of the enemy. We oppose reproachful criticism with a fearless faith. When confidence in God is considered vile, we determine to be viler still.

And I have hated every false way. Love of the truth resulted in hatred for falsehood. He who values a robe despises the moth that would devour it. This godly man was not indifferent to anything in the moral and spiritual world, but what he didn't love, he hated. He was not lukewarm regarding the truth. He loved well and hated well, but he was never a waverer. He knew what he felt and expressed it plainly. He was no Gallio, for *he cared for none of those things* (Acts 18:12-17). He was as strong in that which he hated as he was in that which he loved. He did not have a good thing to say about any practice that did not bear the light of truth. The fact that such large multitudes follow the broad road had no influence on this holy man, except to make him more determined to avoid every form of error and sin.

May the Holy Spirit so rule in our hearts that our affections can be in the same unquestionable state toward the precepts of the Word. May we take our place on the side of God and righteousness and never bear the sword in vain. We don't want to be quarrelsome, but we dare not be sinfully indifferent. We must hate all sin, for if it is indulged by even one of the whole community of believers, it will be our ruin. To arms! To arms, you soldiers of the cross!

Psalm 119:129-136

PE

Thy testimonies are wonderful; therefore does my soul keep them.

The exposition of thy words gives light; it gives understanding unto the simple.

I opened my mouth and panted; for I longed for thy commandments.

Look thou upon me and be merciful unto me, as thou didst use to do unto those that love thy name.

Order my steps with thy word; and let not any iniquity have dominion over me.

Ransom me from the violence of men, and I will keep thy precepts.

Make thy face to shine upon thy slave and teach me thy statutes.

Rivers of waters ran down my eyes because they did not keep thy law.

All the verses in this section begin with the seventeenth letter of the Hebrew alphabet, but each verse begins with a different word. This seventeenth letter is the letter *P*. The section is precious, practical, profitable, and powerful; peculiarly so. Let us pray for a blessing upon the reading of it.

129. *Thy testimonies are wonderful; therefore does my soul keep them.*

Thy testimonies are wonderful, full of wonderful revelations, commands, and promises. God's *testimonies are wonderful* in their nature, being free from all error and conveying overwhelming self-evidence of their truth. They are wonderful in their effects, such as instructing, elevating, strengthening, and comforting the soul. Jesus the eternal Word is called Wonderful, and all the spoken words of God are wonderful in their degree. Those who know them best wonder at them most. It is wonderful that God would have given testimony at all to sinful men, and more wonderful still that His testimony would be of such heavenly character – so clear, so full, so gracious, and so mighty.

Therefore does my soul keep them. Their wonderful character so impressed itself upon his mind that David kept them in his memory. Their wonderful excellence so delighted his heart that he kept them in his life. Some people wonder at the words of God and use them for their speculation, but David was always practical, and therefore, the more he wondered, the more he obeyed. Note that his religion was soul work; he did not just keep the testimonies with his head and hands, but his soul – his truest and most real self – held fast to them. The psalmist took such pleasure in the revealed will of God that he felt bound to exhibit its power in his daily life. His wondering and pondering produced reverential obedience.

130. *The exposition of thy words gives light; it gives understanding unto the simple.*

The exposition of thy words gives light. No sooner do God's words gain admission into the soul than they enlighten it, and what light can be expected from their continued indwelling! Their very entrance floods the mind with instruction because they are so full and clear. What brightness must their abiding bring!

On the other hand, there must be such an "entrance," or there will be no illumination. The mere hearing of the Word with the external ear is of little value on its own, but when the Word of God enters into the chambers of the heart, then light is scattered on all sides. This is the work of God; He alone can give entrance to His Word. We knock at the door in vain until grace opens it. The Word finds no entrance into some minds because they are blocked up with self-conceit, prejudice, or indifference; but where right and proper attention is given, divine insight must surely follow upon a knowledge of the mind of God. O Lord, make a clear entrance into my soul! Grant that Your words, like the beams of the sun, may enter through the window of my understanding and dispel the darkness of my mind.

> *Those whom the world calls fools are among the truly wise if they are taught of God.*

It gives understanding unto the simple. True disciples of the Word are sincere and candid. To such people the Word gives not only knowledge, but it also gives understanding. These simple-hearted people are frequently despised, and their simplicity is made the theme of ridicule; but what does it matter? Those whom the world calls fools are among the truly wise if they are taught of God. What a divine power rests in the Word of God, since it not only gives light, but even gives the mental eye by which the light is received – *It gives understanding.* This is the value of the words of God to the simple, who cannot receive mysterious truth unless their minds are aided to see it and prepared to grasp it.

131. *I opened my mouth and panted; for I longed for thy commandments.*

I opened my mouth and panted. An enlarged desire is one of the first fruits of an understanding given to us from the Lord. The psalmist's desire was so full of spirit that he looked into the animal world to find a picture of it. Humans restrain their expressions, but in the animal world everything is natural, and therefore it is truthful and forceful. Therefore, being filled with an intense longing, holy David was not ashamed to describe it using a most expressive, natural, and yet singular symbol. Like a stag that has been hunted in the chase and is hard-pressed and pants for breath, so did the psalmist pant for the entrance of God's Word into his soul. Nothing else could satisfy him. All that the world could generate still left him panting with open mouth. His soul panted for God – for the living God – and for grace to walk with Him in the way of holiness.

For I longed for thy commandments. David longed to know them, longed to obey them, longed to be conformed to their spirit, and longed to teach them to others. He was a servant of God, and his industrious mind longed to receive orders. He was a learner in the school of grace, and his eager spirit longed to be taught of the Lord. Oh, for more of this eager hungering, thirsting, yearning, and panting!

132. *Look thou upon me and be merciful unto me, as thou didst use to do unto those that love thy name.*

Look thou upon me. A godly man cannot go without prayer for very long. During the previous verses, David expressed his love for God's Word, but here he is on his knees again. This prayer is especially short, but is exceedingly pious. *Look thou upon me.* While he stood with open mouth panting for the commandments, he begged the Lord to look on him and let his condition and his unexpressed longings plead for him. He desires to be known by God and daily observed by Him. He wishes also to be favored with the divine smile that is included in the word *look*. If a look from us to God can be effective to save us, what may we not expect by way of a look from God to us?

And be merciful unto me. Christ's look at Peter was a look of mercy, and all the looks of the heavenly Father are of the same kind. If He looked on us with stern justice, His eyes would not tolerate us; but looking in mercy, He spares and blesses us. If God looks and sees us panting, He will not fail to be merciful to us.

As thou didst use to do unto those that love thy name. Look on me as You look on those who love You. Be merciful to me as You are accustomed to be toward those who truly serve You. There is a way that God is accustomed to observe towards those who love Him, and David craved to experience it. He did not want the Lord to deal better or worse with him than He was accustomed to deal with His saints, for to deal with him worse would not save him, and it could not be better. In effect he prays, "I am Your servant; treat me as You treat Your servants. I am Your child; deal with me as You deal with the rest of Your children."

It is especially clear from the context that David wanted the Word to enter him in such a way that he would gain such a clear understanding of it, as God usually gives to His own according to the promise, *And all thy sons shall be taught of the LORD* (Isaiah 54:13).

Reader, do you love the name of the Lord? Is His character most honorable in your sight? Is He most dear to your heart? This is a sure indicator of grace, for no soul ever loved the Lord except as the result of love received from the Lord Himself.

133. *Order my steps with thy word; and let not any iniquity have dominion over me.*

Order my steps with thy word. This is one of the Lord's customary mercies to His chosen: *He keeps the feet of his saints* (1 Samuel 2:9). This He does for those who love His name. By His grace, He enables us to put our feet step-by-step in the very place that His Word ordains. This prayer seeks a very special favor, namely, that every distinct act, every step, might be arranged and governed by the will of God. This does not stop short of perfect holiness, and neither will the believer's desires be satisfied with anything less than that blessed object.

And let not any iniquity have dominion over me. This is the negative side of the blessing. We ask to do all that is right and not to fall under the power of anything wrong. God is our sovereign, and we desire to have every thought in subjection to His authority. Believers have no pet sins to which they would be willing to bow. They pant for perfect deliverance from the dominion of evil, and being conscious that they cannot obtain it themselves, they cry unto God for it.

> Believers have no pet sins to which they would be willing to bow.

When we take this in connection with the former clause, we learn that to avoid all sin we must observe all duty. Only by actual obedience can we be preserved from falling into evil. Omissions lead to commissions; only an ordered life can save us from the disorder of wickedness.

134. *Ransom me from the violence of men, and I will keep thy precepts.*

Ransom me from the violence of men. David had tasted all the bitterness of this great evil. It had forced him into exile from his country and banished him from the sanctuary of the Lord. Because of this, he pleads to be saved from it. It is said that oppression makes a wise man insane, and no doubt it has made many a righteous man sinful. Oppression is in itself wicked, and it drives men to wickedness. We little know how much of our virtue is due to our liberty. If we had been in bonds under arrogant tyrants, we might have given in to them. Instead of being confessors of the faith, we might now have been apostates and have denied the faith. He who taught us to pray, *Lead us not into temptation*, will approve this prayer to be delivered from oppression, since it is of much the same tone. To be oppressed is to be tempted. Lord, preserve us from it.

And I will keep thy precepts. When the stress of oppression was taken off, he would go his own way, and that way would be the way of the Lord. Although we should not give in to the threatenings of men, many do so. In many instances, a wife is compelled to act against her conscience by the oppression of her husband. Children and servants, families and societies, and even whole nations have been brought into the same difficulty. Sins committed through intimidation will be largely laid at the oppressor's door, and it usually pleases God before long to overthrow those powers and people who compel others to do evil. The worst of it is that some people, when the pressure is taken off, follow after unrighteousness by their own choice. These people give evidence of being sinners by nature. As for the righteous, it happens to them as it did for the apostles of old: *And being let go, they went to their own company* (Acts 4:23). When saints are freed from tyrants, they joyfully offer praise to their Lord and King.

135. *Make thy face to shine upon thy slave and teach me thy statutes.*

Make thy face to shine upon thy slave. Oppressors frown, but the Lord smiles upon me. They darken my life, but when You shine upon me, all will be bright. The psalmist again declares that he is God's servant, and therefore he values his Master's smile. He seeks no favor from others, but only from his own Lord and Master.

And teach me thy statutes. He seeks holy instruction as the foremost token of divine love. This is the favor that he considers to be the shining of the face of God upon him. If the Lord will be exceedingly gracious and make him his favorite, he will ask no higher blessing than still to be taught the royal statutes. See how David craves after holiness! He values this as the greatest of all gems. We say that a good education is a great treasure, and so it is that to be taught of the Lord is a gift of special grace. The most favored believer needs teaching; even when he walks in the light of God's countenance, he still has to be taught the divine statutes or he will sin.

136. *Rivers of waters ran down my eyes because they did not keep thy law.*

David wept in sympathy with God when he saw the holy law despised and broken. He wept in pity for people who drew down the fiery wrath of God upon themselves in this manner. His grief was such that he could scarcely express his feelings. His tears were not simply drops of sorrow, but they were rivers of waters and torrents of woe.

In this sacred grief, the man of God became like the Lord Jesus, who beheld the city of Jerusalem and wept over it (Matthew 23:37-39; Luke 19:41-44). He acted in part like Jehovah himself, who does *not desire the death of the wicked but that the wicked turn from his way and that he live* (Ezekiel 33:11). The experience of this verse indicates a great advance upon anything we have read previously in this divine song. The psalm and the psalmist are both growing. David is a mature believer who sorrows because of the sins of others. Mourners in Zion are among the chief of the saints. In verse 120, his flesh trembled at the presence of God, but here it seems to melt and flow away in floods of tears.

Teach me thy statutes is followed by an expression of great tenderness of heart. No people are so affected by heavenly things as those who are much in the study of the Word, and are thereby taught the truth and essence of things. Worldly people are afraid of brute force, and they weep over losses and crosses; but those who are spiritual feel a holy fear of the Lord Himself, and lament most of all when they see dishonor cast upon His holy name.

> "Lord, let me weep for naught but sin,
> And after none but thee,
> And then I would, O that I might!
> A constant weeper be."
> – Benjamin Beddome

Psalm 119:137-144

TZADDI

Righteous art thou, O LORD, and upright are thy judgments.

Thou hast commanded righteousness, which consists of thy testimonies and thy truth.

My zeal has consumed me, because my enemies have forgotten thy words.

Thy word is very pure; therefore thy slave loves it.

I am small and despised; yet I have not forgotten thy precepts.

Thy righteousness is eternal righteousness, and thy law is the truth.

Trouble and anguish found me; but thy commandments were my delights.

Thy testimonies are eternal righteousness; give me understanding, and I shall live.

This passage deals with the perfect righteousness of Jehovah and His Word, and it expresses the struggles of a holy soul in reference to that righteousness. The first letter of every verse in this section begins with a sound that reminded the Hebrew reader of the word for *righteousness*. The main theme of this section is righteousness. Oh, for grace to delight ourselves in righteousness!

137. *Righteous art thou, O LORD, and upright are thy judgments.*

Righteous art thou, O LORD. The psalmist has not often used the name of Jehovah in this vast composition. The whole psalm shows David to have been a deeply religious man, thoroughly familiar with the things of God, and such people never use the holy name of God carelessly, nor do they even use it at all frequently in comparison with the thoughtless and the ungodly.

Familiarity brings about reverence in this case. Here David uses the sacred name in worship. He praises God by attributing perfect righteousness to Him. God is always right, and He is always actively right, or righteous. This quality is bound up in our very idea of God. We cannot imagine an unrighteous God. Let us praise Him by crediting righteousness to Him, even when His ways to us are painful to flesh and blood.

And upright are thy judgments. Here David praises God's Word, or recorded judgments, as being right, just as their Author is righteous. That which comes from the righteous God is itself righteous. Jehovah both says and does that which is right, and that only. This is a great support to the soul in time of trouble. When we are severely afflicted and cannot see the reason for the act of divine providence, we can fall back on the certain fact that God is righteous, and His dealings with us are righteous too. It would be our glory to sing this brave confession when everything around us suggests the opposite. When worldly reason mutters about excessive severity and the like, this is the richest adoration that can rise from the lips of faith.

138. *Thou hast commanded righteousness, which consists of thy testimonies and thy truth.*

All that God has testified in His Word is right and truthful. His testimonies are righteous and can be relied on for the present. They are faithful and can be trusted in for the future. There is a divine authority about every portion of the inspired testimonies. They are published by God's command and they carry the mark of the royal style that carries omnipotence in it. Not only the precepts, but also the promises are commanded by the Lord, as are all the teachings of Scripture. It is not left to our choice whether we will accept them or not. They are issued by royal command and are not to be questioned. Their characteristic is that they are like the Lord who has proclaimed them. They are the essence of justice and the soul of truth. God's Word is righteous and cannot be impeached. It is faithful and cannot be questioned. It is true from the beginning, and it will be true to the end.

Thy testimonies that thou hast commanded are righteous and very faithful (Psalm 119:138 KJV). Dwell on that sweet phrase – *very faithful*. What a mercy that we have a God to deal with who is meticulously faithful, true to every item and detail of His promises, punctual regarding time, and steadfast during all time! We can certainly risk all on a Word that is "ever faithful, ever sure."[11]

Since the psalmist dwells on the righteousness of God and His words in these verses, it benefits us to consider the divine character and to attempt to imitate it. *If ye know that he is*

---

11 John Milton, "Ever Faithful, Ever Sure." This is a hymn written by Milton in 1645 in which each of the hymn's seven stanzas ends with "Ever faithful, ever sure."

righteous, also know that any one that does righteousness is born of him (1 John 2:29).

In the last two verses David spoke concerning his God and His law; here he speaks about himself, saying:

139. *My zeal has consumed me, because my enemies have forgotten thy words.*

This was no doubt prompted by his having such a clear sense of the admirable character of God's Word. His zeal was like a fire burning within his soul. The sight of man's forgetfulness of God acted like a fierce blast to excite the fire to a more vehement flame, and it blazed until it was ready to consume him.

David could not bear that people would forget God's words. He was ready to forget himself – to consume himself – because these people forgot God. The ungodly were David's enemies; they hated him for his godliness, and he abhorred them for their ungodliness. These people had gone so far in iniquity that they not only violated and neglected the commands of God, but they also appeared to actually have forgotten them. This stirred up David's passion, and he burned with indignation. How dare they trample on sacred things! How could they completely ignore the commands of God Himself? He was astonished and filled with holy anger.

Don't we have some who profess to be Christians, who know the truth, but live as if they have forgotten it?

140. *Thy word is very pure; therefore thy slave loves it.*

Thy word is very pure. It is truth distilled, the embodiment of holiness. In the Word of God there is no mixture of error or sin. It is pure in its sense, pure in its language, pure in its spirit, pure in its influence, and all this to the very highest degree – *very pure*.

Therefore thy slave loves it. This is evidence that David himself was pure in heart, for only those who are pure love God's Word because of its purity. His heart was knit to the Word because of its glorious holiness and truth. He admired it, delighted in it, sought to practice it, and longed to come under its purifying power.

141. *I am small and despised; yet I have not forgotten thy precepts.*

That fault of forgetfulness that he condemned in others (verse 139) could not be charged to himself. His enemies did not think much of him, and they regarded him as a man without power or ability. Therefore, they looked down on him. He appears to accept the situation and humbly takes the lowest position, but he carries God's Word with him.

How many people have been driven to some unkind action in order to reply to the contempt of their enemies! By either speaking or acting in a manner which they cannot justify, they have made a spectacle of themselves. The beauty of the psalmist's piety was that it was calm and well-balanced, and since he wasn't influenced by flattery, he was not overcome by shame. If small, he more jealously paid attention to the smaller duties; if despised, he more earnestly kept the despised commandments of God.

142. *Thy righteousness is eternal righteousness, and thy law is the truth.*

Thy righteousness is eternal righteousness. Having attributed righteousness to God in a previous verse, he now goes on to declare that the righteousness is unchanging and endures from age to age. This is the joy and glory of the saints. What God is, He always will be, and His method of dealing with the sons of men is unchanging. Both the righteousness and the unrighteousness of people come to an end, but the righteousness of God is without end.

And thy law is the truth. As God is love, so His law is the truth – the very essence of truth: truth applied to ethics, truth in action, and truth on the judgment seat. We hear great disputes about "What is truth?" The Holy Scriptures are the only answer to that question. Note that they are not only true, but they are the truth itself. We cannot say that they contain the truth, but that they are the truth: *thy law is the truth.*

There is nothing false about the law or precepts of Scripture. Those who are obedient to this will find that they are walking in a way consistent with fact, while those who act contrary to it walk in a vain show. Because the Word is true, it has an everlasting righteousness about it. To alter, diminish, or add to it is to lie against God.

143. *Trouble and anguish found me; but thy commandments were my delights.*

Trouble and anguish found me. This affliction may have arisen from his circumstances, from the cruelty of his enemies, or from his own internal conflicts, but it is certain that he was the subject of much distress – a distress that seized him and carried him away as a captive to its power. His griefs, like fierce dogs, had taken hold of him; he felt their teeth. He had double trouble: trouble externally and anguish within himself. The apostle Paul put it this way: *We were troubled on every side; without were fightings, within were fears* (2 Corinthians 7:5).

But thy commandments were my delights. As a result, he

became a riddle. He was troubled, and yet delighted; he was in anguish, and yet content. The child of God can understand this enigma, for he well knows that while he is cast down on account of what he sees within himself, he is all the more lifted up by what he sees in the Word. He is delighted with the commandments, although he is troubled with his imperfections. He finds abundant light in the commandments, and by the influence of that light he discovers more of his own darkness, and he mourns over it.

Only the person acquainted with the struggles of the spiritual life will understand this statement. Let the reader find a balance with which to weigh himself. Does he find, even when he is surrounded by sorrow, that it is a delightful thing to do the will of the Lord? Does he find more joy in being sanctified than sorrow in being chastised? If so, then the spot of God's children is upon him.

> *The more we say in praise of the Bible, the more we may say, and the more we can say.*

144. *Thy testimonies are eternal righteousness; give me understanding, and I shall live.*

Thy testimonies are eternal righteousness. First, David said that God's testimonies were righteous, then that they were everlasting, and now that their righteousness is everlasting. In this way, he gives us a larger and more detailed account of the Word of God as he proceeds. The longer he is engaged in writing about it, the more he has to write. The more we say in praise of the Bible, the more we may say, and the more we can say.

God's testimonies to man cannot be assailed; they are righteous from beginning to end, and though ungodly men have opposed divine justice, they have always failed to establish any accusation against the Most High. As long as the earth stands, as long as there is a single intelligent creature in the universe, it will be confessed that God's plans of mercy are in all respects marvelous proof of His love of justice, and even though He may be gracious, Jehovah will not be unjust.

Give me understanding, and I shall live. This is a prayer that David constantly prayed – that God would give him understanding. Here he evidently considers that such a gift is essential to his living. To live without understanding is not to live the life of a man, but to be dead while we live. Only as we know and understand the things of God can we be said to enter into life. The more the Lord teaches us to admire the eternal rightness of His Word, and the more He quickens us with the love of such rightness, the happier and better we will be.

As we love life and seek many days in which we see good, it is proper for us to seek immortality in the everlasting *word of God, which lives and abides for ever* (1 Peter 1:23), and to seek good in that renewal of our entire nature that begins with the enlightenment of the understanding and continues on to the regeneration of the entire person. Here is our need of the Holy Spirit, the Lord and Giver of life, and the Guide of all those who have been made alive spiritually, who will lead us into all truth. Oh, for the visitations of His grace at this good hour!

We live by the Word of God in the sense that it preserves us from those sinful ways that would be death to us. To understand and copy the righteousness of God is the best preservative from all our deadly foes. If the Lord will give us understanding so that we do this, we will indeed live in the highest and best sense, despite the powers of death and hell.

Psalm 119:145-152

KOPH

I cried with my whole heart; answer me, O LORD, and I will keep thy statutes.

I cried unto thee; save me, and I shall keep thy testimonies.

I arose before the dawning of the morning and cried: I waited in thy word.

My eyes anticipate the night watches that I might meditate in thy spoken word.

Hear my voice according to thy mercy; O LORD, cause me to live according to thy judgment.

Those that persecute me draw near unto evil; they have strayed from thy law.

Thou art near, O LORD; and all thy commandments are truth.

Concerning thy testimonies, I have known of old that thou hast founded them for ever.

This section is devoted to memories of prayer. The psalmist describes the time and the manner of his supplication, and he pleads with God for deliverance from his troubles. He who has been with God in the closet will find God with him in the furnace. If we have cried to Him, we will be answered. Delayed answers may drive us to more earnest and persistent prayer, but we don't need to fear the ultimate result, since God's promises aren't uncertain, but are established forever.

The entire passage shows us: how he prayed (verse 145), what he prayed for (verse 146), when he prayed (verse 147), how long he prayed (verse 148), what he pleaded (verse 149), what happened (verse 150), how he was rescued (verse 151), and what his witness was regarding the whole matter (verse 152). May the Lord bless our meditations on this instructive passage!

145. *I cried with my whole heart; answer me, O LORD, and I will keep thy statutes.*

I cried with my whole heart. His prayer was a sincere, mournful, painful, and natural expression, like that of a creature in pain. We cannot tell whether he used his voice every time he cried out in this way, but we do know something of much greater consequence: he cried with his heart. Heart-cries are the essence of prayer, and he mentions the unity of his heart in this holy engagement. His whole soul pleaded with God. All his affections, his united desires, all was poured out toward the living God.

It is good when a person can say things such as this about their prayers, but I'm afraid many never cried to God with their whole heart in all their lives. There may be no eloquent beauty about such prayers, no length of expression, depth of doctrine, or accuracy of diction, but if the whole heart is in them, they will find their way to the heart of God.

Answer me, O LORD. David desires of Jehovah that his cries won't die in the air, but that God would honor them. True supplicants aren't satisfied with just the exercise of praying; they have an end and objective in praying, and they watch for it. If God doesn't hear prayer, we pray in vain.

The word "hear" (or "answer" in this verse) is often used in Scripture to express attention and consideration. In one sense God hears every sound made on earth and every desire of every heart, but David meant much more. He desired a kind, sympathetic hearing, such as a physician gives to his patient when he tells him his sad story. He asked that the Lord would draw near and listen with a friendly ear to the voice of his complaint, with the view of being sympathetic to him and helping him. Note that his wholehearted prayer goes to the Lord alone. David has no second hope or help. *Answer me, O LORD* is the full range of his petition and expectation.

I will keep thy statutes. He could not expect the Lord to hear him if he did not hear the Lord, nor would it be true that he prayed with his whole heart unless it was obvious that he labored with all his might to be obedient to the divine will. His objective in seeking deliverance was that he might be free to fulfill his religion, free to carry out every ordinance of the law, and free to serve the Lord.

Note that a holy resolution goes well with earnest supplication. David is determined to be holy. His whole heart goes with that resolve as well as with his prayers. He will keep God's statutes in his memory, in his affections, and in his actions. He will not willfully neglect nor willingly violate any one of the divine laws.

> 146. *I cried unto thee; save me, and I shall keep thy testimonies.*

I cried unto thee. Again he mentions that his prayer was to God alone. The sentence signifies that he prayed fervently and very often and that it had become one of the greatest facts of his life that he cried unto God.

Save me. This was his prayer. It was very short, but very full. He needed saving. No one but the Lord could save him, and so to the Lord he cried out. *Save me* from the dangers that surround me, from the enemies that pursue me, from the temptations that assail me, from the sins that accuse me.

He didn't use many words, but only cried, *Save me.* People are never wordy when they are downright serious. He didn't ask for a number of things, but asked only for salvation. People are seldom lengthy when they are intent upon the one thing needful.

And I shall keep thy testimonies. His great objective in desiring salvation was that he might be able to continue in a blameless life of obedience to God, that he might be able to believe the witness of God, and that he might himself become a witness for God. It is a great thing when people seek salvation for such a high purpose.

David did not ask to be delivered so that he could sin without punishment. His cry was to be delivered from sin itself. He had vowed to keep the laws of God, and here he resolves to keep the testimonies or doctrines of God, and to have a sound mind as well as clean hands. Salvation brings all these good things along with it. David had no idea of a salvation that would allow him to live in sin or abide in error. He knew quite well that there is no saving a man while he lives in disobedience and ignorance.

147. *I arose before the dawning of the morning and cried: I waited in thy word.*

I arose before the dawning of the morning and cried. David was up before the sun and began pleading to the Lord before the dew began to evaporate. Whatever is worth doing is worth doing promptly. This is the third time that he mentions that he *cried*. He cried, and cried, and cried again. His supplications had become so frequent, fervent, and intense that it might be said that he did little else from morning to night but cry to his God. His desire after salvation was so strong that he could not rest in his bed. He so eagerly sought it that at the first possible moment he was on his knees.

I waited in thy word. Hope is a very powerful means of strengthening us in prayer. Who would pray if he had no hope that God would hear him? Who would not pray when he has a good hope of a blessed delivery of his requests? His hope was fixed on God's Word. This is a sure anchor, because God is true, and in no situation has He ever run back from His promise or altered a thing that has gone forth from His mouth. He who is diligent in prayer will never be deprived of hope. Observe that as the early bird gets the worm, so the early prayer is soon refreshed with hope.

148. *My eyes anticipate the night watches that I might meditate in thy spoken word.*

My eyes anticipate the night watches. Before the watchman cried the hour, David was crying to God. He did not need to be informed about how the hours were flying by, for every hour his heart was flying toward heaven. He began the day with prayer, and he continued in prayer through the watches of the day and the watches of the night. The soldiers changed guard, but David did not change his holy activity. At night, however, he especially kept his eyes open and drove sleep away so that he could maintain intimacy with his God. He worshipped from watch to watch in the same way that travelers journey from one destination to the next.

That I might meditate in thy spoken word. This had become

meat and drink to him. Meditation was the food of his hope and the comfort of his sorrow. His thoughts ran on one theme – the blessed Word which he continually mentions and in which his heart so greatly rejoices. He preferred study to sleep, and he learned to give up his necessary sleep for much more necessary devotion. It is instructive to find meditation so constantly connected with fervent prayer. It is the fuel that sustains the flame. How rare a thing it is these days! When do we meet anyone who spends nights in meditation? Have we done so ourselves?

149. *Hear my voice according to thy mercy; O LORD, cause me to live according to thy judgment.*

Hear my voice according to thy mercy. People find it very helpful to use their voices in prayer. It is difficult to maintain the intensity of devotion for long unless we hear ourselves speak. That is why David broke through his silence at last. He arose from his quiet meditations and began crying with voice as well as heart to the Lord his God. Note that he does not plead his own worth, nor does he even for a moment appeal for payment of a debt on account of his merit. He takes the way of free grace, and says, *according to thy mercy*. When God hears prayer according to His mercy, He overlooks all the imperfections of the prayer. He forgets the sinfulness of the one praying, and in compassionate love He grants the desire, even though the supplicant is unworthy.

When God hears prayer according to His mercy, He overlooks all the imperfections of the prayer.

It is according to God's lovingkindness to answer quickly, to answer frequently, to answer abundantly – yes, *exceeding abundantly above all that we ask or think* (Ephesians 3:20). Lovingkindness is one of the sweetest words in our language.

Kindness has much in it that is most precious, but lovingkindness is doubly dear; it is the cream of kindness.

O LORD, cause me to live according to thy judgment. This is another of David's wise and fervent prayers. He first cried, "Save me," then, "Hear me," and now, *Cause me to live*, or quicken me. This is often the very best way of delivering us from trouble – to give us more life so we can escape from death, and to add more strength to that life so we will not be overloaded with its burdens. See how he asks for life according to God's judgment, or in such a way as would be consistent with infinite wisdom and prudence.

God's methods of transmitting greater vigor to our spiritual life are exceedingly wise. It would probably be in vain for us to attempt to understand them, and it would be wise for us to wish to receive grace, not according to our idea of how it should come to us, but according to God's heavenly method of granting it. It is His prerogative to make alive as well as to kill, and that sovereign act is best left to His infallible judgment. Has He not already granted us to have life and to have it more abundantly? (John 10:10). In this gift He has *abounded in us in all wisdom and prudence* (Ephesians 1:8).

150. *Those that persecute me draw near unto evil; they have strayed from thy law.*

Those that persecute me draw near unto evil. He could hear their footsteps close behind him. They are not following him for his benefit, but for his harm; therefore, the sound of their approach is to be dreaded. They are not prosecuting a good thing, but they are persecuting a good man. As if they did not have enough evil in their own hearts, they hunted after more. He sees them running a steeplechase over hedge and ditch in order to harm him, and he points them out to God and asks the

Lord to fix His eyes upon them and to deal with them to their confusion. They were already upon him, and he was almost in their grip, so he cries more earnestly.

They have strayed from thy law. A wicked life cannot be an obedient one. Before these people could become persecutors of David, they were obligated to get away from the restraints of God's law. They could not hate a saint and still love the law. Those who keep God's law neither do harm to themselves nor to others. Sin is the greatest of all troublemakers. David mentions the character of his adversaries to the Lord in prayer, feeling some kind of comfort in the fact that those who hated him hated God also, and they broke the law when they sought to do him harm. When we know that our enemies are God's enemies, and they are ours because they are His, we can certainly take comfort in that.

151. *Thou art near, O LORD; and all thy commandments are truth.*

Thou art near, O LORD. Near as the enemy might be, God was nearer. This is one of the best comforts for the persecuted child of God. The Lord is near to hear our cries and to quickly provide us aid. He is near to chase away our enemies and to give us rest and peace.

And all thy commandments are truth. God neither commands a lie nor lies in His commands. Virtue is truth in action, and this is what God commands. Sin is falsehood in action, and this is what God forbids. If all God's commands are truth, then the true man will be glad to stay near to them, and in them he will find the true God near to him.

This sentence will be the persecuted man's protection from the false hearts that seek to do him harm. God is near and God is true, and therefore His people are safe. If at any time we fall into danger through keeping the commands of God, we don't need to suppose that we have acted unwisely. On the contrary, we can be quite sure that we are on the right path, for God's teachings are right and true, and for this very reason wicked men come against us. False hearts hate the truth, and therefore they hate those who do the truth. Their opposition may be our consolation, while God's presence at our side is our glory and delight.

152. *Concerning thy testimonies, I have known of old that thou hast founded them for ever.*

David learned long ago that God had founded His testimonies in ancient times and that they would stand firm throughout all ages. It is a very blessed thing to be taught about God so early in life that we know the main doctrines of the gospel even from our youth. Those who know the eternal truth in their early days will look back upon such knowledge with pleasure when they are older.

Those who think that David was a young man when he wrote this psalm will find it rather difficult to reconcile this verse with their theory, because it is much more probable that he had now grown gray and was looking back on what he had known long before. At the very beginning he knew that the doctrines of God's Word were settled before the world began, that they had never changed, and they could never by any possibility be altered.

David had begun by building on a rock, by knowing that God's testimonies were *founded*, or grounded, laid as a foundation, and settled and established. David knew that they were settled with a view to all the ages to come and all the changes that would happen. It was because David knew this that he had such confidence in prayer and was so unrelenting in it.

It is sweet to plead unchanging promises with an unchanging God. It was because of this that David learned to hope. A person cannot expect much from a friend who changes, but he can certainly have confidence in a God who cannot change. It was because of this that David delighted in being near the Lord, for it is a most blessed thing to keep up close communication with a Friend who never varies.

Let those who are not satisfied with God choose to follow after the modern school of thought and look for fresh light to break out that will put the old light out of view. As for us, we are satisfied with the truth that is as old as the hills and as fixed as the great mountains. *Thus hath the LORD said, Stand ye in the ways and see and ask for the old paths, where the good way is and walk therein, and ye shall find rest for your souls* (Jeremiah 6:16).

Let "cultured intellects" invent another god, more gentle and effeminate than the God of Abraham. We are well content to worship Jehovah, who is eternally the same. Things everlastingly established are the joy of established saints. Bubbles that float upon the air please boys, but men value those things that are solid and substantial, with a foundation and a bottom to them that will bear the test of the ages.

Psalm 119:153-160

RESH

Consider my affliction and deliver me; for I have not forgotten thy law.

Plead my cause and redeem me; quicken me according to thy spoken word.

Saving health is far from the wicked, for they do not seek thy statutes.

Many are thy tender mercies, O LORD: cause me to live according to thy judgments.

Many are my persecutors and mine enemies; yet I do not deviate from thy testimonies.

I beheld the transgressors and was grieved because they did not keep thy words.

Consider, O LORD, that I love thy precepts; cause me to live according to thy mercy.

The beginning of thy word is truth, and every one of the judgments of thy righteousness is eternal.

In this section, the psalmist seems to draw still nearer to God in prayer and to state his case and invoke the divine help with more boldness and expectation. It is a pleading passage, and the keyword is *consider*. With much boldness, he pleads his intimate union with the Lord's cause as a reason why he should be helped. The special aid he seeks is personal quickening, for which he cries to the Lord again and again.

153. *Consider my affliction and deliver me; for I have not forgotten thy law.*

Consider my affliction and deliver me. The writer has a good case, though it is a grievous one, and he is ready, and even anxious, to submit it to divine arbitration. His matters are right, and he is ready to lay them before the supreme court. His manner is that of someone who feels safe at the throne, yet there is no impatience. He does not ask for hasty action, but for consideration. In effect, he cries, "Look into my grief and see that I need to be delivered. See my sorrowful condition and judge the proper method and time for my rescue."

The psalmist desires two things, and these things are blended together. First, David desires a full consideration of his sorrow. Secondly, he desires deliverance, and that this deliverance would come with a consideration of his affliction. It should be the desire of every gracious person experiencing adversity that the Lord would look upon his need and relieve it in such a way as will be most for the divine glory, and for his own benefit.

The words *my affliction* are vivid. They seem to portion off a special spot of woe as the writer's own inheritance. He possesses it like no one else has ever done, and he begs the Lord to have that special place under His care, like a husbandman looking over all his fields may take special care of a certain selected plot. David's prayer is eminently practical, for he seeks to be delivered; that is, he seeks to be brought out of his trouble and protected from sustaining any serious damage by it. For God to *consider* is to act in due season. We might consider and do nothing, but such is never the case with our God.

For I have not forgotten thy law. David's affliction with all its bitterness was not enough to drive out the memory of God's law from his mind; nor could it lead him to act contrary to the divine command. He forgot prosperity, but he did not forget obedience. This is a good plea when it can be honestly urged. If we are faithful to keep God's precepts, we can be sure God will remain faithful to His promises. If we do not forget His law, the Lord will not forget us. He will not leave that person in trouble for long whose only fear in trouble is that he might leave the way of righteousness.

154. *Plead my cause and redeem me; quicken me according to thy spoken word.*

Plead my cause and redeem me. In the last verse David prayed, *Deliver me,* and here he specifies one method in which that deliverance might be granted; namely, by the support of his cause. In providence, the Lord has many ways of clearing the slandered of the accusations brought against them. He can make it clear to everyone that these accusations have been disproved, and in this way, He can practically plead their cause. He can also raise up friends for the godly who will leave no stone unturned until their characters are cleared, or He can strike their enemies with such fearfulness of heart that they will be forced to confess their lies, and in this way, the righteous will be delivered without striking a blow.

> *If we are faithful to keep God's precepts, we can be sure God will remain faithful to His promises.*

Dr. Alexander reads it, "Strive my strife, and redeem me." That is, stand in my place, bear my burden, fight my fight, pay my price, and bring me out to freedom. When we find ourselves silent before the foe, this is a prayer made for our situation.

What a comfort to know that if we sin, we have an Advocate, and if we do not sin, that same One is engaged on our side!

Quicken me. We saw this prayer in the last section, and we will see it again and again in this section. It is a desire that cannot be felt and expressed too often. Just as the soul is the center of everything, so to be quickened is the central blessing. More life (quickening) means more love, more grace, more faith, more courage, and more strength, and if we get these, we can hold up our heads before our adversaries. Only God can give this quickening, but to the Lord and Giver of life, the work is easy enough, and He delights to perform it.

According to thy spoken word. David had found the blessing of quickening among the promised things, or at least he perceived that it was according to the general tone of God's Word that believers who were going through trials would be quickened and brought up again from the dust of the earth. Therefore, he pleads the Word and desires the Lord to act according to the usual course of that Word. It is an implied, if not an expressed, promise, that the Lord will quicken His people. What a mighty plea this is: *according to thy spoken word*! No gun in all our arsenals can match it.

155. *Saving health is far from the wicked, for they do not seek thy statutes.*

Saving health is far from the wicked. By their perseverance in evil, they have almost put themselves beyond hope. They talk about being saved, but they cannot know anything about it or they wouldn't remain wicked. Every step they have taken on the path of evil has removed them further from the kingdom of grace. They go from one degree of hardness to another until their hearts become like stone. When they fall into trouble it will be impossible to fix. Yet they talk big, as if they don't need salvation or could save themselves whenever they have the notion to do so. They are so far from salvation that they don't even know what it means.

For they do not seek thy statutes. They do not try to be obedient, but quite the reverse. They seek themselves, they seek evil, and therefore they never find the way of peace and righteousness. When people have broken the statutes of the Lord, their wisest course is to seek forgiveness by repentance, and by faith to seek salvation. Then salvation is so near them that they will not miss it, but when the wicked continue to seek after disobedience, salvation is set further and further from them. Salvation and God's statutes go together. Those who are saved by the King of grace love the statutes of the King of Glory. The main reason people are not saved is that they get away from the Word of God.

> *Those who are saved by the King of grace love the statutes of the King of Glory.*

156. *Many are thy tender mercies, O LORD: cause me to live according to thy judgments.*

This verse is very much like verse 149, yet it is no vain repetition. There is such a difference in the main idea that the one verse stands out distinct from the other. In the first case, David mentions his prayer, but leaves the method of its accomplishment with the wisdom or judgment of God. In this verse, he pleads no prayer of his own, but simply the mercies of the Lord, and he begs to be quickened by judgments rather than to be left to spiritual weariness. We can take it for granted that an inspired author is never so short of thoughts as to be obliged to repeat himself. In the places where we think we have a repetition of the same idea in this psalm, we are misled by our neglect of careful study. Each verse is a distinct pearl. Each blade of grass in this field has its own drop of heavenly dew.

Many are thy tender mercies, O LORD. Here the psalmist pleads the largeness of God's mercy and the immensity of His tender love. He speaks of *mercies* – many mercies, tender mercies, and great mercies. With the glorious Jehovah, he makes this a plea for his one leading prayer – the prayer for quickening. This quickening is a great and tender mercy, and it is many mercies in one. Shall one so greatly good permit His servant to die? Will not one so tender breathe new life into him?

Cause me to live according to thy judgments. A measure of awakening comes with the judgments of God. They are startling and arousing, and therefore the believer is quickened by them. David wanted every serious blow sanctified to his benefit, as well as every tender mercy. The first part of this verse says, *Many are thy tender mercies, O LORD.* David remembers this in connection with the "many persecutors" whom he speaks about in the next verse. By all these many mercies, he pleads for revitalizing grace, and so he has many strings to his bow. We will never be short of arguments if we draw them from God Himself and desire both His mercies and His judgments as reasons for our quickening.

157. *Many are my persecutors and my enemies; yet I do not deviate from thy testimonies.*

Many are my persecutors and my enemies. Those who actually assault me, or who secretly despise me, are many. David sets this against the many tender mercies of God. It seems a strange thing that such a truly godly man as David would have many enemies, but it was inevitable. The disciple cannot be loved where his Master is hated. The seed of the serpent must oppose the seed of the woman. It is their nature. *And the LORD God said unto the serpent, Because thou hast done this, thou art cursed above all beasts and above every animal of the field; . . . and I will put enmity between thee and the woman and between thy seed and her seed* (Genesis 3:14-15).

Yet I do not deviate from thy testimonies. David did not deviate from the truth of God, but proceeded on the straight path, no matter how many adversaries might endeavor to block his path. Some people have been led astray by one enemy, but here is a saint who held his way in the teeth of many persecutors. There is enough in the testimonies of God to reward us for pushing forward against all the multitudes that might combine against us. As long as they cannot drive or draw us into a spiritual decline, our enemies have done us no great harm. Truly, they have accomplished nothing by their malice. If we don't decline, they are defeated. If they can't make us sin, they have missed their mark. Faithfulness to the truth is victory over our enemies.

158. *I beheld the transgressors and was grieved because they did not keep thy words.*

I beheld the transgressors. I saw the traitors. I understood their character, their objective, their way, and their purpose. I could not help seeing them, for they pushed themselves into my path. As I was forced to see them, I watched them closely to learn what I could from them.

And was grieved. I was sorry to see such sinners. I was sick of them, disgusted with them, and I could not put up with them. I found no pleasure in them, for they were a sad sight to me, no matter how fine their clothing or how witty their conversation. Even when they were most jovial, the sight of them made my heart heavy. I could not tolerate either them or their actions.

Because they did not keep thy words. My grief was brought

about more by their sin against God than by their hostility and hatred against myself. O Lord, I could bear their evil treatment of my words, but not their neglect of Your Word. Your Word is so precious to me that those who will not keep it move me to indignation. I cannot keep the company of those who do not keep God's Word. That they would have no love for me is a triviality, but to despise the teaching of the Lord is detestable.

159. *Consider, O LORD, that I love thy precepts; cause me to live according to thy mercy.*

Consider, or see, *that I love thy precepts.* He asks for consideration a second time. As he said before, *Consider my affliction,* so now he says, "Consider my affection." He loved the precepts of God – loved them indescribably – and loved them so much as to be grieved by those who did not love them. This is a sure test: many people warmly accept the promises, but they cannot endure the precepts.

The psalmist so loved everything that was good and excellent, that he loved all that God had commanded. All of the precepts are wise and holy, and therefore the man of God loved them tremendously. He loved to know them, to think about them, to proclaim them, and mostly to obey them. He asked the Lord to remember and consider this, not upon the ground of merit, but that it would serve as an answer to the slanderous accusations that at this time were the sting of his sorrow.

Cause me to live according to thy mercy. Here he comes back to his former prayer, *Quicken me* (verse 154), and *cause me to live* (verse 156). He prays again the third time, using the same words. There is no harm in using repetition. The thing forbidden is the using of *vain repetitions,* as unbelievers do (Matthew 6:7).

David felt half stunned with the assaults of his enemies, ready to faint under their incessant malice and hatred. That is why he cries, *Cause me to live!* What he wanted was revival, restoration, and renewal, so he pleaded for more life. Oh, You who caused me to live when I was dead, quicken me again, so I may not return to the dead! Quicken me so I may outlive the blows of my enemies, the faintness of my faith, and the swooning of my sorrow. This time he does not say, *Cause me to live according to thy judgments*, but *Cause me to live according to thy mercy*.

David places his last and greatest reliance on the love and mercy of God. This is the great gun that he brings up last to the conflict. It is his ultimate argument. If this does not succeed, he will fail. He has long been knocking at mercy's gate, and with this plea he strikes his heaviest blow. When he had fallen into great sin, his plea was *Have mercy upon me, O God, according to thy mercy* (Psalm 51:1), and now that he is in much trouble, he hurries to the same worthwhile reasoning. Because God is love, He will give us life; because He is kind, He will again kindle the heavenly flame within us.

> *The ungodly are false, but God's Word is true.*

160. *The beginning of thy word is truth, and every one of the judgments of thy righteousness is eternal.*

The sweet singer finishes up this section in the same way as the last, by dwelling upon the sureness of the truth of God. It will be good for the reader to note the likeness between verses 144, 152, and the present one.

Thy word is truth. Whatever the transgressors may say, God is true, and His Word is true. The ungodly are false, but God's Word is true. They charge us with being false, but our comfort is that God's true Word will clear us.

The beginning. God's Word has been true from the first moment in which it was spoken. It has been true throughout all of history, true to us from the moment we believed it, and yes, true to us before we were true to it. Some read it, "Thy word is true from the head," or true as a whole, true from top to bottom. Experience had taught David this lesson, and experience is teaching us the same. The Scriptures are as true in Genesis as in Revelation, and the five books of Moses are as inspired as the four Gospels.

And every one of the judgments of thy righteousness is eternal. What God has decided remains irreversible in every case. No writ of error can be demanded against decisions of the Lord,[12] and neither will any of the acts of His sovereignty ever be repealed. There is not one single mistake either in the Word of God or in the providential dealings of God. There will never be any need to point out a single line of error in either the book of revelation or of providence, for no error exists. The Lord has nothing to regret or to retract, nothing to amend or to reverse. All God's judgments, decrees, commands, and purposes are righteous, and as righteous things are lasting things, every one of them will outlive the stars. *Until heaven and earth pass away, not one jot or one tittle shall pass from the law until all is fulfilled* (Matthew 5:18). God's justice endures forever. This is a cheering thought, but there is a much sweeter one, that which was the song of the priests of old in the temple; let it be ours: *His mercy endures for ever* (Psalm 136).

---

12   A writ of error is sometimes issued by a court of appeals requiring that the record of a trial from a lower court be sent to the court of appeals so it could be examined for alleged errors committed during the trial.

Psalm 119:161-168

SCHIN

Princes have persecuted me without a cause, but my heart stands in awe of thy words.

I rejoice at thy spoken word, as one that finds great spoil.

I hate and abhor lying, but I love thy law.

Seven times a day do I praise thee because of the judgments of thy righteousness.

Those who love thy law have great peace, and nothing shall cause them to stumble.

LORD, I have waited for thy saving health and done thy commandments.

My soul has kept thy testimonies, and I have loved them exceedingly.

I have kept thy precepts and thy testimonies, for all my ways are before thee.

We are drawing near to the end. The pulse of Psalm 119 beats more quickly than usual. The sentences are shorter, the sense is more vivid, the tone is more full and deep. The veteran of a thousand battles and the receiver of ten thousand mercies rehearses his experience and again declares his loyalty to the Lord and His law. Oh, that when we come to the close of life we might be able to speak like David does as he closes his life-psalm! Not boastfully, but still boldly, he places himself among the obedient servants of the Lord. Oh, to be clear in conscience when life's sun is setting!

161. *Princes have persecuted me without a cause, but my heart stands in awe of thy words.*

Princes have persecuted me without a cause. Such people should have known better. They should have had sympathy with one of their own rank. A man expects a fair trial at the hands of his peers. It is shameful for anyone to be prejudiced, but worst of all for noblemen to be so. If honor were banished from all other hearts, it should remain in the bosom of kings, and certainly honor forbids the persecution of the innocent.

Princes are appointed to protect the virtuous and avenge the oppressed, and it is a shame when they become the assailants of the righteous. It was a sad case when the man of God found himself attacked by the judges of the earth, for their eminent position added weight and venom to their enmity. It was good that the sufferer could truthfully assert that this persecution was *without a cause*. He hadn't broken their laws, injured them, or even desired to see them injured. He hadn't been an advocate of rebellion or lawlessness. He had neither openly nor secretly opposed their power, and therefore, while this made their oppression more inexcusable, it took away a part of its sting, and it helped the brave-hearted servant of God to bear up under their oppressions.

But my heart stands in awe of thy words. David might have been overcome by awe of the princes if it not been that a greater fear drove out the less, so that he was swayed by awe of God's Word. How insignificant crowns and scepters are in the judgment of that man who perceives a more majestic royalty in the commands of his God! We are not likely to be disheartened by persecution nor driven by it into sin if the Word of God exerts supreme power over our minds.

162. I rejoice at thy spoken word, as one that finds great spoil.

His awe did not prevent his joy. His fear of God was not the kind that perfect love casts out, but was of the sort that it nourishes. He trembled at the Word of the Lord, and yet rejoiced at it. He compares his joy to that of one who has been long in battle and has finally won the victory and is dividing the spoil. This usually falls to the lot of princes, and though David was divided from other monarchs by their persecution of him, he still had victories of his own, which they did not understand, and he had treasures in which they could not share. He could say:

> "With causeless hate by princes chased,
>   Still on thy word my heart is placed.
> That word I dread; that word I hold
>   More dear than heaps of captured gold."[13]

David's spoil was more than equal to the greatest gains of all the mighty men. His holy loot taken by his intense contention for the truth of God was greater than all the trophies that can be gained in war. Grace divides greater spoil than falls to the portion from sword or bow.

In the evil times, we have to fight hard for divine truth. Every doctrine costs us a battle. But when we gain a full understanding of eternal truth by personal struggles, it becomes doubly

---

13 Reverend Richard Mant, *The Book of Psalms in an English Metrical Version* (Oxford: W. Baxter, 1824), 413.

precious to us. If we have uncommon battling for the Word of God, may we have for our spoil a firmer hold upon the priceless Word!

Perhaps the passage means that the psalmist rejoiced like someone who comes upon hidden treasure for which he has not fought. In this case, we find the analogy in the man of God who, while reading the Bible, makes grand and blessed discoveries of the grace of God stored up for him – discoveries which surprise him, for he had not looked to find such a prize. Whether we come by the truth as finders or as warriors fighting for it, the heavenly treasure should be equally dear to us. With quiet joy the plowman slips home with his golden find! How victors shout as they share the plunder! How glad that person should be who has discovered his portion in the promises of Holy Scripture and is able to enjoy that portion for himself, knowing by the witness of the Holy Spirit that it is all his own!

163. *I hate and abhor lying, but I love thy law.*

I hate and abhor lying. This is a double expression for an inexpressible loathing. Falsehood in doctrine, in life, or in speech – falsehood in any form or shape – had become totally detestable to the psalmist. This was a remarkable statement for him to make, for generally, at the time, lying was the pleasure of Easterners, and the only wrong they saw in it was when their skill was at fault and the lie was found out.

David had made much progress when he had come to this, for he, too, had practiced deceit in his day. However, he doesn't just refer to falsehood in conversation, but evidently includes wrong ways in faith and teaching. He wrote down all opposition to the God of truth as lying, and then he turned his whole soul against it with the most intense form of indignation. Godly people should detest false doctrine in the same way that they abhor any other lie.

But I love thy law. He did not merely yield to it, but he had great pleasure in it. A bad-tempered obedience is essentially rebellion. Only a wholehearted love will secure sincere loyalty to law. David loved the law of God because it is the foe of falsehood and the guardian of truth. His love was as passionate as his hate. He intensely loved the Word of God, which is in itself pure truth. True men love truth and hate lying. It is good for us to know which way our hates and loves run. We can perform vital service to others by declaring what are the objects of our admiration and detestation. Both love and hate are contagious, and when they are sanctified, the wider their influence the better.

> *David loved the law of God because it is the foe of falsehood and the guardian of truth.*

164. *Seven times a day do I praise thee because of the judgments of thy righteousness.*

He thoroughly worked to praise his perfect God, and therefore he fulfilled the perfect number of songs – that number being seven. He reached a Sabbath in his praise, and before he rested on his bed he found sweet rest in the joyful adoration of Jehovah. Seven may also signify noteworthy frequency. He frequently lifted his heart in thanksgiving to God for His divine teachings in the Word and for His divine providential actions.

With his voice, David praised the righteousness of the Judge of all the earth. As often as he thought of God's ways, a song leaped to his lips. At the sight of the oppressive princes and at the hearing of the abounding falsehood around him, he felt all the more compelled to adore and magnify God, who in all things is truth and righteousness. When others slander us or in any other way rob us of our just reward of praise, it should be a warning to us not to fall into the same behavior toward our God, who is so much more worthy of honor.

If we praise God when we are persecuted, our music will be all the sweeter to Him because of our faithfulness during suffering. If we keep clear of all lying, our song will be all the more acceptable because it comes from honest lips. If we never flatter other people, we will be in a better condition for honoring the Lord. Do we praise God seven times a day? Sadly, the question we should probably ask is: Do we praise Him once in seven days? O shameful fraud that deprives the Ever Blessed One of the music of this lower sphere!

The excellent holiness of Jehovah's laws and acts should bring forth from us continued praise. Holy people are happy to be ruled by a righteous governor who never errs. Each lover of righteousness will say in his heart:

> "Just are thy laws; I daily raise
> The sevenfold tribute of my praise."[14]

165. *Those who love thy law have great peace, and nothing shall cause them to stumble.*

Those who love thy law have great peace. What a charming verse this is! It does not deal with people who perfectly keep the law, for where would such people be found? Rather, it deals with those who love it, whose hearts and hands are conformed to its precepts and demands. These people always strive with all their hearts to walk in obedience to the law, and even though they are often persecuted, they have peace, yes, *great peace,* for they have learned the secret of the reconciling blood, they have felt the power of the comforting Spirit, and they stand before

---
14   Mant, *The Book of Psalms*, 413.

the Father as people accepted. The Lord has granted them to feel His peace, *which passes all understanding* (Philippians 4:7). They have many troubles and are likely to be persecuted by the proud, but their usual state of mind is that of deep calm – a peace too great for these light afflictions to break.

And nothing shall cause them to stumble, or, shall really injure them. *And we now know that unto those who love God, all things help them unto good, to those who according to the purpose are called to be saints* (Romans 8:28). These offenses must come, but these lovers of the law are peacemakers, and so they do not give or take offense. The peace that is founded upon conformity to God's will is a living and lasting one, worth writing about with enthusiasm, like the psalmist does here.

166. *LORD, I have waited for thy saving health and done thy commandments.*

Here we have salvation by grace, and the fruits of it. All David's hope was fixed upon God; he looked to Him alone for salvation, and then he tried most earnestly to fulfill the commands of His law. Those who place least reliance on good works are very frequently those who have the most of them. That same divine teaching that delivers us from confidence in our own doings leads us to abound in every good work to the glory of God.

In times of trouble, there are two things to be done. The first is to hope in God, and the second is to do what is right. The first without the second is just presumption; the second without the first is mere formalism. It is good if we look back and can claim to have acted in the way commanded by the Lord. If we have acted rightly toward God, we are sure that He will act kindly toward us.

167. *My soul has kept thy testimonies, and I have loved them exceedingly.*

My soul has kept thy testimonies. Outwardly, my life has kept Your precepts, and my inward life, my soul, has kept Your testimonies. God has given testimony to many sacred truths, and these we hold fast with all our heart and soul, for we value them like life itself. The gracious man stores up the truth of God within his heart like a treasure exceedingly dear and precious. He keeps it. His secret soul, his inmost self, becomes the guardian of these divine teachings that are his only authority in soul matters. To him it becomes a great joy in his old age to be able to say, *My soul has kept thy testimonies.*

And I have loved them exceedingly. This was why he kept them, and having kept them, this was the result of the keeping. He did not merely store up revealed truth because of duty, but because of a deep, unspeakable affection for it. He felt that he would sooner die than give up any part of the revelation of God. The more we store heavenly truth within our minds, the more deeply we will be in love with it. The more we see the surpassing riches of the Bible, the more our love will exceed measure and expression.

168. *I have kept thy precepts and thy testimonies, for all my ways are before thee.*

I have kept thy precepts and thy testimonies. David had stored up, preserved, and followed both the practical and doctrinal parts of God's Word. It is a blessed thing to see the two forms of the divine Word equally known, equally valued, and equally confessed. There should be no picking and choosing as to the mind of God. We know those who try to be careful regarding the precepts, but who seem to think that the doctrines of the gospel are mere matters of opinion that they can form for themselves. This is not a perfect condition of things.

We have known others who are very rigid as to the doctrines and painfully careless with reference to the precepts. This also is far from right. When the two are kept with equal earnestness, then we have the perfect person.

For all my ways are before thee. Here he probably means to say that this was the motive of his effort to be right both in head and heart, because he knew that God saw him, and under the sense of the divine presence he was afraid to err. Or else he is appealing to God like this in order to bear witness to the truth of what he has said. In either case, it is no small consolation to feel that our heavenly Father knows all about us, and that if princes speak against us and worldly people fill their mouths with cruel lies, He can still vindicate us, for there is nothing secret or hidden from Him.

We are struck with the contrast between this verse, which is the last of its octave, and verse 176, which is similarly placed in the next octave. This verse is a protest of innocence – *I have kept thy precepts*, and verse 176 is a confession of sin – *I have gone astray like a lost sheep*. Both are sincere, and both are accurate. Experience makes many a paradox clear, and this is one. Before God, we might be clear of any open fault, and yet at the same time mourn over a thousand heart-wanderings that need His restoring hand.

Psalm 119:169-176

TAU

Let my cry come near before thee, O LORD; give me understanding according to thy word.

Let my supplication come before thee; deliver me according to thy spoken word.

My lips shall overflow with praise when thou hast taught me thy statutes.

My tongue shall speak thy words; for all thy commandments are righteousness.

Let thine hand help me, for I have chosen thy precepts.

I have longed for thy saving health, O LORD, and thy law is my delight.

Let my soul live, and it shall praise thee, and let thy judgments help me.

I have gone astray like a lost sheep; seek thy slave; for I have not forgotten thy commandments.

The psalmist is now at the last section of the psalm, and his petitions gather still more force and fervency. He seems to break into the inner circle of divine fellowship and to even come to the feet of the great God for whose help He is pleading. This nearness creates the lowliest view of himself and leads him to close the psalm, prostrate in the dust, in deepest self-humiliation, begging to be sought out like a lost sheep.

169. *Let my cry come near before thee, O LORD; give me understanding according to thy word.*

Let my cry come near before thee, O LORD. He is tremblingly afraid for fear that he might not be heard. He is conscious that his prayer is nothing better than the cry of a poor child or the groan of a wounded beast. He dreads that it could be shut out from the ear of the Most High, but he very boldly prays that it may come before God so He will hear and take notice, and that it will be looked upon with His acceptance.

David goes even further when he pleads, *Let my cry come near before thee, O LORD.* He wants the Lord's attention to his prayer to be very close and considerate. He uses a figure of speech and personifies his prayer. We can picture his prayer like Esther, venturing into the royal presence, pleading to an audience, and begging to find favor in the sight of the blessed and only king. It is a very sweet thing to a praying person when he knows for certain that his prayer has obtained an audience – when it has walked the sea of glass before the throne and has come even to the footstool of the glorious seat around which heaven and earth adore. This prayer is expressed to *Jehovah* with trembling earnestness. Our translators, filled with holy reverence, translate the word *Jehovah* as *O LORD*. We crave an audience with no one else, for we have confidence in no other besides Him.

Give me understanding according to thy word. This is the prayer about which the psalmist is so extremely anxious. Of all that he could get, he wants to get understanding, and no matter what else he misses, he is determined not to miss this priceless blessing. He desires spiritual light and understanding, as it is promised in God's Word, as it proceeds from God's Word, and as it produces obedience to God's Word. He pleads as though he had no understanding whatsoever of his own, and he asks to have it given to him. *Give me understanding.*

In truth, he had understanding according to the judgment of men, but what he sought was understanding according to God's Word, which is quite another thing. To understand spiritual things is the gift of God. To have a judgment enlightened by heavenly light and conformed to divine truth is a privilege that only grace can give. Many people who are considered wise by this world's standards are fools according to the Word of the Lord. May we be among those happy children who will be taught of the Lord!

> *May we be among those happy children who will be taught of the Lord!*

170. *Let my supplication come before thee; deliver me according to thy spoken word.*

Let my supplication come before thee. It is the same appeal with a slight change of words. David humbly calls his cry a *supplication*, a sort of beggar's petition, and again he asks for an audience and for an answer. There might be hindrances standing in the way of an audience, and he begs for their removal – *Let my supplication come.* Other believers are heard by the Great Lord Himself. Let my prayer come before You, and let me also have an audience with my God.

Deliver me according to thy spoken word. Rid me of my adversaries, rid me of my slanderers, preserve me from my tempters, and bring me up out of all my afflictions, even as Your Word has led me to expect You to do. In the previous verse David sought understanding. His enemies would succeed through his foolishness, if they succeeded at all; but if he exercised sound discretion, they would be confused and he would escape from them. The Lord, in answer to prayer, frequently delivers His children by making them wise as serpents and harmless as doves (Matthew 10:16).

171. *My lips shall overflow with praise when thou hast taught me thy statutes.*

David will not always be pleading for himself; he will rise above all selfishness and offer thanks for the benefit received. He promises to praise God when he has gained practical instruction in the life of godliness. This is something to praise for, and no blessing is more precious. The best possible praise is that which proceeds from people who honor God, not only with their lips, but also with their lives. We learn the music of heaven in the school of holy living. He whose life honors the Lord is sure to be a person of praise. David could not be silent in his gratitude, but he wanted to express it appropriately. His lips wanted to utter what his life had practiced. Eminent disciples are accustomed to speak well of the master who instructed them, and this holy man, when taught the statutes of the Lord, promises to give all the glory to Him to whom it is due.

172. *My tongue shall speak thy words; for all thy commandments are righteousness.*

My tongue shall speak thy words. When David had finished singing, he began preaching. God's tender mercies are such that they can be either said or sung. When the tongue speaks about God's Word, it has a most fruitful subject. Such speaking will be like a tree of life, the leaves of which will be for the healing of the people (Ezekiel 47:12; Revelation 22:2). People will gather together to listen to such talk, and they will treasure it up in their hearts.

The worst about us is that for the most part we are full of our own words and speak only a little about God's Word. Oh, that we could come to the same determination as this godly man, and say from this day forward, *My tongue shall speak thy words*! Then we would break through our sinful silence. We would no longer be cowardly and halfhearted, but we would be true witnesses for Jesus.

It is not only about God's works that we are to speak, but also about His Word. We can praise its truth, its wisdom, its preciousness, its grace, and its power; and then we can tell all it has revealed, all it has promised, all it has commanded, and all it has accomplished. The subject gives us plenty of which to speak. We can speak on forever; the tale is forever telling, yet untold.

For all thy commandments are righteousness. David appears to have been mainly captivated by the teaching parts of God's Word, and regarding the instruction, his main delight lay in its purity and excellence. When a man can speak in this way from his heart, his heart is certainly a temple of the Holy Spirit.

David has said earlier, *Thou hast commanded righteousness, which consists of thy testimonies and thy truth* (verse 138), but here he declares that they are righteousness itself. The law of God is not only the standard of right, but it is also the essence of righteousness. This the psalmist affirms about each and every one of the precepts without exception. He felt like Paul when he wrote, *So the law is truly holy, and the commandment holy and just and good* (Romans 7:12). When a man has such a high opinion of God's commandments, it is little wonder that his lips are ready to praise the ever-glorious One.

173. *Let thine hand help me, for I have chosen thy precepts.*

Let thine hand help me. Give me practical help. Don't hand me over to my friends or to Your friends, but put Your own hand to the work. Your hand has both skill and power, readiness and strength. Display all these qualities on my behalf. I am willing to do all that I am able to do, but what I need is Your help, and this is so urgently required that if I do not have it, I will fall. Do not refuse to help me. Great as Your hand is, let it rest on me – even me. The prayer reminds us of Peter walking on the sea and beginning to sink; he, too, cried, *Lord, save me* (Matthew 14:30), and the hand of his Master stretched out for his rescue.

For I have chosen thy precepts. This is a good argument. It is suitable for someone to ask help from God's hand when he has dedicated his own hand entirely to the obedience of the faith. *I have chosen thy precepts.* David's choice was made. His mind was made up. In preference to all earthly rules and ways, in preference even to his own will, he had chosen to be obedient to the divine commands. Will not God help such a man in holy work and sacred service? Certainly He will. If grace has given us the heart with which to will, it will also give us the hand with which to perform. Whenever, under the constraints of a divine call, we are engaged in any high and lofty enterprise and feel it to be too much for our strength, we can always invoke the right hand of God in words like these.

174. *I have longed for thy saving health, O LORD, and thy law is my delight.*

I have longed for thy saving health, O LORD. David speaks like old Jacob on his deathbed. Certainly all saints, both in prayer and in death, perform as one in word, deed, and mind. He knew God's salvation, and yet he longed for it; that is to say, he had experienced a measure of it and he was therefore led to desire something still higher and more complete.

The holy hunger of the saints increases as it is satisfied. There is a salvation yet to come, when we will be completely delivered from the body of this death, set free from all the turmoil and trouble of this mortal life, raised above the temptations and assaults of Satan, and brought near to our God, to be like Him and with Him forever and ever.

> *The holy hunger of the saints increases as it is satisfied.*

I have longed for thy saving health, O LORD, and thy law is my delight. The first clause tells us what David longs for, and the second informs us of his present satisfaction. God's law, contained in the Ten Commandments, gives joy to believers. God's law, that is, the entire Bible, is a wellspring of consolation and enjoyment to all who receive it. Though we have not yet attained the fullness of our salvation, we still find so much in God's Word concerning a present salvation that we are delighted even now.

175. *Let my soul live, and it shall praise thee, and let thy judgments help me.*

Let my soul live. Fill it full of life, preserve it from wandering into the ways of death, allow it to enjoy the indwelling of the Holy Spirit, let it live to the fullness of life, to the greatest possibilities of its newly created being.

And it shall praise thee. It will praise you for life, for new life, for eternal life, for You are the Lord and Giver of life. The more it lives, the more it will praise, and when it lives in perfection, it will praise You in perfection. Spiritual life is prayer and praise.

And let thy judgments help me. While I read the record of

what You have done, in terror or in love, let me be quickened and strengthened. While I see Your hand at work upon me and upon others, punishing sin and smiling on righteousness, let me be helped both to live right and to praise You properly. Let all Your deeds in providence instruct me, and help me in the struggle to overcome sin and to practice holiness.

This is the second time David has asked for help in this section. He was always in need of it, and so are we.

> 176. *I have gone astray like a lost sheep; seek thy slave; for I have not forgotten thy commandments.*

This is the *finale*, the conclusion of the whole matter. *I have gone astray like a lost sheep* – often, willfully, shamelessly, and even hopelessly except for Your intervening grace. In the past, before I was afflicted and before You had fully taught me Your statutes, I went astray. *I have gone astray* from the practical precepts, from the instructive doctrines, and from the heavenly experiences that You have set before me. I lost my way, and I lost myself. Even now, I have a tendency to wander, and in fact, have strayed already; therefore, Lord, restore me.

> "Am not I thy wilder'd sheep?
>   Seek me, O thou Shepherd good,
> Find, and for thy service keep
>   The dear purchase of thy blood;
> Lost again if thou depart,
>   Hide me, Savior, in thy heart."[15]

Seek thy slave. David was not like a dog that somehow or other can find its way back. He was like a lost sheep, which

---

15 Charles Wesley, *A Poetical Version of Nearly the Whole of the Psalms of David* (London: John Mason, 1854), 237.

goes farther and farther away from home; yet still he was a sheep, and the Lord's sheep, His property, and precious in His sight. Therefore, he hoped to be sought in order to be restored. However far he might have wandered, he was still not only a sheep, but also God's servant, and therefore he desired to be in his Master's house again, and once again to be honored with duties for his Lord. If he had been only a lost sheep, he would not have prayed to be sought; but being also a servant, he had the power to pray. He cries, *Seek thy slave*, and he hopes not only to be sought, but also to be forgiven, accepted, and taken into work again by his gracious Master.

Notice this confession. Many times in this psalm David has defended his own innocence against foul-mouthed accusers; but when he comes into the presence of the Lord his God, he is more than ready to confess his transgressions. Here he sums up not only his past, but even his present life, under the image of a sheep which has broken from its pasture, forsaken the flock, left the shepherd, and brought itself into the wilderness, where it has become lost. The sheep bleats, and David prays, *Seek thy slave*.

His argument is a forcible one: *for I have not forgotten thy commandments*. I know what is right, and I approve and admire what is right. What is more, I love what is right and long for it. I cannot be satisfied to continue in sin. I must be restored to the ways of righteousness. I am homesick for my God. I yearn after the ways of peace. I do not and I cannot forget Your commandments, nor do I cease to know that I am always happiest and safest when I carefully obey Your law and find my joy in doing so.

If the grace of God enables us to maintain the loving memory of God's commandments in our hearts, it will surely yet restore us to practical holiness. That person whose heart is still with God cannot be utterly lost. If he has gone astray in many respects, and yet is still true in his soul's inmost desires, he will be found again and will be fully restored.

Yet let the reader still remember the first verse of the psalm while he reads the last. The key blessedness lies not in being restored from wandering, but in being upheld in a blameless way even to the end. It is our obligation to keep to the center of the road, never leaving the King's highway for By-Path Meadow[16] or any other flowery path of sin. May the Lord uphold us even to the end. Yet even then, we will not be able to boast with the Pharisee, but will still pray with the publican, *God, reconcile me, a sinner* (Luke 18:13), and with the psalmist, *Seek thy slave.*

Let the last prayer of David in this psalm be ours as we close this book and lift our hearts to the Chief Shepherd of the sheep. Amen.

---

16   In John Bunyan's *The Pilgrim's Progress*, By-Path Meadow represents us trying an easier way than the way of the cross to get to heaven.

Charles H. Spurgeon –
A Brief Biography

Charles Haddon Spurgeon was born on June 19, 1834, in Kelvedon, Essex, England. He was one of seventeen children in his family (nine of whom died in infancy). His father and grandfather were Nonconformist ministers in England. Due to economic difficulties, eighteen-month-old Charles was sent to live with his grandfather, who helped teach Charles the ways of God. Later in life, Charles remembered looking at the pictures in *Pilgrim's Progress* and in *Foxe's Book of Martyrs* as a young boy.

Charles did not have much of a formal education and never went to college. He read much throughout his life though, especially books by Puritan authors.

Even with godly parents and grandparents, young Charles

resisted giving in to God. It was not until he was fifteen years old that he was born again. He was on his way to his usual church, but when a heavy snowstorm prevented him from getting there, he turned in at a little Primitive Methodist chapel. Though there were only about fifteen people in attendance, the preacher spoke from Isaiah 45:22: *Look unto me, and be ye saved, all the ends of the earth.* Charles Spurgeon's eyes were opened and the Lord converted his soul.

He began attending a Baptist church and teaching Sunday school. He soon preached his first sermon, and then when he was sixteen years old, he became the pastor of a small Baptist church in Cambridge. The church soon grew to over four hundred people, and Charles Spurgeon, at the age of nineteen, moved on to become the pastor of the New Park Street Church in London. The church grew from a few hundred attenders to a few thousand. They built an addition to the church, but still needed more room to accommodate the congregation. The Metropolitan Tabernacle was built in London in 1861, seating more than 5,000 people. Pastor Spurgeon preached the simple message of the cross, and thereby attracted many people who wanted to hear God's Word preached in the power of the Holy Spirit.

On January 9, 1856, Charles married Susannah Thompson. They had twin boys, Charles and Thomas. Charles and Susannah loved each other deeply, even amidst the difficulties and troubles that they faced in life, including health problems. They helped each other spiritually, and often together read the writings of Jonathan Edwards, Richard Baxter, and other Puritan writers.

Charles Spurgeon was a friend of all Christians, but he stood firmly on the Scriptures, and it didn't please all who heard him. Spurgeon believed in and preached on the sovereignty of God, heaven and hell, repentance, revival, holiness, salvation through Jesus Christ alone, and the infallibility and necessity of the Word of God. He spoke against worldliness and hypocrisy among Christians, and against Roman Catholicism, ritualism, and modernism.

One of the biggest controversies in his life was known as the "Down-Grade Controversy." Charles Spurgeon believed that some pastors of his time were "down-grading" the faith by compromising with the world or the new ideas of the age. He said that some pastors were denying the inspiration of the Bible, salvation by faith alone, and the truth of the Bible in other areas, such as creation. Many pastors who believed what Spurgeon condemned were not happy about this, and Spurgeon eventually resigned from the Baptist Union.

Despite some difficulties, Spurgeon became known as the "Prince of Preachers." He opposed slavery, started a pastors' college, opened an orphanage, led in helping feed and clothe the poor, had a book fund for pastors who could not afford books, and more.

Charles Spurgeon remains one of the most published preachers in history. His sermons were printed each week (even in the newspapers), and then the sermons for the year were re-issued as a book at the end of the year. The first six volumes, from 1855-1860, are known as *The Park Street Pulpit*, while the next fifty-seven volumes, from 1861-1917 (his sermons continued to be published long after his death), are known as *The Metropolitan Tabernacle Pulpit*. He also oversaw a monthly magazine-type publication called *The Sword and the Trowel*, and Spurgeon wrote many books, including *Lectures to My Students*, *All of Grace*, *Around the Wicket Gate*, *Advice for Seekers*, *John Ploughman's Talks*, *The Soul Winner*, *Words of Counsel for Christian Workers*, *Cheque Book of the Bank of Faith*, *Morning and Evening*, his autobiography, and more, including some commentaries, such as his twenty-year study on the Psalms – *The Treasury of David*.

Charles Spurgeon often preached ten times a week, preaching

to an estimated ten million people during his lifetime. He usually preached from only one page of notes, and often from just an outline. He read about six books each week. During his lifetime, he had read *The Pilgrim's Progress* through more than one hundred times. When he died, his personal library consisted of more than 12,000 books. However, the Bible always remained the most important book to him.

Spurgeon was able to do what he did in the power of God's Holy Spirit because he followed his own advice – he met with God every morning before meeting with others, and he continued in communion with God throughout the day.

Charles Spurgeon suffered from gout, rheumatism, and some depression, among other health problems. He often went to Menton, France, to recuperate and rest. He preached his final sermon at the Metropolitan Tabernacle on June 7, 1891, and died in France on January 31, 1892, at the age of fifty-seven. He was buried in Norwood Cemetery in London.

Charles Haddon Spurgeon lived a life devoted to God. His sermons and writings continue to influence Christians all over the world.

Similar Titles

ANEKO
PRESS

Words of Warning, by Charles H. Spurgeon

This book, *Words of Warning*, is an analysis of people and the gospel of Christ. Under inspiration of the Holy Spirit, Charles H. Spurgeon sheds light on the many ways people may refuse to come to Christ, but he also shines a brilliant light on how we can be saved. Unsaved or wavering individuals will be convicted, and if they allow it, they will be led to Christ. Sincere Christians will be happy and blessed as they consider the great salvation with which they have been saved.

Available where books are sold.

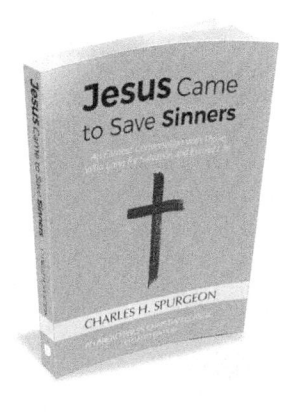

Jesus Came to Save Sinners, by Charles H. Spurgeon

This is a heart-level conversation with you, the reader. Every excuse, reason, and roadblock for not coming to Christ is examined and duly dealt with. If you think you may be too bad, or if perhaps you really are bad and you sin either openly or behind closed doors, you will discover that life in Christ is for you too. You can reject the message of salvation by faith, or you can choose to live a life of sin after professing faith in Christ, but you cannot change the truth as it is, either for yourself or for others. As such, it behooves you and your family to embrace truth, claim it for your own, and be genuinely set free for now and eternity. Come and embrace this free gift of God, and live a victorious life for Him.

Available where books are sold.

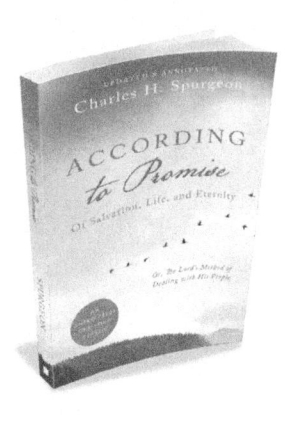

According to Promise, by Charles H. Spurgeon

The first part of this book is meant to be a sieve to separate the chaff from the wheat. Use it on your own soul. It may be the most profitable and beneficial work you have ever done. He who looked into his accounts and found that his business was losing money was saved from bankruptcy. This may happen also to you. If, however, you discover that your heavenly business is prospering, it will be a great comfort to you. You cannot lose by honestly searching your own heart.

The second part of this book examines God's promises to His children. The promises of God not only exceed all precedent, but they also exceed all imitation. No one has been able to compete with God in the language of liberality. The promises of God are as much above all other promises as the heavens are above the earth.

Available where books are sold.

Life in Christ (Vol. 1), by Charles H. Spurgeon

Men who were led by the hand or groped their way along the wall to reach Jesus were touched by his finger and went home without a guide, rejoicing that Jesus Christ had opened their eyes. Jesus is still able to perform such miracles. And, with the power of the Holy Spirit, his Word will be expounded and we'll watch for the signs to follow, expecting to see them at once. Why shouldn't those who read this be blessed with the light of heaven? This is my heart's inmost desire.

    I can't put fine words together. I've never studied speech. In fact, my heart loathes the very thought of intentionally speaking with fine words when souls are in danger of eternal separation from God. No, I work to speak straight to your hearts and consciences, and if there is anyone with faith to receive, God will bless them with fresh revelation.

    – Charles H. Spurgeon

Available where books are sold.

Words of Counsel, by Charles H. Spurgeon

Is there any occupation as profitable or rewarding as that of winning souls for Christ? It is a desirable employment, and the threshold for entry into this profession is set at a level any Christian may achieve – you must only love the Lord God with all your heart, soul, and mind; and your fellow man as yourself. This work is for all genuine Christians, of all walks of life. This is for you, fellow Christian.

Be prepared to be inspired, challenged, and convicted. Be prepared to weep, for the Holy Spirit may touch you deeply as you consider your coworkers, your neighbors, the children you know, and how much the Lord cares for these individuals. But you will also be equipped. Charles Spurgeon knew something about winning souls, and he holds nothing back as he shares biblical wisdom and practical application regarding the incredible work the Lord wants to do through His people to reach the lost.

Available where books are sold.

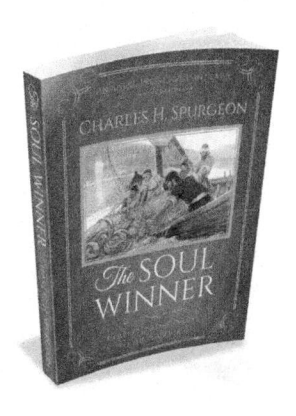

The Soul Winner, by Charles H. Spurgeon

As an individual, you may ask, How can I, an average person, do anything to reach the lost? Or if a pastor, you may be discouraged and feel ineffective with your congregation, much less the world. Or perhaps you don't yet have a heart for the lost. Whatever your excuse, it's time to change. Overcome yourself and learn to make a difference in your church and the world around you. It's time to become an effective soul winner for Christ.

As Christians, our main business is to win souls. But, in Spurgeon's own words, "like shoeing-smiths, we need to know a great many things. Just as the smith must know about horses and how to make shoes for them, so we must know about souls and how to win them for Christ." Learn about souls, and how to win them, from one of the most acclaimed soul winners of all time.

Available where books are sold.

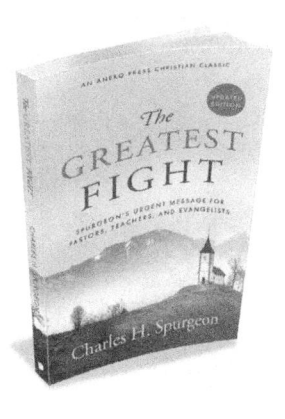

The Greatest Fight, by Charles H. Spurgeon

This book examines three things that are of utmost importance in this fight of faith. The first is *our armory*, which is the inspired Word of God. The second is *our army*, the church of the living God, which we must lead under our Lord's command. The third is *our strength*, by which we wear the armor and use the sword.

The message in this book, when originally presented by Charles Spurgeon in his final address to his own Pastor's College, was received rapturously and enthusiastically. It was almost immediately published and distributed around the world and in several languages. After Charles Spurgeon's death in 1892, 34,000 copies were printed and distributed to pastors and leaders in England through Mrs. Spurgeon's book fund. It is with great pleasure that we present this updated and very relevant book to the Lord's army of today.

Available where books are sold.

Come Ye Children, by Charles H. Spurgeon

Teaching children things of the Lord is an honor and a high calling. Children have boundless energy and may appear distracted, but they are capable of understanding biblical truths even adults have a hard time grasping. Children's minds are easily impressed with new thoughts, whether good or bad, and will remember many of their young lessons for the rest of their life. Adults and churches tend to provide entertainment to occupy the children, but children ought to have our undivided attention. Jesus said, let the little children come to me. They were worthy of His time and devotion, and they are worthy of ours.

Expect to be challenged and inspired as you read this classic from Charles H. Spurgeon. Learn how to enlarge your heart for all types of children, learn what lessons are best, and learn what results to expect. May this helpful little book be the catalyst for many new or improved shepherds of the Lord's lambs.

Available where books are sold.

Made in United States
North Haven, CT
27 November 2024